Geography in the Early
2nd Edition

This completely revised and updated 2nd Edition of *Geography in the Early Years* presents a lively and comprehensive overview of teaching and learning in geography. Theoretical aspects of early years teaching in geography are complemented by up-to-date research findings and illustrated with discussion, a wealth of case studies, and suggestions for the development and implementation of sound geographical work in practice.

In a practitioner-friendly style, this book provides:

- an examination of the essence of geography in terms of children's conceptions of the physical environment;
- a detailed description of geography in the National Curriculum and of the place and nature of environmental education within early years teaching;
- guidelines for taking a whole-school approach in policy, planning and organisation of geographical learning;
- examples of initial teacher training and continuing professional developments.

This highly accessible, illuminating book will be immensely helpful to teachers, student teachers, policy-makers and all other providers of education for children aged 3 to 7 years.

Joy Palmer is Pro-Vice-Chancellor of the University of Durham.
Joanna Birch is Senior Research Associate at the University of Durham.

Teaching and Learning in the Early Years
Series Editor *Joy Palmer*

This innovatory and up-to-date series is concerned specifically with curriculum practice in the first three years of school. Each book includes guidance on:

- subject content
- planning and organisation
- assessment and record-keeping
- in-service training

This practical advice is placed in the context of the National Curriculum and the latest theoretical work on how children learn at this age and what experiences they bring to their early years in the classroom.

Books in the series:

Geography in the early years, 2nd edition
Joy Palmer

History in the early years, 2nd edition
Hilary Cooper

Mathematics in the early years
Wendy Clemson and David Clemson

Music in the early years
Aelwyn Pugh and Lesley Pugh

Physical education in the early years
Pauline Wetton

RE in the early years
Elizabeth Ashton

Special educational needs in the early years, 2nd edition
Ruth A. Wilson

Geography in the Early Years
2nd Edition

Joy A. Palmer
and
Joanna C. Birch

RoutledgeFalmer
Taylor & Francis Group

London and New York

First edition published 1994 by Routledge

This edition published 2004 by RoutledgeFalmer
11 New Fetter Lane, London EC4P 4EE

Simultaneously published in the USA and Canada
by RoutledgeFalmer
270 Madison Avenue, New York, NY 10016

RoutledgeFalmer is an imprint of the Taylor & Francis Group

© 1994, 2004 Joy Palmer and Joanna Birch

Typeset in Times by Keyword Typesetting Services Limited
Printed and bound in Great Britain by MPG Books Ltd, Bodmin

British Library Cataloguing in Publication Data
A catalogue record for this book is available from the
British Library

Library of Congress Cataloging in Publication Data
Palmer, Joy, 1951–
    Geography in the early years / Joy A. Palmer and Joanna C. Birch. – 2nd ed.
       p. cm.
    Includes bibliographical references and index.
    I. Geography–Study and teaching (Elementary)   I. Birch, Joanna C.   II. Title.
    G73. P235 2004
    372.89′1–dc22   2004001370

ISBN 0-415-32070-4

Contents

List of illustrations   vi
The authors   viii
Editor's preface   ix
Acknowledgements   xi

1 The young child in the geographical world   1

2 Geographical and environmental education   28

3 Policy, planning and organisation   44

4 Policy into practice   86

5 Training and professional development   165

6 Resources   193

Postscript   206
References   209
Name index   213
Subject index   214

Illustrations

Figures

3.1   Components of a school policy: geography/environmental
education   45
3.2   A sequence of mapwork activities   76–7
3.3   Planning matrix: knowledge, skills and understanding   81
3.4   Key Stage 1: Medium-term planning sheet for geography   82
3.5   Topic plan: Go Bananas!   83
3.6   Geography KS1: Bananas: Lesson planning sheet   84
4.1   My desk   90
4.2   Worksheet outline (a)   91
4.3   Worksheet outline (b)   91
4.4   Worksheet outline (c)   92
4.5   Worksheet outline (d)   93
4.6   Great North Park Nature Trail: Teacher's Notes   109
4.7   Creature Feature: Pupil worksheet   110
4.8   Planning: Areas of study and activities   127
4.9   My favourite place in school   131
4.10   A letter to Grandad   133
4.11   Children's mapwork from Red Fox (a) Atif   141
4.12   Children's mapwork from Red Fox (b) Louis   142
4.13   Children's mapwork from Red Fox (c) Chloe   143
4.14   Progression in National Curriculum Geography through
Programmes of Study and level descriptions   155
4.15   Recording listening: suggested format   159
4.16   Summary of teacher's questions and cognitive processes
related to Key Stage 1 geography   160
4.17   Questioning: individual recording sheet   161
4.18   Thinking about the street   163
4.19   Questions to ask on a trail   164
5.1   The stages involved in topic refining   168

5.2   Example (a) of children's work which might be used for
      assessment purposes   170
5.3   Example (b) of children's work which might be used for
      assessment purposes   171
5.4   Example (c) of children's work that might be used for
      assessment purposes   172
5.5   Example (d) of children's work that might be used for
      assessment purposes   173

Plates

4(i)   A tiled map of the school grounds is one of the imaginative
         features of the outdoor environment   99
4(ii)   Looking over the pond to the stone wall and the end of the
         school field   100
4(iii)   Eco-Schools Corner: Noticeboard and can crusher bin   121
4(iv)   Violet Lane nursery garden and wall, painted by adjacent
         secondary school pupils   122
4(v)   Collage artwork of a town environment   134
4(vi)   Collage artwork of a countryside environment   134
4(vii)   The Willow Cat   149
4(viii) The Book of Herbs   150

Table

2.1   Extract from a planning model   43

The authors

Joy A. Palmer is Professor of Education and Pro-Vice-Chancellor of the University of Durham. She has researched and published extensively in the fields of geographical and environmental education and is sole author of the first edition of this volume, published in 1994. Recent works include *Environmental Education in the 21st Century* and *50 Key Thinkers on the Environment*.

Joanna C. Birch is post-doctoral Research Associate at the University of Durham. She has recently completed a review of the education provision of The Wildlife Trusts in the UK and is currently working on a major European Commission funded project on the Integrated Management of European Wetlands.

Editor's preface

Each book in this series focuses on a specific curriculum area or theme. The series relates relevant learning theory and a rationale for early years learning to the practical development and implementation of subject-based schemes of work, topics and classroom activities at the appropriate level. Volumes address teaching and learning related to the age range 3 and 4 to 7 years; that is, the Foundation Stage and Key Stage 1 of the National Curriculum for Schools in England.

Each volume is intended to be an up-to-date, judicious mix of theory and practical classroom application, offering a wealth of background information, ideas and advice to all concerned with planning, implementing, monitoring and evaluating teaching and learning in the first three years in school. Theoretical perspectives are presented in a lively and interesting way, drawing upon recent classroom research findings wherever possible. Case studies and activities from a range of classrooms and schools illuminate many of the substantial issues related to the subject area in question.

Readers will find a similar pattern of contents in all the books in the series. Each discusses the early learning environment, transition from home- to school-based learning, and addresses the key questions of what this means for the early years teacher and the curriculum. Such discussion inevitably incorporates ideas on the knowledge which young children may have of subjects and an overview of the subject matter itself which is under scrutiny. As the thrust of the series is towards young children learning subjects, albeit in a holistic way, no doubt readers will wish to consider what is an appropriate content or rationale for the subject in the early years. Having considered young children as learners, what they are bringing into school in terms of prior knowledge, the teacher's task and the subject matter itself, each book then turns its attention to appropriate methods of planning, organising, implementing and evaluating teaching and learning activities. Crucial matters such as assessment, evaluation and record-keeping are dealt with in their own right, and are also referred to and discussed in ongoing examples of good practice. Each book concludes with useful suggestions for further staffroom discussion/INSET activities and advice on resources.

While following this general format and indeed the format of the series' original book on *Geography in the Early Years* (Palmer 1994), this completely re-worked and revised edition takes into account changes required by the revised National Curriculum and introduction of the Foundation Stage and new literature and research related to early years geography teaching and learning. It also reflects recent changes in training for teachers and professional development courses, and the importance of cross-curricular links with education for sustainable development and environmental education in particular; also with the national literacy strategy, information and communication technology, personal, social and health education, and values education. It recognises the importance of special educational needs, inclusion, community and parental involvement, links with other education providers and schools' partners in training and professional development. It concludes with an extensive and updated list of resources.

As a whole, the series aims to be inspirational and forward-looking. As all readers know so well, the National Curriculum is not 'written in concrete'. Education is a dynamic process. While taking due account of the essential National Curriculum framework, authors go far beyond the level of description of rigid content guidelines to highlight *principles* for teaching and learning. Furthermore, they incorporate two key messages which surely underpin successful, reflective education, namely 'vision' and 'enthusiasm'. It is hoped that students and teachers will be inspired and assisted in their task of implementing successful and progressive plans which help young learners to make sense of their world and the key areas of knowledge within it.

Joy A. Palmer

Acknowledgements

The authors gratefully acknowledge the advice, support and contributions received from many individuals, schools and other organisations. In particular, thanks are due to Steve Ashton, People and Wildlife Manager, Tees Valley Wildlife Trust; Katherine Packer, Education Manager, and Linda Baldwin, The Great Outdoors Project Co-ordinator, Education Team, Sheffield Wildlife Trust; Diane Barker, Headteacher, and Carol Dyche, Geography Co-ordinator, ECO Co-ordinator and Reception Class Teacher, Violet Lane Infants School, Burton-upon-Trent; Imogen Berisford for the case study 'The use of study' as prepared for the first edition of this book; Kate Carey, Headteacher, and Lesley Brebner and Melodie Buckley, Class Teachers, Kindergarten, Derby High School for Girls; Richard Coombes, Headteacher, Jo Talbot, Class Teacher, and Debbie Dickson, Classroom Assistant at Ebchester Church of England Primary School, Ebchester, County Durham; Dorothy Douglas, Acting Headteacher, Eglingham Church of England First School, Eglingham, near Alnwick, Northumberland; Derrick Golland, Adviser for Environment and Sustainable Development and e-learning Manager, for Quality Learning Services, and Kate Russell, Geography Adviser for Quality Learning Services, Staffordshire County Council Education Department; Lily Horseman, Wildplay Officer, Hereford Wildlife Trust; Jim McManners, Headteacher and Nicola Woolley, Class Teacher, Cassop Primary School, Cassop, County Durham; Justine Millward, Education Manager, Norfolk Wildlife Trust; David Owen, Head of Centre of Education and Foundation Studies and Subject Leader for Geography, and Alison Ryan, BA Year One Co-ordinator and Primary Admissions Tutor, School of Education, Sheffield Hallam University; John Rhymer, Head of Bishops Wood Environmental Education Centre, Teacher Adviser for Worcester LEA and Programme Co-ordinator for the UK branch of the Institute for Earth Education; Margaret Westmore, Education Officer, Gloucestershire Wildlife Trust; and Jan White, Early Years Development Officer for the North of England, Learning Through Landscapes (Sheffield).

We are greatly indebted to Tina Andrews, secretary to Pro-Vice-Chancellors at the University of Durham, for her assistance with the preparation of the manuscript.

Chapter 1

The young child in the geographical world

INTRODUCTION

While the content of the National Curriculum for Schools in England underpins and guides the structure of the forthcoming text, this volume also discusses general principles of teaching and learning in geographical education that are transferable and applicable to all 'early years' children of nursery and school age. It is relevant to teachers, student teachers, policy-makers and all other providers of education for children aged 3 and 4 to 7 years; that is, the Foundation Stage and Key Stage 1 in the language of the National Curriculum.

We consider it to be both a difficult and inappropriate task to pursue any discussion of learning experiences relating to the subject matter of geography in the early years of schooling without making reference to the cross-curricular theme of education for sustainable development, closely allied to the area of learning which many know as environmental education. These two curriculum components are to a large extent inextricably linked in the work of nursery, reception and early primary classes; therefore, their inter-relationships are considered, and practical examples throughout the book take account of teaching and learning across the whole spectrum of geography and what might be termed 'environmental geography'.

The chief aim of this volume is to provide a text which is interesting, illuminative and, above all, helpful to teachers who are going about the complex task of developing worthwhile geographical education for children in nursery, reception, and Years 1 and 2 in primary school.

Essentially it sets about providing an overview of some of the more theoretical aspects of early years learning in geography, illuminated by up-to-date research findings; and illustrates these with discussion, case studies and suggestions for the development and implementation of sound geographical work in practice. It is intended, therefore, to be a judicious mix of theory and practice, enlivened throughout by practical examples deriving from a wide range of schools, classrooms and other educational settings.

Beyond a consideration of theoretical perspectives on learning and links between the subject matter of geography and education for sustainable development/environmental education, the text considers the critical topics of policy-making, organisation and planning, assessment and record-keeping, resources and activities for training and continuing professional development.

While geography in the early years of schooling is inevitably planned at the level of whole-school policy and approach, and implemented with class or year groups, the individual child is also inevitably at the heart of the learning process. Each child has a unique relationship with the world in which he or she is growing up: a relationship based on feelings, experiences and interactions with people, places, objects and events. It is hoped that this focus on 'the young child in the geographical world' extends beyond the heading for the book's opening chapter, and permeates readers' reflections on the text in its entirety.

It seems, therefore, only appropriate that the opening words of text set the scene by focusing on what young learners actually do think about aspects of our geographical world.

VIEWS OF THE WORLD

Stanley, from the north-east of England, aged 4

Researcher	We're going to look at pictures of a special place – what can we see?
Stanley	Trees and water.
Researcher	Good boy. What do we call a place where there's lots and lots of trees?
Stanley	A rain forest.
Researcher	How do you know that?
Stanley	Because my mummy tells me.
Researcher	Your mummy tells you. Good. Yes, that's a rain forest. A tropical rain forest in a country a long way away. So, Stanley, what do you know about rain forests?
Stanley	It's got snakes and jaguars and . . . I've been to a rain forest.
Researcher	You've been to a rain forest?
Stanley	Yes. I've seen snakes and rattlesnakes and nice green trees.
Researcher	Where did you go to a rain forest?
Stanley	In Spain.
Researcher	In Spain. Your mummy's told you about them. So you know about some of the animals in the forest?
Stanley	Yes.
Researcher	Have you seen rain forests in books?
Stanley	Yes. I've got a rain forest book.

Researcher	Let's look at some of the animals who live in a rain forest. Let's see if you know these rain forest animals. What do we have here?
Stanley	Gorilla, and jaguar. Don't know.
Researcher	Very good. This one's called a cheetah.
Stanley	Cheetah.
Researcher	And that one's called an orang-utan. And that one's called a chimpanzee. Do you think people live in rain forests?
Stanley	Some people live in rain forests who's in charge of it.
Researcher	Sometimes people come and cut down the trees. Is that a good idea or a bad idea?
Stanley	A bad idea.
Researcher	Right, Stanley, it's a bad idea. Why shouldn't we cut rain forests down?
Stanley	Because we won't be able to see the flowers, because the trees will fall on top of the flowers.
Researcher	Why else is it wrong to cut down all the trees in the forest?
Stanley	Because we won't see the flowers any more. The flowers get pulled off the branches, and then they go a different colour if you leave them on the park, on the grass.
Researcher	So we should look after rain forests, shouldn't we?
Stanley	Yes.
Researcher	Forests are important in the world. Do you know why forests are so important?
Stanley	Because there's nice things in there and good things. . . .
Researcher	Let's look at one more place. This isn't a rain forest – what do we have here?
Stanley	North Pole, that is.
Researcher	North Pole! Very good. What's this?
Stanley	Ice.
Researcher	Ice and snow. If the weather at the North Pole got hot, what would happen to all the snow at the North Pole?
Stanley	It would just melt.
Researcher	Well done. Do you know where the snow would go to? What would happen to it?
Stanley	It would just go and be gone for ever.
Researcher	Do you know where it would go? Would it just disappear?
Stanley	Yes. . . .
Researcher	Good boy. So we've got some beautiful places in our world, rain forests and the North Pole, and beautiful places with flowers. And we have to take care of them, don't we?
Stanley	Yes.
Researcher	Sometimes people spoil the world by throwing rubbish all over it.
Stanley	Yes, throwing rubbish all over the flowers and all on the floor to make it dirty.

Researcher	Is that wrong?
Stanley	Uh-huh.
Researcher	What should we do with the rubbish?
Stanley	Just throw it in the bin.
Researcher	Do you know where rubbish goes when it's in the bin?
Stanley	The bin men put it in their big truck.
Researcher	They do, and the truck takes it away. Do you know where the truck takes it?
Stanley	To their place.
Researcher	And do you know what happens to it? Can you guess?
Stanley	They put it into a black bin, and then give it to another bin man.
Researcher	Can you think of any other ways we can take care of our beautiful world?
Stanley	From not cutting down the trees.
Researcher	Not cutting down the trees, that's right.
Stanley	Not spoiling the flowers, not treading on the flowers, not going on to the grass and treading all on the flowers.
Researcher	That's right. Why should we look after our world?
Stanley	Yes, it's a very beautiful world.
Researcher	Do you take care of our world?
Stanley	Yes, I do.
Researcher	How could we help other people to know that they must take care of the world?
Stanley	But bad people kill elephants because of their tusks.
Researcher	So . . . do you think we should ever kill animals?
Stanley	No, we should look after them.
Researcher	Because they're part of our world, aren't they?
Stanley	But bull fights aren't very nice, are they?
Researcher	No.
Stanley	Yes, because they try and kill all the bulls, don't they?
Researcher	That's right.
Stanley	They tease them.
Researcher	That's right. And we shouldn't tease animals, should we?
Stanley	No, because that's naughty, isn't it?
Researcher	Do you think that when you grow up you will always want to take care of the world?
Stanley	Yes. When I grow up, I'm going to be an animal doctor.
Researcher	Right. That's a very good thing to want to be. So you're going to work very hard at school?
Stanley	Yes. I have to go to London to learn about it.
Researcher	Do you?
Stanley	Uh-huh.
Researcher	Right. So when you grow up, you're going to go to London. . . .
Stanley	Uh-huh.

| Researcher | ... and learn more about animals, because you want to learn how to look after them. |
| Stanley | Yes. |

Daniel, from the USA, aged 4

Researcher	So ... do you have any idea where those places may be?
Daniel	I think that's Hawaii.
Researcher	It's like Hawaii, isn't it? Good boy, Daniel. What can you see on the picture?
Daniel	Trees and bushes ...
Researcher	Well done.
Daniel	And a river.
Researcher	Lots of trees. This is a place called a forest. It's called a tropical rain forest.
Daniel	That's ... is that a tropical rain forest?
Researcher	Yes – do you know about them?
Daniel	'Cos I've seen Ronald McDonald, and he's in a tropical rain forest.
Researcher	Who's been in a tropical rain forest?
Daniel	Ronald McDonald.
Researcher	Who's that?
Daniel	He's a guy ... and it's a place where you can go and get happy meals ...
Researcher	Right. So you've seen pictures of a tropical rain forest there. In McDonald's?
Daniel	Yes.
Researcher	Good boy. So ... do you know what it's like in the forest, Daniel?
Daniel	Uh-huh. Sometimes you can see tigers.
Researcher	Good boy. What else might you see there?
Daniel	And lions ... and, and ... and frogs that are coloured. And ... toucan.
Researcher	Great.
Daniel	Tree frogs.
Researcher	You're an expert.
Daniel	Fox.
Researcher	Have you seen all these things in pictures in McDonald's?
Daniel	Yes.
Researcher	That's wonderful. Well, I have one or two pictures of things which live in the forest.
Daniel	That's, um ... that's an orang-utan.
Researcher	Well done!
Daniel	That ... those are chimpanzees.
Researcher	Daniel, you're an expert.

Daniel	That is um . . . a . . . called a cheetah.
Researcher	OK. And one of the big problems in rain forests is that people sometimes cut the trees down.
Daniel	Yeah – they shouldn't do that.
Researcher	Good boy. Do you know why they do it?
Daniel	Because they need wood to build their houses.
Researcher	Excellent, Daniel.
Daniel	And firewood for them.
Researcher	And do you know what else they do with the wood they cut down?
Daniel	They make stuff out of it.
Researcher	Right. Why is it a real bad idea to cut the trees down?
Daniel	Because then the rain forest just becomes a whole all dead place.
Researcher	Well done, Daniel. That is right. So what would happen to the animals?
Daniel	They'd die.
Researcher	And the people who live there?
Daniel	They'd die too. . . .
Researcher	And my other place we have . . .
Daniel	Ugh!
Researcher	This place. Now that's not like a rain forest, is it?
Daniel	That is . . . um . . . er . . . that looks like . . . um . . . that looks like . . . um . . . Iceland.
Researcher	Well done. It's a very very snowy land, so that isn't like a rain forest. A rain forest is hot hot, and this is cold cold.
Daniel	I like cool air.
Researcher	Do you? Yes, I do too. If this place got hot like a forest, what would happen to the snow?
Daniel	All of it would melt.
Researcher	What happens to snow when it melts?
Daniel	It becomes . . . everything becomes clean.
Researcher	Right. And where would the snow go?
Daniel	It just evaporates . . .
Researcher	I can see that you like looking at pictures and reading a lot of books.
Daniel	I read . . . I read stories. And I even have . . . been reading a story about a man named Stuart Liddell. What's the next picture?
Researcher	That's another snowy place.
Daniel	Hey, it has some flowers.
Researcher	Right. So this is such a beautiful world that we live in, and some people don't take care of it. Do you know how people can spoil the world?
Daniel	Like chopping down all the trees and stepping on all the flowers.

Researcher	That's right. Any other ways?
Daniel	Yes. Killing animals . . . killing people.
Researcher	That's good, Daniel. Those are wrong things to do. Another way people can spoil the world is by throwing trash and garbage around the place. That's not a good idea, is it?
Daniel	They should either throw it away or recycle it.
Researcher	Excellent! And do you recycle yours?
Daniel	Sometimes. And we . . . and we throw it away, and give it to the garbage van.
Researcher	Right. So . . . could you just tell me about recycling, 'cos you're an expert on all these things. What does recycling mean?
Daniel	Recycling means saving the trash, and make old things into new things.
Researcher	That's wonderful. What sort of things can we make into new things?
Daniel	Cans.
Researcher	Right.
Daniel	. . . bottles . . . newspaper . . . comics.
Researcher	Right, right. And do you know why we need to make new things out of . . .
Daniel	Old things.
Researcher	. . . waste things.
Daniel	'Cos that helps the world be healthy.
Researcher	That's a wonderful answer, Daniel. It does help the world be healthy. Could you just say a little bit more about that? How does recycling help the world be healthy?
Daniel	By keeping all the trackways in the world clean. And by saving trees and animals.

Stanley and Daniel know a great deal about the world in which they are growing up. They know that forests contain trees, animals and birds. They can identify a number of species. They appreciate that places can be hot or cold, and that if snow gets warmer it melts away or evaporates. They also appreciate that the correct place for waste materials is in rubbish bins. Daniel is even capable of explaining the concept of recycling.

There are, of course, obvious gaps and errors in the knowledge of Stanley and Daniel. This subject will be returned to later in the chapter.

But before pursuing this intriguing topic of knowledge expressed by 4 year olds themselves, attention first focuses on rather more theoretical perspectives on the young child in the geographical world.

As attention turns to this context, perhaps it should be emphasised that the 'essence' of geography in the early years is concerned with children's developing understanding and appreciation of the human and physical dimensions of the world in which they are growing up. Early years geographical education must therefore take account of wide-ranging theoretical perspectives relating to developing conceptions of the physical environment and understanding of the world, which combine to influence children's thinking and learning in this curriculum area. In short, early years geography is fundamentally about the development of the concepts of 'space' and 'place' and, as we shall see later in this book, a wide range of classroom tasks and related learning activities can contribute to effective learning of these concepts. Practical tasks with which children may engage to promote meaningful learning in geography draw upon a complex theoretical framework. Present space clearly does not allow for a comprehensive overview and analysis of this. Thus it is intended to highlight a number of key elements of the framework and to illuminate these with recent and relevant research evidence.

CONCEPTION OF THE PHYSICAL ENVIRONMENT

Surprisingly little has been written for early years teachers about the origins of children's subject knowledge and conceptual development in the areas of geography and environmental education; that is, areas concerned with cognition of physical systems, spatial relationships, processes and environmental issues. Existing research literature defines and describes the term 'environmental cognition', or the ability to imagine and think about the spatial world, encompassing general ways of thinking about, recognising and organising the physical layout of an environment.

The most substantial body of research on children's conception of the physical environment has been undertaken by Jean Piaget (1960a, 1960b, 1954). His general findings were replicated with much larger samples by Laurendeau and Pinard (1962). Piaget's initial research consideration relating to a child's conception of the world is 'realism', that is, whether external reality is as external and objective for a child as it is for adults. In other words, can a child distinguish the self from the external world? Realism equates to ignoring the existence of self; to drawing boundaries between one's internal world and the physical world. Piaget (1954) describes three processes involved in the evolution of the construction of reality between the ages of 3 and 11. The first of these is the progressive differentiation of the self from physical surroundings, so that an individual can distinguish what comes from within oneself and what is part of the external world.

The second process involved in the evolution of the construction of reality is 'greater reciprocity' or recognising other points of view. In the early years, children take their immediate perceptions to be true instead of recognising the uniqueness of their own perspective. Piaget uses the example of the young child who thinks that the sun and moon are small globes following us as we walk along; the question does not arise as to whether these globes also follow other people.

Piaget's third process is 'from realism to relativity'. Young children think of everything as absolute substance and quality. Gradually, they come to see objects and phenomena as dependent on each other and relative to us. The clouds provide an example: at first, these are thought to move by themselves. Gradually, children become aware that they move with the wind, but still believe that they have their own energy and direct themselves. Later, they come to realise that there are other forces which determine the motion of natural objects (e.g. the wind) and that in turn these are dependent upon other external forces. Ultimately, the idea of the existence of a universe of relationships is established. Parallel to this growing relativity of children's understanding of physical properties, objects and qualities is the developing conception that their own ideas are relative to themselves and to their own evaluations of things.

Piaget's account of children's developing understanding of physical causality (Piaget 1960b) follows a similar pattern to his account of developing conception of reality. In both these processes, the young begin by recognising only their personal point of view, thus confusing themselves and the external environment. Gradually, they move towards greater objectivity, reciprocity and relativity.

The essence of Piaget's developmental theory has been challenged and criticised in more recent years, notably by the development psychologist Vygotsky, who claims that the developmental uniformities found by Piaget are not laws of nature but are 'historically and socially determined' (Vygotsky 1979). His extensive work reveals that cognitive development is influenced by the materials which children experience and the cultural situations in which they are interpreted (see also Donaldson 1978 and 1992). While recent research calls Piaget's stages of development into question, the misinterpretations of reality first described by Piaget have been repeatedly found, a fact relevant to the development of programmes of work for teaching and learning experiences in geography and environmental education. Children have a definite tendency to accept the world around them as it is perceived or 'given' through observation. Their own feelings and abilities are also projected into an interpretation of physical entities and space. Thus confusions are created which may lead to erroneous understandings about objects and places. A teacher's role clearly involves having some understanding of such confusions and misinterpretations, and the ability to design learning tasks which take account of them.

UNDERSTANDING THE WORLD

Planning a curriculum and learning experiences about the geographical world need to take account of the learners' understanding of their environment, their interactions with it and sources of information about it. The chief source of environmental knowledge is a child's own direct experience of people, objects and places, supplemented by indirect information such as that from photographs, maps, other people's descriptions and media images (see, for example, Vosniadou and Brewer, 1992; Wiegand, 1992). From this combination of sources the child can build up a knowledge of where places and objects are in the world, and a set of ideas and attitudes about such places. In general, the ability to imagine and think about the world around us is referred to as environmental cognition. Environmental knowledge that an individual has already acquired is often described as a 'cognitive map', or mental model of the environment (see, for example, Stea *et al.* 1996). Such maps or models are personal representations of the world, and their form is complex and controversial. Perhaps the word 'map' is misleading – cognitive maps are not the same as cartographic maps either in physical form or in content. They are sketchy, incomplete, distorted, simplified and idiosyncratic (Devlin 1976; Evans 1980). It is possible to think of them as composed of three elements: places, the spatial relations between places and travel plans (Garling *et al.* 1984). Places refer to the basic spatial units that we attach information to, such as name, function and perceptual characteristics. A place may be a room, building, neighbourhood, town, nation or the whole world. Spatial characteristics of cognitive maps include the distance and direction between places and the inclusion of one place within another (a room is inside a particular building, in a town, in a nation and so on). The concept of travel plans refers to the crucial bridge between the mental world of cognitive maps and practical behaviours (such as finding our way from one place to another) which they support. As would be anticipated, research studies have shown that the more familiar an individual is with an environment, the more accurate and detailed his or her cognitive map will be (Appleyard 1970; Garling *et al.* 1982). The quantity of information stored in memory about a place increases with experience of that place. Inevitably, children have far less direct contact with places than adults, and many environments of the world will be outside their personal experience. Furthermore, differences between children's and adults' cognitive maps reflect not merely differing levels of experience but also different approaches to problem-solving. Again, the research findings of Piaget and his associates are highly relevant to any discussion on the acquisition of cognitive maps. The research of Piaget and Inhelder (1967) probably provides the most influential theory of cognitive development as applied to spatial cognition. This incorporates a study wherein children were asked to sit on a chair and look at a table on which were placed three model mountains. Three other chairs were placed around the table, and a doll was seated on one of them. From a set of drawings each child was asked to select a view of the scene as the doll would see it. Children below the ages of 7 or 8 typically described the scene as they saw it rather than from the perspective of the doll. Piaget termed this phenomenon egocentrism. During this developmental phase of egocentricity, the child's frame of reference is him/herself. The environment is fragmented and features of it are disconnected. At a later stage, a child's cognitive map is orientated around fixed places in the environment that the child has experience of, but not necessarily the place in which he or she is now situated. Finally, the child's frame of reference assumes more objective representation with accurate spatial connections. Hart and Moore (1973) propose an elaboration of Piaget's findings and suggest that, when developing cognitive mapping abilities, children progress through three sequential stages involving progressively more complex frames of reference. First, there is an undifferentiated 'egocentric reference system' in which the image consists only of those elements in the environment that are of great personal significance. Second, there is a 'partially co-ordinated reference system' in which several clusters of points demonstrate a knowledge of the relationships between landmarks (e.g. distinctive features such as buildings, monuments) and paths (e.g. streets, footpaths, rivers), but where these clusters are not related to each other. Finally, children develop an 'operationally co-ordinated and hierarchically integrated reference system' in which the environmental image is organised into a single spatial reference system.

Subsequent studies have generally confirmed Piaget's observations that pre-school children demonstrate egocentrism, though there is debate and controversy on whether this is a reflection of a truly different way of thinking or a slow increase in the quantity of environmental information and cognitive skills (Bell *et al.* 1990). Research done in large-scale environments has found young children to be more capable of accurate cognitive mapping than that done in studies using models (Cousins *et al.* 1983). Further work on the accuracy and complexity of cognitive maps (Siegel and White 1975) suggests that there are four sequential developmental stages in children's representations of the spatial environment. First, landmarks (distinctive features which are important to the child) are noticed and remembered, followed by paths between landmarks. At stage three, landmarks and paths are organised into clusters or minimaps, and, finally, these clusters along with other features are correctly co-ordinated into an overall framework or complete representation of the environment. Thus Siegel and White's evidence, which draws on a number of different empirical studies, supports the existence of a series of developmental stages in cognitive mapping ability. Despite widespread support for this theory, it should be noted that related evidence derives in the main from indirect methods of testing children's memories and knowledge of their environment, such as maps and models. Other studies, which have directly tested environmental cognition (e.g. Cornell and Heth 1983) by taking children on walks outdoors, have revealed the ease with which young subjects can accurately retrace a route, having only walked along it once before. Darvizeh and Spencer (1984) show that children's memory for a route can be significantly improved when their attention is drawn to appropriate landmarks along the way. Thus they conclude that, instead of explaining children's developing environmental cognition by a series of fixed stages, it may be more appropriate to consider their achievement in terms of their ability to apply efficient strategies for selecting appropriate information from the environment. Even very young children can remember a great deal about a route after limited experience of it, but they may not be as aware of or knowledgeable about the route as older subjects because of their more limited ability to note information about it as they travel along. A detailed review and discussion of research on the development of spatial knowledge and a child's changing environmental needs is provided by Spencer *et al.* (1989). They emphasise the processes of environmental cognition (cognitive mapping, acquisition of spatial information, images of places) as well as its development. Further reference to each of these processes will be made in the context of discussion of practical examples, throughout the remaining chapters of this volume.

NEAR AND FAR

The development of environmental cognition covers a range of space-related concepts, including the child's developing body-image, the location of objects in close space and understanding of geographical scale space, and the emergence of concepts about distant places. Examples in this book cover this range and illuminate the young child's ever-expanding awareness of the physical world. Some researchers (Welsh and Blasch 1980) have stressed the importance of a developmental sequence of spatial understanding, wherein the child must first achieve an 'integrated image' of body-layout with body-part co-ordination, extend this framework of reference to the immediate world, with a focus on location of objects in near space, and then proceed outward from this to consider and understand the spatial inter-relationships between objects and places. Others (Pick and Lockman 1981) argue that an individual does not have to achieve complete mastery of the first frame of reference before proceeding to the next. Furthermore, once mastered, we can use any one or a combination of these reference systems. Spencer *et al.* (1989) provide a detailed review of each stage/frame of reference with discussion of further research evidence that illuminates this developmental question.

One of the most important messages that emerges from research done in this general field of environmental cognition and development of spatial awareness is that young children are remarkably good at learning. They are certainly ready for and are indeed using geographical concepts and understandings as early as 4–5 years of age. They have thought about their immediate space and local environment: about routes and landmarks, about distant places, about our planet, and have acquired skills of investigation and understanding. The following brief glimpse at research evidence certainly reveals a strong basis for the foundation of geographical understanding in the early years.

Cornell and Hay (1984) show the success of personal experience or active exploration in route learning. Children aged 5–8 were asked to view a route either by a slide presentation, a video-tape or by walking the route with a leader. The route was viewed only once, then they had to retrace it in the same medium. Results showed little difference between children using slide or video-tape, but significantly fewer errors were made by the children who actively experienced the route. Landmarks and directions were recalled, and subjects could find their way back to the start.

Blaut (1997) and Spencer *et al.* (1997) demonstrate the ability of young children to learn about mapping from aerial photographs. It is clear that young children can readily understand and work with aerial images and that these images are conceptually within their grasp (Spencer 1998). Also in the realm of early years mapwork, Atkins (1981) taught children aged 4–5 about maps, globes and compass directions, then compared this group to another which had not received instruction. The experimental group performed better than the control group in tests immediately after the instruction and again a year later. The Blaut, Spencer and Atkins studies demonstrate abilities in the field of 'graphicacy' in children much younger than the age that many have associated with the commencement of mapwork understanding. Blades and Spencer (1986) report similar findings and conclude that children may well be able to learn skills of mapwork before they reach the 'projective' stage of spatial development at the age of 7–8. Following on from this early study, Blades and Spencer (1987a) carried out an experiment to test children's understanding of maps and their ability to cope with symbols: 4–6 year olds were asked to name features on a specially designed map.

> Although imaginary, the map was intended to represent a possible urban environment, with roads (grey) lined by small and large houses (red). There were two roundabouts at road junctions. To the south-west two roads crossed by bridges over a river (blue) and to the east there was a road bridge over a railway line (black). In the north-east, a large irregular area was coloured green to represent a park or playing field. The map also included symbols for particular buildings; two 'churches' (shown as black crosses), two 'schools' (shown in 'playgrounds') and in the south-east corner, three black oblongs to represent a 'station' next to the railway lines.
>
> (Blades and Spencer 1987a)

One hundred and eight children between the ages of 4 and 6 took part in this experiment. Half were asked to name the symbols as each one was pointed out to them on the map. There were ten symbols altogether (road, river, park, roundabout, bridge, school, church, railway, station and house). The other half of the children were given the names of each feature and were asked to point to an example of the symbol representing that feature on the map. By the age of 6, nearly all the children could identify the majority of the symbols on the map. Even the 4 year olds could recognise at least half of the symbols.

> Very few children failed to recognise anything at all on the map or describe it simply in terms of lines, shapes or colours. It was easier for children to find examples of named features than to have to suggest names for the symbols on the map. Not all the symbols were of equal difficulty; roads, river, and park were easily identified by nearly all the children, but the symbols for station, church and school were harder to identify, though by the age of 6, children were able to suggest quite appropriate definitions (such as 'hospital' or 'factory').
> The results from this experiment and the findings from the research into children's ability to understand aerial photographs indicate that young children can appreciate a view of the world from above, even when, as in the case with the map, the view is one that is conventionalised and includes symbols.
>
> (Spencer *et al.* 1989)

A further element of mapwork that has come under research scrutiny is co-ordinates. Many maps use co-ordinate reference systems so that particular locations can be identified by a grid reference relating to a series of horizontal and vertical grid lines. While some research (Piaget *et al.* 1960) has suggested that children cannot accurately locate a point in space until around the age of 8, other findings reinforce the view that much younger children are capable of demonstrating skills of graphicacy. Somerville and Bryant (1985) show that 4–6 year olds are capable of using co-ordinates in simple tasks. In their studies, children were shown an opaque square board that was placed over two rods; one rod protruded from the left or right side of the board, thus providing a horizontal co-ordinate, and the other protruded from the top or bottom of the board, providing a vertical co-ordinate. The subjects were asked to extrapolate from the visible portions of the rods and indicate where they thought the rods crossed under the board by selecting one of four given points marked on top of the board. Results showed that children as young as 4 and a half years could do this task successfully, and that most aged 6 and a half could be successful in a number of variations on the basic task. Further experiments by Blades and Spencer (1987a) investigate whether young children can use a grid reference system: 4–6 year olds were tested using a board that incorporated 16 sunken squares in a 4 × 4 layout. Each square contained a different picture, hidden by a cardboard cover. Vertical and horizontal co-ordinate lines were drawn across the board and intersected over the centre of each covered picture. The vertical co-ordinates were numbered 1, 2, 3, 4, and the horizontal co-ordinates were lettered a, b, c, d. The children were given a grid reference card (e.g. 4a, 1c) and a copy of the correct hidden picture was fixed to the back of the card. The children's task was to find the appropriate square on the board for a given grid reference. After a square had been selected, the cover could be removed so that its picture could be checked for match with that on the back of the grid reference card. Results showed that the majority of the 6 year olds could perform this task successfully; but only a small percentage of the younger children could do so.

A follow-up experiment was performed with another group of children of similar age. This time each grid co-ordinate was labelled with a different colour. (It was hypothesised that perhaps in the original experiment the younger children may have been confused because they were not proficient with the alphabet or numbers.) The grid reference in this second experiment was a card with two colours on it, one for the horizontal co-ordinate and one for the vertical co-ordinate. Results this time showed that half the 4 year olds and the majority of 5 and 6 year olds were successful in the given task, confirming the hypothesis that results in the previous experiment may have been affected by inability to read letters or numbers. The combined results of Somerville and Bryant and Blades and Spencer suggest that 4 year olds are capable of using a grid co-ordinate reference system. As with other elements of mapwork, we may conclude that young children's competence in this area has for a long time been underestimated and underdeveloped in school-based learning tasks.

A similar trend emerges in the area of map use. Bluestein and Acredolo (1979) showed children aged 3 to 5 a map of a small rectangular room with table, chairs and four identical green boxes which could serve as hiding places for a small toy. The boxes were placed at the mid-point of each wall. In one corner of the room was a door and in each of the other three corners were objects, e.g. a red box. The children were shown on a map the box that contained the hidden toy. Then they were asked to find the correct box in the actual room. The children were shown the map either inside or outside the room and it was either correctly orientated with the room or rotated through 180 degrees relative to it. Of the children who saw the map in the room correctly orientated, half the 3 year olds, three-quarters of the 4 year olds and all the 5 year olds could find the toy successfully. Only the 5 year olds could use the map correctly when it was rotated. A key conclusion from this work is that children as young as 3 years can use a map in certain circumstances.

Other experiments confirm that children of a very young age can use a map to find a particular object or place. In so doing, they show a tendency to refer to landmarks on the map or on the 'ground'. The ability to use landmarks effectively has been demonstrated by indoor 'laboratory' experiments as well as by studies of children finding their way in actual environments (Darvizeh and Spencer 1984). Blades and Spencer (1986) also suggest that it is possible to teach 4 year olds how to orientate simple maps. They showed children how to align an incorrectly orientated map so that it corresponded to a layout before they attempted to use the map to find a place in the layout. The majority of the children who were shown how to align the map learnt to do this speedily and could apply the same skills in different situations. A more complex test has been devised (Blades and Spencer 1987b) to find out if young children can use a map to navigate through an environment that is not completely visible. A 25-metre-long maze was drawn on the surface of a school playground. Within this maze were three T-junctions, and large screens were placed across the pathways in front of the junctions in order to limit the children's view across the maze. Wooden boxes were placed across the paths to serve as 'roadblocks' and the position of these was hidden by the screens. Thus the children could not see them before making a route choice at each of the T-junctions. The subjects were then given a map of the maze showing the positions of the roadblocks. This map was attached to a clipboard so that it could be carried as they walked through the maze. Their task was to navigate through the maze without bumping into any of the roadblocks: 60 children in five age groups between 3 and 6 years had six trials each at the maze. For each trial, the positions of the roadblocks were changed. The majority of children in all age groups except the very youngest were able to use their maps effectively to find their route through the maze.

> The maze experiment demonstrated that from the age of 4 years children could use a simple map to follow a route, and their improved performance when the landmarks were present suggests that the children were sensitive to any additional information provided by the map.
>
> (Spencer *et al.* 1989)

Thus a number of studies demonstrate that very young children can use simple maps to find places, to follow routes and to locate landmarks.

> Untrained children from the age of 3 or 4 years have an appreciation of a two-dimensional representation of a given area. This is considerably earlier than might be expected from the interpretations of Piaget's theory of spatial development, which imply that such young children are too limited in their understanding of spatial relationships.
>
> (Spencer *et al.* 1989)

The concluding message for educators is, of course, that it is feasible to start teaching elements of mapwork and aspects of the use of maps to children as young as 4 years of age.

Further illumination of young children's capacity for geographical/environmental learning is provided by research on their images and understanding of distant places, of which they have no direct experience. Once again, a similar pattern of conclusions emerges: children are remarkably good at learning about other lands and peoples, albeit from secondary source materials. They have a 'world inside their heads', derived from constant interactions with the media (TV, films, newspapers), travel advertisements, books and descriptions by other people. Young children know that there is a 'world out there' – from the news, from international take-away food shops, from foreign presenters of children's TV programmes and from story books, among numerous other incidental contacts with distant places and people of other nationalities. This topic will be explored at greater depth in Chapter 4, but at this stage further dimensions of young children's geographical learning must be introduced.

Considerable evidence has already been referred to which demonstrates that children are efficient learners and bring a sound basis of geographical knowledge into the classroom as and when they start school. Yet they also bring gaps in knowledge, erroneous knowledge and perhaps biased/stereo-typical knowledge which the teacher needs to be well aware of in order to design appropriate learning tasks. Research on children's images of distant lands illustrates this point well.

Piaget made a substantial contribution to the understanding of a child's developing concepts of his or her own area, town, region and country, paying attention to conceptual development rather than sources of information. According to Piaget's study (1960a) there are three broad stages in the child's development of the idea of country. In the first instance, a country is 'simply a unit along with towns and districts', which the child believes are of similar size. Next is a stage in which the child knows that a district is within a country and yet it is spoken of as if it were a piece of land 'enclosed within a foreign country'. In the third stage, the child acquires a correct idea of the relationship – one can belong to a town, a district and a country at the same time. This work does not consider yet more distant places. Later studies have replicated and extended Piaget's work. Piché (1981) interviewed 5–8 year olds on their expanding understanding of the world, from most local to most distant places. It was found that 5 year olds will describe a building, a district, a city and a country as the same kind of place because one can go there. For many children of this age, all places that are not home are in a category of 'elsewhere'. This fact aside, a great deal of information is acquired by young minds about 'elsewhere' from the media and other incidental contacts. The question must then be asked – what is the status of this 'knowledge' that is acquired? Tajfel (1981) argues that children are capable of absorbing attitudes and prejudices about other people and nations well before they have any factual information about them:

> The young child is at an early, but important stage in the development of a social identity – related to the in-and-out groups as specified by the surrounding culture; and the acquisition and interpretation of factual information about own group and other groups will be related to this frame of reference. In other words, information will be selectively sought, received and remembered, in ways that are supportive of pre-existing (pre-judged) categories.
>
> (Tajfel 1981)

Stillwell and Spencer (1974) demonstrated the role of educational media in changing children's knowledge of and feelings for other countries. They investigated the influence of wallcharts and classroom displays on the development of primary school pupils' attitudes towards other nations. Nine year olds were interviewed about their knowledge of and feelings towards four countries: India, Germany, the USA and the USSR. Displays of wallcharts depicting street scenes, transport, local dress and the world position of those countries were then put up in the classroom for a week, with no accompanying teaching or discussion. After this time, the children were interviewed once again, and revealed a significant increase in information about all four countries. Of noticeable importance was the children's changing preferences for these countries. In the initial interviews they had been strongly pro-USA and anti-German, with India and the USSR being on the positive side of neutral. After the displays and increased knowledge about these places, the USA remained popular, Germany became strongly positive, the USSR remained relatively neutral, and India moved to a position of negative preference. Children initially stressed the differences between Britain and Germany, claiming that towns, clothes and skin colour were 'different from here'. The USA was strongly supported initially as it was believed to be 'like us, only better'. These findings are in line with those of Jaspars *et al.* (1963) who found that children preferred the countries that they saw as near to their own in cognitive space. In the Stillwell and Spencer experiment, initially the USSR and India had been largely unknown lands – neither apparently like us nor obviously different. The effect of the displays was remarkable – children who had previously perceived great differences between Britain and Germany saw photographs of similar environments. Thus preferences were shifted from the negative to the positive. The USA was confirmed as 'bigger and better', and the USSR was confirmed as being just a little different from Britain. India shifted its position to being negative, through pictures that set a scene of being 'not like us'. From this study, it may be concluded that the provision of accurate information in educational circumstances may not necessarily increase understanding and resultant positive acceptance of a nation and its people. This study was conducted with 9 year olds, but its results are transferable to a younger age. Stereotypes exist in young minds, and knowledge and information may be used to measure the similarity of a nation against our own, which is inevitably valued.

The popular media also provide a strong influence on the development of the 'world inside children's minds'. A survey of American children's images of Africa (Birns in Spencer *et al.* [1989]) reveals words such as 'wild animals, jungles, witch doctors, and Daktari' as being uppermost in their minds – conjured up largely by a popular television programme. Along similar lines, Storm (1984) reported word-association tests with children of primary school age. Results showed that the words most commonly associated with 'Africa' were 'lions', 'heat', 'snakes', 'elephants', 'trees', 'tigers', 'palm trees' and 'black people', conjuring up images of the exotic, colour and perhaps the excitement of Africa derived from 'jungle' films and programmes on TV – images far removed from many of the realities of everyday life there today in the shape of poverty and cities.

Crucial issues to bear in mind when approaching and planning the study of distant lands with young children are thus stereotyping, bias and often incomplete or erroneous subject knowledge which may be brought to the classroom. Perhaps it should also be pointed out that the situation may not be helped by a teacher's genuine ignorance of particular facts or biased viewpoint about a place, perhaps arising from specific media coverage or a holiday in an atypical part of the land. The teacher's task is thus a complex and difficult one. It is to build upon the existing knowledge base of the children, yet the teacher has to bear in mind the problems and limitations of this as identified. In an ideal world, by being provided with appropriate accurate information, leading to an appreciation of environmental conditions different from our own, and by building up a more coherent and complete picture of the place being studied, the confused infant will emerge into an adult with accurate and unbiased views of people and places. Unfortunately, the world of school classrooms is perhaps not that ideal.

KNOWLEDGE OR CONCERN?

So far this chapter has illuminated and discussed aspects of children's early learning about the geographical world. It has, we hope, delivered the powerful message that young children are remarkably good at learning about their surroundings, even though elements of this resultant subject knowledge may be incomplete, biased or prejudiced. Research evidence has traditionally concentrated on what children know and can do: the development of those elements of knowledge, skills and concepts which underpin geographical and environmental understanding. Yet if environmental education is at least in part about the development of awareness and positive attitudes towards taking care of the world, it follows that an equally important area for consideration in the planning of appropriate teaching and learning tasks should be the development of children's attitudes towards and concern *for* the environment. An ongoing research study at the University of Durham (Palmer and Suggate 2004) provides some interesting and important insights into the development of both subject knowledge and concern. This research study as a whole investigates 'emergent environmentalism', that is, the development of subject knowledge and concern for the environment in both children and adults. The element of the study involving pre-school children illuminates many issues relevant to geographical and environmental education in the early years that underpin a good deal of the case study work outlined in this book.

Present space allows for only a brief overview of this extensive work, yet provides a 'flavour' of its findings. Young children attending nursery schools in a number of countries, including the UK, USA, Greece and Slovenia, have been interviewed on an individual basis about global environmental issues including rain forests/deforestation, polar lands/global warming and waste management. An autobiographical, discussion approach was used to find out as much as possible about the 4-year-olds' knowledge of and concern for these issues. Photographs were used to stimulate discussion between each child and the researcher. The aims of the semi-structured interviews were to ascertain:

- what the children knew and understood about these issues, if anything;
- the sources of their knowledge;
- the extent to which the children were aware of these topics as issues about which people should be concerned.

A second substantive ongoing project, related to the above, focuses on young children's developing understanding of local wetland environments [A European Commission funded research study entitled The Integrated Management of European Wetlands]. Based at the University of Durham and linking with researchers in Romania, Greece, Finland and Lithuania, this inter-disciplinary study incorporates an investigation into 4-year-olds' emerging knowledge and understanding of wetlands and of the inter-relationships that exist among people, fish, birds and other elements of such habitats.

Extracts from the interviews with Stanley (UK) and Daniel (USA) were provided at the beginning of the chapter. There now follows a series of abbreviated extracts illuminating aspects of other children's thinking on issues discussed.

On rain forests, trees and animals

John (USA)

Researcher	What do you see there?
John	A lake . . .
Researcher	Right. And . . .?
John	Palm trees.
Researcher	Lots of trees. So do you know what sort of place this is?
John	A desert?
Researcher	Ah, no, not a desert. Deserts don't have too many trees and water. It's called a forest.
John	I wanted to say that.
Researcher	Right, no problem. And this forest is called a tropical rain forest. Not heard of one of those?
John	No.

Researcher	Right. I wonder what lives in a tropical rain forest. I wonder why it's called a rain forest. Could you guess the answer: Why do you think it's called a rain forest?
John	Because there's lots of . . . like, rain.
Researcher	That's right, John. And I wonder who lives in the forest. Can you think?
John	A lion?
Researcher	May do. Right. Good boy. Lots of animals live here.
John	Tiger?
Researcher	Lots and lots of animals, and here's some of them. So what do we see here?
John	A cheetah.
Researcher	Well done! Good boy – how did you know that was a cheetah?
John	Because my brother is older than me . . .
Researcher	And he shows you pictures of them?
John	Yes.
Researcher	Good. And what sort of animals are here that live in the forest?
John	Monkeys.
Researcher	They're monkeys – and these are another sort of monkey, these are chimpanzees. And the forest has frogs and birds and beautiful flowers.
John	At Rhode Island I found lots of frogs . . .
Researcher	You know, John, these forests have got problems because sometimes people chop the trees down. Do you know why they do that?
John	Why?
Researcher	Well, they use the wood.
John	Oh, yeah – to use wood for fire.
Researcher	To make a fire. What else may they use the wood for?
John	Make a house.
Researcher	Right. And do you think it's a good idea to chop the trees down?
John	No.
Researcher	No it isn't. Why is it a bad idea?
John	Because the trees will die and we need them to breathe air.
Researcher	We need them to . . . ?
John	To breathe air.
Researcher	How do you know about that?
John	My mom told me.

Jeffrey (USA)

Researcher	What can you see here?
Jeffrey	Um . . . I can see some water.
Researcher	Right. And what else can you see here?

Jeffrey	Um . . . trees.
Researcher	Lots of trees. So this is a place where we have lots and lots of trees. Do you know what we call a place where there are lots of trees?
Jeffrey	Water?
Researcher	We call this a forest.
Jeffrey	Forest . . .
Researcher	This place is called a tropical rain forest.
Jeffrey	A tropical rain forest.
Researcher	I wonder why it's called a rain forest?
Jeffrey	Because it rains so much.
Researcher	That's very good – because it has lots of rain. It's very hot and it has lots of rain. And . . . I wonder who lives in the forest?
Jeffrey	Ah . . . snakes, foxes . . . and wolves.
Researcher	And wolves.
Jeffrey	Specially in the dark . . . specially when it's night time.
Researcher	How do you know about forests, Jeffrey?
Jeffrey	Because I've seen pictures.
Researcher	You've seen pictures. Pictures in books?
Jeffrey	Yes.
Researcher	Let's look at some pictures of some of the animals who live in the forest.
Jeffrey	A gorilla . . . I think I've seen him when I've been to the zoo.
Researcher	You saw him in the zoo? Right, good boy.
Jeffrey	And I saw these . . . ah . . .
Researcher	They're called cheetahs . . .
Jeffrey	Cheetahs . . . I saw some cheetahs. Do they have any . . . do you have any snakes?
Researcher	There are snakes in the forest . . .
Jeffrey	My dad's seen snakes . . . he's seen snakes . . . when he's been running . . . [more discussion about animals, birds, flowers]
Researcher	Do you know why they might do that? [cut down trees]
Jeffrey	Why? To make a house or a cabin.
Researcher	Right, good boy. So they might use the wood from the trees to make their house. So is that a good idea to cut down trees?
Jeffrey	No. [shakes head]
Researcher	Why is it not a good idea?
Jeffrey	Because then you waste wood.
Researcher	That's very good.

On warming of the world

Carl (UK)

Researcher	What do you think this place is like?

Carl	Snowy.
Researcher	So is it hot or cold?
Carl	Cold.
Researcher	If it got hot, what do you think would happen to the snow?
Carl	Melt.
Researcher	Well done, that's very good. And what happens to snow when it melts?
Carl	It would be gone.
Researcher	Do you know where it would go to?
Carl	To the forest.
Researcher	You think the snow would go to the forest?
Carl	Everywhere.
Researcher	Right. So the snow would go from the North Pole . . . and where would it go to?
Carl	To Santa Claus' house.
Researcher	To Santa Claus' house?
Carl	'Cos Santa Claus makes the snow, doesn't he?

Jocelyn (USA)

Researcher	What do you think this place is like?
Jocelyn	Snowy.
Researcher	So is this a hot place?
Jocelyn	No!
Researcher	If this place got hot, what would happen to the snow?
Jocelyn	Melt!
Researcher	Right. You know about that . . .
Jocelyn	I like deep, fresh snow.
Researcher	If the snow melts, do you know where it goes?
Jocelyn	Where?
Researcher	Do you know? What may happen to it?
Jocelyn	Turns into water.
Researcher	Right. And where does the water go?
Jocelyn	Into bays.
Researcher	Well done! Do you know what a bay is?
Jocelyn	Place where a lot of water runs, and where people come to sit on the sand.
Researcher	Right. And then . . . where does the water in the bays go to?
Jocelyn	Well, I don't really know that.
Researcher	Well, that's part of the sea, you know, the big oceans in our world.

Eleanor (USA)

Researcher	. . . What do you think would happen to the snow?
Eleanor	The snow would melt.

Researcher	Well done. Where would it go?
Eleanor	Where?
Researcher	Mmm. Where does snow go when it melts? What happens to it?
Eleanor	It . . . it disappears.
Researcher	Right. Do you know where it disappears to?
Eleanor	The water.
Researcher	Into the water. And where's the water?
Eleanor	It's the sea.
Researcher	That's right. So if that place got warm, there would be no snow.
Eleanor	There'd be water . . . it would all be water.

On waste materials

Kelly (USA)

Kelly	Yeah – they throw litter on the ground and in the water . . .
Researcher	Right.
Kelly	. . . and that's so bad.
Researcher	Right. What do you do with your litter?
Kelly	Er . . . you throw it in the trash can.
Researcher	Good girl. Do you know what happens to it when it's in the trash can?
Kelly	Er . . . The garbage man came and makes new stuff out of it.
Researcher	That's very good. Do you know what we call it when we make new stuff out of it?
Kelly	Er . . .
Researcher	There's a special word for it.
Kelly	It calls . . . recycling.
Researcher	Well done, Kelly. You know a lot about these things. How do you know all this?
Kelly	Mm . . . 'cos my daddy told me about it.
Researcher	And how do you know about recycling?
Kelly	Er . . . heard it on TV.
Researcher	OK. Is your family really good at recycling?
Kelly	Yeah.
Researcher	Do you know why recycling is very, very important?
Kelly	Uh-huh . . . 'Cos it makes . . . it can make new paper out of newspaper, that calls recycling.

Danielle (UK)

Researcher	What happens to the rubbish in the bin?
Danielle	You keep it in there.
Researcher	You keep it in the bin. And then does someone empty the bin?

Danielle	Yes.
Researcher	Who empties the bin?
Danielle	The bin man.
Researcher	The bin man. And do you know where the bin man takes it?
Danielle	To a rubbish man.
Researcher	Do you know what the rubbish man does with the rubbish?
Danielle	Puts it in a hole.

On wetlands

Delia (Romania)

Researcher	So, here we have fish, birds and other creatures. Do they all live here all of the time?
Delia	The birds don't live here all year long, they go to warm countries.
Researcher	What is this person doing?
Delia	This person is fishing birds and fish.
Researcher	Why is he doing this?
Delia	To eat them.
Researcher	Is this a good thing to do or a bad idea?
Delia	It is good, otherwise people here will not have what they have to eat.
Researcher	What is this lady in the picture doing?
Delia	Milking a cow.
Researcher	Why is she doing this?
Delia	To give milk to her children.
Researcher	Is this a good thing to do?
Delia	It is a little worse, because the cow won't have milk for her children.
Researcher	We have seen pictures of birds and fish and people. Do they all get on happily together?
Delia	They are happy because it is beautiful.
Researcher	What would happen to the creatures if the people changed this environment here – if they drained some of the water, or built more villages and roads?
Delia	Something terrible. They might get run over by cars or their homes destroyed.
Researcher	Would it be good or bad for people if more roads and villages were built?
Delia	Bad for the people.
Researcher	Is there anything you don't like about living here?
Delia	No, everything is beautiful here.
Researcher	If you were in charge of this place, would you make any changes to it?
Delia	No change!

Analysis

Three categories of information emerged from the great wealth of data provided by the conversations:

1   Details of the children's knowledge and understanding about people, places and environmental issues – including their accurate knowledge, gaps in knowledge and erroneous thinking. Such details provided substantial insight into the development of basic scientific concepts needed to understand the issues being focused upon.
2   Insights into the children's levels of awareness and concern for the world in which they are growing up, and problems which affect our planet.
3   Details of the origins and sources of knowledge and concern in these pre-school children who had received no formal education programmes.

To consider the first of these categories, we see, for example, that the majority of children correctly associated trees with forests and animal and plant life. Some could identify specific animals and birds – cheetah, chimpanzee, gorilla, and so on. Jeffrey could explain that wood makes houses and cabins and that trees have various uses for people; also that wood must not be wasted. John linked the use of trees with making fire and houses, and knew that they are linked to the atmosphere. The majority of children interviewed could explain that if snow gets warm it melts. Eleanor explained that melting snow makes water (linking it with the sea), and Jocelyn explained that melting snow goes into bays, where water runs and people sit on the sand. A number of children, notably in California, had a relatively sophisticated understanding of recycling waste materials. Some linked this process with not making things 'over and over again', and many clearly knew that we should not waste things in the world. Delia possessed an idea about creatures migrating. Already at the age of 4 she demonstrated a sense of beauty and some notion of balance – i.e. that people need some things in the environment for food but this can come at a cost to animals.

Alongside this array of accurate knowledge, we are provided with examples of false knowledge, gaps in knowledge, naive preconceptions, and biased, stereotypical knowledge: John said that trees 'breathe air' but offered no further explanation of this; Jeffrey believed that rain forests are inhabited by creatures of temperate woodlands; Carl talked of snow going to the home of Santa Claus (he makes it) and Delia believes that all elements of a food chain live happily together with no competition among them.

The data derived from these conversations thus provide insights into the development of basic concepts needed to understand our geographical world and related environmental issues. We are also provided with insights into the development of awareness of problems and concern for the world. Many children talked of the need to protect trees and flowers; they knew that wood can be wasted, and that rubbish should be sensibly dealt with.

Sources of knowledge about the world were various, and included books, the media, parents, other relatives, and indeed a well-known 'happy food' restaurant.

The research projects briefly outlined above aim to provide a detailed analysis of the categories of information illuminated by the data. Researchers are also comparing the knowledge and concern of children entering school with that of 6–7 year olds, thus illustrating aspects of development in geographical and environmental thinking during the first three years in school. The ultimate aim is to inform the development of curriculum materials and schemes of work for use with children during these early years of learning. In the context of this volume, analysis provides fascinating insights into 'the world of the 4 year old', which can illustrate and inform many of the practical issues addressed on forthcoming pages.

This chapter has therefore set the scene for discussion of appropriate learning tasks and methods of organising the curriculum for teaching and learning in geographical education.

Chapter 2

Geographical and environmental education

Structure, content and issues

STRUCTURE AND CONTENT

Overview

In order to help readers understand the richness, relevance and context of the many examples of 'principles into practice' incorporated in the remaining chapters of this book, we include here a brief overview of the structure and content of the National Curriculum for Schools in England and of the Foundation Stage, a more detailed description of the particular requirements for geography, and a discussion of the place and nature of environmental education/education for sustainable development. For some readers the basic facts will be very familiar but we hope they will nevertheless serve as a useful *aide memoire* for considering issues raised and discussed. For overseas readers and others not familiar with implementing the English National Curriculum, such background is essential for understanding the case studies of interpretation which follow.

The National Curriculum for schools in England is organised on the basis of four key stages following on from the Foundation Stage. The Foundation Stage, introduced in September 2000, is part of the statutory National Curriculum for England and covers education for children aged from 3 to the end of the Reception year in school. It is intended as a valuable educational stage in its own right; also one of preparation for learning in the first of the key stages of schooling that commences at the end of the Reception year and proceeds through Years 1 and 2. Many children attend one or more forms of nursery or pre-school at the age of 3 and so follow this distinctive stage which addresses central aspects of early childhood learning and experience.

The four key stages which follow are defined precisely with the Education Act of 1996. The age range 5–7, or Year Groups 1 and 2 constitute Key Stage 1. Geography is one of seven statutory non-core Foundation subjects (the others being Design and Technology, Information and Communication Technology, History, Art and Design, Music and Physical Education) to be included within the curriculum for Key Stage 1, alongside the statutory core subjects of English, Mathematics and Science.

For each subject and for each key stage, programmes of study set out what pupils should be taught, and attainment targets set out the expected standards of pupils' performance. It is for schools to choose how they organise their school curriculum to include the programmes of study (DfEE 1999).

The 1996 Education Act defines a programme of study as the 'matters, skills and processes' that should be taught to pupils of different abilities and maturities during the key stage. This programme provides the basis for planning schemes of work. An attainment target sets out the 'knowledge, skills and understanding which pupils of different abilities and maturities are expected to have by the end of each key stage'. Attainment targets consist of a series of level descriptions of increasing difficulty (up to level 8) plus a description of exceptional performance above level 8. Each level description describes the types and range of performance that pupils working at that level should characteristically demonstrate (DfEE 1999). The level descriptions provide the basis for making judgements about pupils' performance at the end of Key Stage 1, as discussed in Chapter 4.

Geography, like all National Curriculum subjects, provides many opportunities within its Programme of Study for learning across the curriculum – that is, inter-disciplinary studies and the development of cross-curricular themes and skills. In particular it provides opportunities for:

- promoting spiritual, moral, social and cultural development;
- promoting personal, social and health education and citizenship;
- promoting skills across the curriculum including communication, application of number, information technology, working with others, problem solving and thinking skills;
- promoting other aspects of the school curriculum, notably education for sustainable development as discussed below.

Let us turn then to the precise requirements of geography within the National Curriculum, beginning with its links to learning in the Foundation Stage.

Foundation Stage

Learning for children in the Foundation Stage is planned and assessed through six areas of learning:

1   Personal, social and emotional development.
2   Communication, language and literacy.
3   Mathematical development.
4   Knowledge and understanding of the world.
5   Physical development.
6   Creative development.

Work in all of these areas paves the way for geographical learning in Key Stage 1. In particular, 'knowledge and understanding of the world' lies at the heart of development of geographical education. In this area, children are developing crucial knowledge, skills and understanding that help them make sense of the world. This forms the foundation for later work in a number of core and foundation subjects including geography. Curriculum guidance for the Foundation Stage suggests that practitioners should give particular attention to:

- activities based on first-hand experiences that encourage exploration, observation, problem-solving, prediction, critical thinking, decision-making and discussion;
- an environment with a wide range of activities indoors and outdoors that stimulate children's interest and curiosity;
- opportunities that help children to become aware of, explore and question issues of differences in gender, ethnicity, language, educational needs and disability issues;
- adult support in helping children communicate and record orally and in other ways;
- supplementary experience and information for children with sensory impairment.

(DfEE/QCA 2001)

As with all other elements of the National Curriculum, discussion on planning at the Foundation Stage, effective learning activities and effective teaching follows in ensuing chapters.

Key Stage I

During Key Stage 1 pupils investigate their local area and a contrasting area in the United Kingdom or abroad, finding out about the environment in both areas and the people who live there. They also begin to find out about the wider world. They carry out geographical enquiry inside and outside the classroom. They ask geographical questions about people, places and environments, and use geographical skills and resources such as maps and photographs (DfEE 1999).

The *Programme of Study* calls upon teachers to ensure that four areas of learning are covered – geographical enquiry and skills, knowledge and understanding of places, knowledge and understanding of patterns and processes, and knowledge and understanding of environmental change and sustainable development.

Geographical enquiry and skills

1   In undertaking geographical enquiry, pupils should be taught to:

a   ask geographical questions [for example, 'What is it like to live in this place?'];

b   observe and record [for example, identify buildings in the street and complete a chart];

c   express their own views about people, places and environments [for example, about litter in the school];

d   communicate in different ways [for example, in pictures, speech, writing].

2   In developing geographical skills, pupils should be taught to:

a   use geographical vocabulary [for example, hill, river, motorway, near, far, north, south];

b   use fieldwork skills [for example, recording information on a school plan or local area map];

c   use globes, maps and plans at a range of scales [for example, following a route on a map];

d   use secondary sources of information [for example, CD-ROMs, pictures, photographs, stories, information texts, videos, artefacts];

e   make maps and plans [for example, a pictorial map of a place in a story].

Knowledge and understanding of places

3   Pupils should be taught to:

a   identify and describe what places are like [for example, in terms of landscape, jobs, weather];

b   identify and describe where places are [for example, position on a map, whether they are on a river];

c   recognise how places have become the way they are and how they are changing [for example, the quality of the environment in a street];

d   recognise how places compare with other places [for example, compare the local area with places elsewhere in the United Kingdom];

e   recognise how places are linked to other places in the world [for example, food from other countries].

Knowledge and understanding of patterns and processes

4   Pupils should be taught to:

a   make observations about where things are located [for example, a pedestrian-crossing near school gates] and about other features in the environment [for example, seasonal changes in weather];

b   recognise changes in physical and human features [for example, heavy rain flooding fields].

Knowledge and understanding of environmental change and sustainable development

5   Pupils should be taught to:

a   recognise changes in the environment [for example, traffic pollution in a street];

b   recognise how the environment may be improved and sustained [for example, by restricting the number of cars].

(DfEE 1999)

These areas of learning should be addressed within an agreed breadth of study:

Breadth of study

6   During the key stage, pupils should be taught the knowledge, skills and understanding through the study of two localities:

a   the locality of the school;

b   a locality *either* in the United Kingdom *or* overseas that has physical and/or human features that contrast with those in the locality of the school.

7   In their study of localities, pupils should:

a   study at a local scale;

b   carry out fieldwork investigations outside the classroom.

(DfEE 1999)

The *Attainment Target* in geography, consisting of eight level descriptions of increasing difficulty plus a level of exceptional performance beyond that, sets out the knowledge, skills and understanding that pupils of varying abilities and maturities should gain from the Programmes of Study for the key stages.

Within Key Stage 1, the majority of pupils are expected to work at levels 1–3 and attain level 2 at the end of the key stage. We therefore detail the descriptors for levels 1, 2 and 3. Clearly these descriptions relate to the four aspects of attainment as stated in the Programme of Study, these being: 1 geographical enquiry and skills; 2 knowledge and understanding of places; 3 knowledge and understanding of patterns and processes; 4 knowledge and understanding of environmental change and sustainable development.

The numbers in parentheses within the level descriptions as detailed below refer to these aspects.

Level 1

Pupils show their knowledge, skills and understanding in studies at a local scale (2; 3; 4). They recognise and make observations about physical and human features of localities (2; 3). They express their views on features of the environment of a locality (1; 4). They use resources that are given to them, and their own observations, to ask and respond to questions about places and environments (1; 2; 3; 4).

Level 2

Pupils show their knowledge, skills and understanding in studies at a local scale (2; 3; 4). They describe physical and human features of places, and recognise and make observations about those features that give places their character (2; 3). They show an awareness of places beyond their own locality (2). They express views on the environment of a locality and recognise how people affect the environment (4). They carry out simple tasks and select information using resources that are given to them (1). They use this information and their own observations to help them ask and respond to questions about places and environments (1; 2; 3; 4). They begin to use appropriate geographical vocabulary (1).

Level 3

Pupils show their knowledge, skills and understanding in studies at a local scale (2; 3; 4). They describe and compare the physical and human features of different localities and offer explanations for the locations of some of those features (2; 3). They are aware that different places may have both similar and different characteristics (2). They offer reasons for some of their observations and for their views and judgements about places and environments (1; 2; 3; 4). They recognise how people seek to improve and sustain environments (4). They use skills and sources of evidence to respond to a range of geographical questions, and begin to use appropriate vocabulary to communicate their findings (1).

(QCA 2001)

Before moving on to see how these guidelines may translate into appropriate planning, organisation and activities, we must consider the geography curriculum's very close link with what many around the globe term 'Environmental Education' and which in the National Curriculum is referred to as 'Education for Sustainable Development'. The evolution of and links between these two terms are complex matters and present space does not allow for a detailed exploration of these. Readers with a particular interest in the development of and links between these areas are advised to consult other more detailed sources, for example, Palmer 1998; Huckle and Sterling 1996.

The Qualifications and Curriculum Authority (QCA 2002) advises that education for sustainable development (ESD) is not a new subject. It is an approach to the whole curriculum and management of a school with its roots in environmental education. The National Curriculum and Government Panel for Sustainable Development Education (QCA 2002) describe ESD as follows:

> Education for sustainable development enables people to develop the knowledge, values and skills to participate in decisions about the way we do things individually and collectively, both locally and globally, that will improve the quality of life now without damaging the planet for the future.

In terms of formal statutory links, requirements for ESD in the geography Key Stage 1 National Curriculum are:

KS1/1c

Geographical enquiry and skills

    c   express their own views about people, places and environment [for example, about litter in the school].

KS1/5a, b

Knowledge and understanding of environmental change and sustainable development

    a   recognise changes in the environment [for example, traffic pollution in a street];
    b   recognise how the environment may be improved and sustained [for example, by restricting the number of cars].

KS1/Breadth of study/7a, b

    a   study at a local scale;
    b   carry out fieldwork investigations outside the classroom.

Without doubt, ESD has a firm 'foothold' in geography, while having a substantial body of knowledge and understanding in its own right. It involves an understanding of key concepts such as interdependence, stewardship, needs and rights of future generations, quality of life, sustainable change and so on. It involves a wide range of skills such as critical thinking, weighing evidence and presenting reasoned argument on sustainable development issues; it involves an awareness of the needs of others, appreciation of diverse viewpoints, and an awareness of the complexity of issues. It involves areas of knowledge and understanding such as climate; soils, rocks and minerals; water; materials and resources, including energy; plants and animals; people and their communities; food and agriculture; buildings, industrialisation and management of waste materials.

Interpretation of these various elements and issues into topics and learning tasks is a matter for individual schools and teachers to pursue. Plans will necessarily build upon and incorporate the three inter-related components of environmental education which ESD builds upon, namely:

1   Education *about* the environment (i.e. basic knowledge and understanding of the environment).
2   Education *for* the environment (concerned with values, attitudes and positive action for the environment).
3   Education *in* or *through* the environment (i.e. using the environment as a resource with emphasis on enquiry and investigation and pupils' first-hand experiences).

These three components are inextricably linked, and are thus essential to the planning of educational programmes and tasks at all levels, including whole-school curriculum plans and specific programmes of work and activities for individuals and class groups. Part of the planning process should take account of the need to help learners understand the inter-relationships that exist among the three elements.

A statement of proposed entitlement of pupils in environmental education was prepared in England by a group convened to examine this theme in the early stages of the development of the National Curriculum (NCC 1990). A summary (unpublished), still relevant today, follows. It is clear that the critical time for commencing an implementation of this entitlement is in the primary phase; indeed, in the early years.

By the age of 16 all pupils should have had educational experiences which range from local to global in scale, and which enable them to:

1   understand the natural processes that take place in the environment, including the ecological principles and relationships that exist;
2   understand that human lives and livelihoods are totally dependent on the processes, relationships and resources that exist in the environment;
3   be aware of the impact of human activities on the environment including planning and design, to understand the processes by which communities organise themselves, initiate and cope with change; to appreciate that these are affected by personal, economic, technological, social, aesthetic, political, cultural, ethical and spiritual considerations;
4   be competent in a range of skills which help them to appreciate and enjoy, communicate ideas and participate in the decision-making processes which shape the environment;

5   view, evaluate, interpret and experience their surroundings critically so
     that a balanced appreciation can be reached;
6   have insights into a range of environments and cultures, both past and
     present, to include an understanding of the ways in which different
     cultural groups perceive and interact with their environment;
7   understand the conflict that may arise over environmental issues, par-
     ticularly in relation to the use of resources, and to consider alternative
     ways to resolve such conflicts;
8   be aware of the interdependence of communities and nations and some
     of the environmental consequences and opportunities of those relation-
     ships;
9   be aware that the current state of the environment has resulted from
     past decisions to which they made a contribution;
10   identify their own level of commitment towards the care of the environ-
     ment.

Underpinning this entitlement is a clear emphasis on values and attitudes. A
decade later the National Curriculum for Schools incorporates a statement
of values which educators should base their teaching and school ethos on.
This statement includes values pertaining to four elements: the self,
relationships, society and the environment. The core value statement for
the environment, underpinning all curriculum work in ESD is 'we value the
environment, both natural and shaped by humanity, as the basis of life and a
source of wonder and inspiration' (DfEE 1999). How easy it is to identify
with this when reading the samples of dialogue in the first chapter of this
book. Pupils of nursery school age clearly identify with such sense of wonder
and inspiration.

   As we have seen, environmental education and ESD have obvious links
with geographical education, with its emphasis on natural processes, human
activity, range of environments and cultures and environmental change. Also
these areas of learning incorporate knowledge, skills and concepts which
inter-relate with other areas of the curriculum, e.g.

1   *Knowledge, understanding and attitudes*

     a   Knowledge about the environment at a variety of levels, ranging
          from local to global.
     b   Knowledge and understanding of environmental issues at a variety
          of levels, ranging from local to global.
     c   Knowledge of alternative attitudes and approaches to environmen-
          tal issues and the value systems underlying such attitudes and
          approaches.

2   *Skills*

   a   Finding out about the environment, either directly or through the environment or by using secondary resources.

   b   Communicating:

      i   knowledge about the environment to others;

      ii   both the pupils' own and alternative attitudes to environmental issues, to include justification for the attitudes or approaches advanced;

   c   Involvement in decision-making.

3   *Concepts*

   a   interdependence;

   b   citizenship and stewardship;

   c   needs and rights of future generations;

   d   diversity;

   e   quality of life;

   f   sustainable change;

   g   uncertainty and precaution.

The success of incorporating worthwhile programmes of ESD into the early years curriculum is dependent upon the inclusion of such knowledge, skills and concepts within the framework of the three inter-related components of environmental education outlined above, and taking account of meaningful integration with other subject areas through carefully constructed cross-curricular tasks.

In summary then, geographical learning in the early years involves the structured content of a foundation subject which has a distinct integrity and identifiable content of its own, while maintaining meaningful and well-planned links with environmental education and education for sustainable development. Furthermore, it involves links with other areas of knowledge and key skills across the curriculum, assumes parental and community involvement and engagement with such overarching matters as values and inclusion. All of these elements are returned to and explored in greater detail in the context of examples of good practice in later chapters.

PRELIMINARY ISSUES

The content and inter-relationships of geography and environmental education/ESD on the curriculum map raise a number of issues relating to the development of children's thinking and organisation of teaching and learning in these areas.

Such issues permeate this book as a whole, but several will now be highlighted before being elaborated upon in the context of practical examples in this and subsequent chapters. Issues raised are in no particular order of priority. Neither do they form a comprehensive list. They do, however, provide a focus for further discussion on the design and implementation of policies and programmes of work in geographical and environmental education in the first three years in school.

The first issue relates to the use of first-hand experiences in the local environment which are essential starting points for the development of classroom tasks. Such organised local experiences will capitalise upon children's spontaneous experiences and previously acquired knowledge of the world around them, while developing this understanding through carefully structured, progressive activities.

Having emphasised the importance of using the locality, a second issue focuses on the need to go beyond the immediate environment, to challenge parochialism and develop children's awareness and understanding of places further afield. Traditionally schools have failed to address aspects of the geography of distant lands; the National Curriculum provides scope for redressing such omission.

This issue is taken up for discussion at a later stage in the context of case studies relating to teaching about distant lands.

Third, teachers need to consider the central role of fieldwork and the process and skills of enquiry in teaching and learning. These are an integral part of any successful topics/schemes of work and progressive attainment in fieldwork and environmental enquiry skills should be recognised as an essential component of geography teaching. Geographical education in the early years requires a wide variety of teaching methods with great emphasis on the enquiry approach. Giving knowledge directly, creative activities, questioning, group and individual tasks, information technology, use of stories/drama/role play, books, maps and other secondary resources all have their part to play. Yet if asked to highlight the most important ingredient of teaching and learning which characterises well-executed geographical schemes, planned fieldwork tasks would be the answer. To many this no doubt conjures up images of mountains, trails, walking boots and backpacks, but no child in school is too young to have a wide variety of learning tasks set in the outdoors, beginning, of course, with the school playground and its immediate environment. All work outside the classroom both uses and extends the world with which young children are familiar, and if trips further afield into the neighbourhood and beyond can be organised, so much the better. Ideally, Year 2 children should have opportunities to visit and investigate contrasting environments, perhaps a farm if the school is in an inner-city area, or a shopping complex/town centre if the school is in a rural community. The inclusion of fieldwork activities should certainly be addressed in all school curriculum plans and policy documents for the teaching of geography.

A fourth issue is a focus in teaching and learning on the concepts of space and place, i.e. on the nature and dynamics of places, spatial relationships in the environment, the human dimension, and environmental impacts and issues. This focus incorporates the all-important dimension of attitude development and the question of making informed value judgements about places.

A fifth issue concerns the context for the planning of teaching and learning in geography. Organisation needs to take account of the context of geographical and environmental learning; that is, the relationship with and the interconnectedness of these areas to other aspects of the curriculum: links should not only be recognised and respected but planned for.

Geography and environmental education can clearly be *supportive* of learning in other areas, and can provide the unifying element in an integrated topic. Furthermore, they can make a *distinctive* contribution to children's learning – particularly in the area of spatial knowledge. Both of these roles – the supportive and the distinctive – cannot be left to chance and must be planned for.

Finally, all schools must address the issue of the resources needed to interpret and develop geographical schemes into worthwhile learning tasks. This significant matter is addressed extensively in this volume, notably in Chapter 6, but it is implicitly addressed in the context of a number of the case studies.

Rather than continue a discussion in abstract, these and other related issues will be considered in context, with specific examples of content. Attention is turned in the first instance to an example of environmental geography in practice, which illustrates the close links between these two subject areas.

Mrs King's class of 7 year olds spent a school term focusing attention on the theme of 'Woodlands'. A series of visits was made to a woodland area, and every opportunity taken to engage the children in first-hand experiences and skills of fieldwork in this habitat. Practical investigatory work was at the forefront of learning. Back in the classroom, these experiences were followed up through integrated topic work, with a discernible core of geography linked to science and environmental understanding. The children were helped to identify the various different types of tree observed in the field with the aid of simple keys and photographs. The trees and their leaves were sketched, and samples of leaves and fruits were taken to the classroom so that leaf prints and sketches could be made. The children wrote creative accounts of the vibrant colours seen in the woodland, and more factual sentences about chronology of change as the autumn progressed. Attention was paid to accuracy and detail as well as imaginative and creative interpretation:

'Now, children, look carefully at the leaves you collected. How many ways are they different from each other? Let's make a list.'
'Little leaves and big leaves, miss.'
'Give me one word that means little and big. The leaves are different . . . ?'
'Sizes, miss.'
'Yes, good boy, Mohammed. Who can spell the word "size"? Tell me another way leaves are different. Tajinder?'
'Shapes – some are wide and some are narrow. Some are one big leaf and some look like they're made up of different bits stuck together.'
'That's right . . . can you tell me another word that means "wide", children?'

[Discussion led to the introduction of the name and the classification 'broadleaf' and leaves were put into sets of broadleaves and conifers.]

'Colours are different too, miss. There are green ones and yellowy ones and most of them are a mixture.'
'I know another way they're different. The edges of the leaves are different – some have jagged edges, and others are straight.'

As continuation of the follow-up to first-hand experiences of the woodland, Mrs King organised various games and classification activities. A tray was set out, containing various different leaves to encourage greater facility in identifying specimens from holly, yew, oak, pine, privet, laurel, beech, larch, sweet chestnut and so on, and then classifying each as either broadleaf or conifer. Posters and sets of commercial cards on the theme of trees and woodlands were available as secondary resource material to reinforce and assist the process. A great deal of emphasis was placed on scientific accuracy, facts and information – trees and leaves, fruits and seeds were identified and classified, and their habits and characteristics discussed and investigated in the field. Field experiences were then linked to human geography.

The value of trees and their usefulness to human life were considered, and samples of numerous woods were displayed alongside a collection of library books on the subject of wood and trees and photographs of important things in our lives made of wood. The more able children were given research tasks using these resources to discover which parts of the world each piece of wood came from.

A number of different issues and sub-topics were covered, including a comparison of differing woodland areas (temperate and tropical) throughout the world and the key conservation/sustainability issue of decline of the world's tropical rain forests. Mrs King incorporated a video recording about 'Pauline's family in Borneo', in order to compare and contrast lifestyles in other parts of the world with the children's own urban surroundings. The pupils investigated the difference in diets, homes and clothing, how food and drink was obtained, and the cost of food in both places. The results were listed, discussed, compared and analysed. Speculation and imagination paralleled accuracy and interpretation of facts. Material contained within the recording lent itself to further factual writing and a great deal of creative art and craft work and imaginative writing ensued.

The children were intrigued by a lifestyle of hunting and living off the land. 'Wish I could live over there,' sighed Abdul, 'I'd have lots of exciting adventures in the jungle.' Further discussion led to opportunities for drama and creative role play. Tropical rain forest scenes were acted out, depicting their wide variety of colourful life, restless atmosphere and sound effects. Vivid accounts accompanied this involvement, describing how different everyday activities would be in Borneo compared with life in an inner city in the UK.

In many ways, the further topic undertaken by Mrs King's pupils followed on from this comparison of rain forest life with that nearer home. A comparison of Borneo and Birmingham led to an investigation into 'wildlife in the city', largely as a response to those children who considered it a barren urban desert, devoid of the colour and excitement of more 'exotic' places. Fieldwork visits to farm and woodland once again provided a focus of first-hand experiences and practical investigations. The children undertook searches on land, in the air and in the water to discover how many species of wildlife inhabited the urban area of the centre. Bird-watching, pond-dipping and land searches of the various habitats led to a good deal of experience in identifying animal life. The activity aroused considerable excitement among the groups of learners, who soon became accustomed to handling petri dishes, magnifying containers, sweep nets, pooters and identification trays.

'Coo, miss, I feel like Sherlock Holmes doing this!'
[New words readily enter the children's vocabulary.]
'Who can tell me what we call a creature without a backbone?'
'A ... invertebrate, miss?'

[The various groups of invertebrates were named, and the children's catches were then examined, counted and classified.]

'This creature has ... how many legs?'
'Eight, miss.'
'So it belongs to ... which group of invertebrates?'
'Arachnids.'

Results of surveys were listed formally and graphs were drawn to illustrate and compare the numbers of creatures found in various classes. One group of interested children spent some time researching the life history and habits of common invertebrates and writing illustrated accounts of these. The whole class drew and painted pictures which were incorporated into a giant panoramic landscape running the length of the classroom wall. Indeed as the year continued, Mrs King involved all the children in contributing towards interactive displays for both classroom and school hallways.

Once again, this topic was skilfully linked to learning about distant environments. Photographs of non-indigenous invertebrates (e.g. giant hissing cockroaches, giant millepedes, African land snails) were studied and a cage of locusts was set up in the classroom for detailed observation and investigatory work. Research was done into the countries of origin of locusts, and the climatic conditions necessary for them to flourish. Much discussion centred around the need to keep locusts in a heated cage, and the (un)likelihood of their survival in our own country because of the nature of our climate. Stories written about 'My Life as a Locust' encouraged empathy with warmer lands and led to reading and discussion of Bible stories involving a locust plague.

This example represents good practice in terms of establishing meaningful links between the core content of geography and components of environmental education. The whole topic was based on fieldwork and skills of practical enquiry. It incorporated all four aspects of geographical content, namely skills and enquiry, knowledge and understanding of places, knowledge and understanding of patterns and processes and knowledge and understanding of environmental change and sustainable development. Furthermore, the topic identified only those other areas of the curriculum with which useful and meaningful links for integration could be achieved, notably science. Environmental education therefore served its planned purpose of providing that cross-curricular link between geography and science.

The Programme of Study of geography and guidelines for ESD were at the forefront of planning; for example, the children's work on tropical rain forests enabled them to ask geographical questions and recognise how places compare with other places. This work also enabled them to have insights into other cultures and an increased understanding of the ways in which different cultural groups perceive and interact with their environment. Attitudes, values and beliefs were recognised as key elements of the learning process. Table 2.1 represents diagrammatically an extract from a simplified version of the planning model used, and is not intended to be comprehensive. Examples of entries are given in each column.

In summary, this example has demonstrated ways in which practical links can be made between the two subject areas of geography and environmental education. It has also exemplified a number of the key issues arising out of the National Curriculum documentation for geography, notably the need for an emphasis on fieldwork and investigatory tasks in the locality, and the need to challenge this parochialism and find tangible ways of teaching and learning about distant lands.

Table 2.1 Extract from a planning model

Topic	Education about the environment	Education for and in the environment	Links with other curriculum areas*	Cross-curricular skills
Woodland past and present	Concern for trees as living things Endangered species and conservation Exploitation of populations of plants and animals Destruction of natural habitats, especially tropical rain forests Prudent and sustainable use of resources	Visit to woodland, study of trees and leaves in their natural habitat Animal and plant life associated with trees Sub-topic on trees in distant lands (using secondary resources) Development of care and 'caretaker ethic'	Science Geography Geography Technology Mathematics Geography English Geography	Observation Problem-solving Study Communication Participation Personal and social

* Specific cross-referencing with programmes of study for the core and foundation subjects of the National Curriculum was documented.

Attention is now turned to a more detailed discussion of the crucial tasks of planning and organising geographical education in the first three years in school (including the Foundation Stage).

Chapter 3

Policy, planning and organisation

SCHOOL POLICY

The aims and purposes of geography teaching embedded within the National Curriculum for Schools are that it offers opportunities to:

- stimulate children's interest in their surroundings and in the variety of human and physical conditions on the Earth's surface;
- foster children's sense of wonder at the beauty of the world around them;
- help children to develop an informed concern about the quality of the environment and the future of the human habitat; and
- thereby enhance children's sense of responsibility for the care of the Earth and its people.

(QCA 1998)

If such aims are to be achieved, and if geographical work is to be implemented successfully, a 'whole-school' approach is essential. This approach requires the headteacher and staff to engage in consultation which results in the articulation of a set of principles, goals and practical statements that provide overall direction for teaching and learning of the subject. In the first instance, a decision must be made as to whether geography and environmental education, or education for sustainable development, are to have separate or linked policy documents. This is a matter for individual schools to decide: perhaps ideally a pair of linked documents is most helpful; that is, a policy for geography, a policy for ESD and a statement giving practical guidance on the overlap between the two, in terms of content, organisation and resources. Whatever approach to document production is used, the following structure and suggested content should be helpful. A whole-school policy will have four key components, as shown in Figure 3.1. During whole-staff consultation meetings, it will be necessary to decide who will assume responsibility for decision-making. This is inevitably linked to the second policy component concerned with leadership. Someone – maybe the headteacher or agreed curriculum co-ordinator for geography – must assume responsibility for

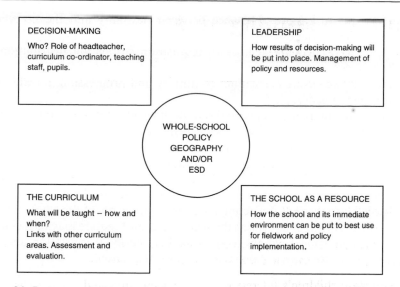

Figure 3.1 Components of a school policy: geography/environmental education.

making decisions based on full-staff discussion, and for translating these into plans for action. Presumably this leader will accept the task of overseeing the production and implementation of policy documentation and the management of resources, including human resources in the school. Once such leadership and management decisions have been made, attention can focus on the curriculum and the environment of the school itself as a major resource for teaching and learning.

A publication of this kind cannot possibly prescribe the content of an individual school's policy document. Every school is unique in its organisation, needs and resources. It is, however, possible to suggest guidelines on issues which should be the subject of staff discussion and 'flesh out' the four components indicated in Figure 3.1. The following issues should be addressed:

- What is our school doing already in the areas of geography and education for sustainable development?
- Who is taking the lead in these areas of the curriculum?
- What should we do next?
- How are geography and education for sustainable development set in the context of the curriculum as a whole?
- What is our common school viewpoint that will give consistent approaches to the implementation and organisation of geographical and environmental learning experiences?
- How will time be organised and prioritised?

- How do we achieve a balance between flexibility and the necessary timetable restrictions?
- Do we have adequate facilities for acquisition, storage and distribution of resources?
- How do we ensure curriculum continuity and progression in children's learning in geography?
- How will pupils be grouped and staff deployed for teaching and learning?
- What forms will assessment and record-keeping take?
- How shall we monitor and evaluate geography and education for sustainable development policy in practice?

A formal document deriving from discussion on each of these areas may be subdivided into sections, reflecting the four components of the whole-school approach. As much or as little as the school and staff require may be included under the following headings, conditioned by national legislation and, of course, the existing curriculum statements for the school:

- decision-making;
- management and implementation of policy;
- aims;
- objectives;
- methods and timing;
- content (knowledge, understanding, skills, concepts, attitudes);
- resources and organisation of resources;
- assessment, record-keeping and evaluation;
- the school itself as a stimulus for geographical work;
- other matters (e.g. links with the community, fieldwork, policy for school grounds development and maintenance).

POLICY INTO PRACTICE

Again, a checklist of elaboration on the stages in the implementation of policy may be helpful. Six key stages are essential in the first instance:

1   Organising leadership and communication.
2   Scrutinising the existing programme.
3   Producing a checklist of requirements.
4   Clarifying content and objectives.
5   Providing a rationale for teaching and learning methods.
6   Establishing mechanisms for evaluation, review and development.

A little more will be said about each of these.

Organising leadership and communication

At an appropriate staff meeting, the headteacher will no doubt initiate discussion on leadership for policy implementation. If a curriculum leader for geography and environmental work is already in place (and initiated policy), so far so good. If not, this person must be identified. The implementation phase may well involve the establishment of a working group of staff (especially in larger schools where early years co-ordinators will liaise with colleagues who teach older pupils) who represent different subject areas. This group may also accept responsibility for working and communicating with other interested parties, including parents, the community and the school's governing body. As so much work in geographical and environmental education will require learning outside the classroom, such liaison is essential.

Scrutinising the existing programme

Work already being done in the school will no doubt form the basis for development. Questions to consider are:

1   What schemes, topics, programmes already contribute to geographical and environmental work?
2   Is the answer to the above question comprehensive? What about extra-curricular activities? What about the hidden curriculum? What messages, both formal and informal, do the pupils receive about quality of the school environment and the need to take care of it?
3   What are the existing views of staff, parents, governors, about the place of geography and environmental education in the curriculum?
4   What links already exist between geographical, environmental work and other curriculum areas?
5   Can we identify areas where overlap of content occurs or repetition?
6   What enthusiasm, expertise, experience and resources already exist in the school for teaching geography and environmental education?
7   What enthusiasm, expertise and experience in these areas can be identified among parents and members of the community, which may be capitalised upon.

Producing a checklist of requirements

By this is meant a list of requirements for implementing policy. Various items will be repetitive of the checklist for producing a policy document. The checklist should include:

- overall rationale for including these curriculum areas in the school's overall programme;
- aims, objectives, content;

- time allocations;
- approach to whole-school organisation of these areas;
- staff responsibilities;
- resource requirements and accessibility;
- monitoring, assessment and recording techniques.

Clarifying content and objectives

This will include helping all staff to understand and appreciate the subject area content and objectives of geography and education for sustainable development, and the structure of these areas of learning as set out in Chapter 2. Both lead to the development of knowledge, understanding, skills and values. A successful policy document may give examples of these components, such as:

Knowledge   of places, of people's homes, of food ingredients, of measuring the weather, of types of farm, of landscape features.

Understanding of links between local and distant places, of ways in which people can harm or destroy parts of the natural world, of the need to manage or protect aspects of our environment.

Skills   of observation, communication, problem-solving, decision-making; of being able to understand issues from the points of view of other people.

Values   having respect for the natural and built environments; having a sense of personal concern for the care of the planet or features within it.

Providing a rationale for teaching and learning methods

Content and objectives, once defined, have implications for teaching and learning methods. The need for emphasis on first-hand, investigatory learning experiences has already been stressed. Successful implementation of policy will no doubt involve the application of this, plus a range of other approaches to teaching and learning. These may include structured input (from the teacher or secondary resources such as books, computer programs, videos), individual research, role plays, group discussions/debate and experiential activities. The rationale statement may emphasise:

- that as geographical and environmental issues are multifaceted and complex, investigatory and co-operative learning is likely to be more successful than competitive learning;

- that relevant skills underpin the acquisition of knowledge and under-standing of geographical concepts;
- that the ethos of the school itself cannot be separated from the content of geographical and environmental education. Does the school environment reflect care and concern? What messages are implicit in the way the school and its grounds are maintained? Does the school community reflect qualities of co-operation, tolerance, respect and empathy?

Establishing mechanisms for evaluation, review and development

By this we mean evaluation, review and development of the whole-school policy. As the delivery of geography and environmental education, or education for sustainable development, is a school-wide matter, it is not sufficient merely to collect data about, assess and record individual pupils' achievements and progress. Overall management, rationale, teaching approaches and the ways in which the whole-school environment has been developed must also be subject to regular review. Once again, it is inappropriate to prescribe a complete set of evaluation and review questions, as individual circumstances should build these into a policy statement. Examples may include:

- Who was involved in working out and writing the school policy and its goals?
- How was the policy communicated to all parties concerned?
- What programme content was included?
- How were individual schemes and programmes evaluated?
- Has an inventory of resources (including human and community resources) been made and kept up-to-date?
- Has the whole-school environment been developed and managed to its full potential for geographical work?
- What future action is planned or needed?

Some final comments on the evaluation and review of school-wide programmes focus attention on the effectiveness of individual schemes or topics, which may have been followed by one or more classes. The curriculum co-ordinator may find the following questions helpful when carrying out or discussing a review of a completed topic:

- Was the topic/scheme based on practical involvement and the pupils' first-hand experiences of the environment? Was the acquisition of geographical skills a starting point or an integral feature of the work done?
- Did the topic/scheme have clear aims, stated both in a conceptual underpinning (e.g. the pupils investigated change through the year on the

local farm) and in a plan of content which included knowledge and understanding from other key curriculum areas?

- Did the topic/scheme identify only those other areas of the curriculum with which useful and meaningful links for integration could be achieved? Did it avoid trying to incorporate every conceivable subject area merely for 'the sake of it'? In other words, did geographical education provide a discernible core of work?

- Did teacher observations and examples of children's writing and other recordings provide an ongoing component of record-keeping and assessment throughout the year?

- Was a wide variety of teaching methods used, including teacher-led discussions and presentations, whole-class activities, and group and individual investigations?

- Was due regard paid to the development of skills, including a wide range of cross-curricular skills (e.g. observation, problem-solving, communication)?

- Were elements of the formal National Curriculum entitlement at the forefront of planning? For example, did planning take account of progression from local to global issues? Were attitudes, values and beliefs recognised as key elements of the learning process? Did content directly relate to National Curriculum guidelines?

- Did planning take account of broader aspects of the National Curriculum and issues which schools must address, for example, special educational needs, general teaching requirements as specified in the official guidelines?

The success of overall policy-making inevitably lies in the details of planning and implementation. Let us then turn to an overview of the context of planning, before seeing the substance of how two primary schools go about the tasks of policy-making and planning at a variety of levels.

PLANNING IN CONTEXT

Planning for the teaching of geography, like all subjects, must inevitably incorporate an understanding of what the learners already know, that is, what they are bringing to the learning situation, and the related ability of a teacher to find this out and to develop it. Perhaps the appropriate place to pursue this discussion is in the context of learning in action in classrooms. It is emphasised that all classroom discussions and descriptions used in this volume are for the purpose of illustrating particular points or issues. They do not necessarily represent examples of 'ideal' or recommended practice – just day-to-day life in schools. Their strengths, and in some cases their weaknesses, are highlighted. Most important, they locate the theoretical and research framework in the real and complex world of children's lives.

Consider the following three examples of geographical learning in action, and the conversations taking place within them.

Mrs Friend's class

Four 5–6 year old children are attempting to reorganise parts of a model village back on to the base that it had occupied the day before. Mrs Friend aims to use this everyday 'play' situation as an opportunity to develop basic geographical concepts concerned with the location of objects in space, and scaled down versions of reality.

Teacher	What's happened to the model? We don't have a village any more. Can you put it back together again?
Simon	The real village?
Teacher	The one we have in our classroom. Why isn't it a real one?
Simon	'Cos the houses are tiny.
Teacher	They're not as big as our houses, are they? Can you think why not?
Fiona	You can't fit a house in a school!
Teacher	Are these houses the same shape as ours? Stand here and look at the top of them … what shape do you see when you look down on them?
Jane	Square.
Carlton	Rectangles.

(Children continue discussing the 'bird's eye view' with interventions by their teacher.)

Teacher	Let's make the village like it was yesterday.
Fiona	What shall we start with?
Carlton	The church.
Simon	I know where the church goes.
Jane	Where?
Simon	There. Over there – by where the trees used to be.
Carlton	Why there?
Simon	'Cos that's where the graveyard is. You have to have a church by the side of the graveyard.
Fiona	Here?
Simon	No. Put it on the other side – that's where the gate is.
Fiona	Right. The church goes – there.
Carlton	Get the houses.
Simon	There's lots of them.
Fiona	They all go round the pond.
Carlton	Yes.
Jane	There was a house next to the church.

Simon	This one?
Carlton	The red one?
Simon	Blue one.
Carlton	And the green one went there.
Jane	I can't remember.
Fiona	I think it was blue. Yes, it was.
Simon	The red house was on the end. The blue one was in between the red house and the church.
Carlton	Let's put the red house on the end . . .
Jane	And the blue house next to the red one.
Fiona	Then the church is next door to the blue one.
Jane	Looks right.
Fiona	Yes, I think so.
Simon	What's left, then?
Carlton	The shop.
Jane	And another house.
Fiona	A green one.
Carlton	The shop was at the other end.
Fiona	On the end?
Simon	Yes. I think it goes there – opposite the red one and the blue one.
Carlton	There's only the green one left.
Jane	Where does that go?
Simon	There.
Fiona	In between the shop and the trees.
Jane	There?
Carlton	Yes.
Jane	Are you sure?
Fiona	Yes.
Simon	How do you know?
Fiona	I just know.
Teacher	The house is the same colour as the trees next to it.

Miss Reynolds' class

A group of children aged 6–7 are pursuing their studies in a topic on tropical rain forests. They are making collage pictures of the forest, and talking about what it would be like to visit a rain forest. This activity is but one of a wide range of practical tasks the children undertake which link various curriculum areas. While geographical education is the core of their work, a great deal of language, art, music, mathematics and science is also incorporated. In this particular lesson, geography leads to some relevant and exciting art and craft work. Its production generates much discussion. The teacher's aim is to establish meaningful links between concepts in science and geography, through the use of art. At the same time she is concerned with establishing levels and accuracy of existing knowledge.

Jed	Wonder what it would be like . . .
Cheryl	What?
Jed	Living in a rain forest.
Teacher	Think of some words to describe the air.
Sebastian	Hot.
Cheryl	And wet, too.
Annette	Must be like a steamy bathroom.
Sebastian	More like a shower. One you've always left running.
Jed	All the time. That's why everything grows so high. Like the trees, see?
Annette	They look as if they're stretching up to touch the sky.
Teacher	Why do they stretch so tall?
Cheryl	Finding the sun, that's why.
Jed	Look how big they are. Taller than telegraph poles. I bet it would take all day to climb one.
Teacher	Would it get lighter or darker as you climbed?
Sebastian	It's dark at the top.
Annette	But the leaves are spreading out to find the sunshine. That's why the light in the forest shines down all greeny-yellow.
Jed	It's sunny outside the forest, but sort of shadowy inside.
Teacher	Can you try and show the shadows in your pictures?
Cheryl	There's still lots of colours, though.
Annette	Yes – red and yellow and green and blue, from all the wildlife you can find.
Jed	Like this parrot I'm painting.
Annette	Parrots don't have colours like those.
Jed	How do you know?
Annette	Well, I've never seen parrots like that.
Sebastian	Yes, but you've never been in a rain forest, have you?
Annette	No.
Sebastian	Well, then. How do you know there won't be parrots this colour in there?
Teacher	Our books help us to understand what colour they are.
Jed	We could find all sorts of strange, new birds there.
Cheryl	Yeah. There must be loads of flowers that we've never seen, 'cos they won't grow anywhere else.
Jed	And lots of tropical plants, too. Just like a jungle.
Cheryl	And fruits. Juicy fruits. Enormous things.
Sebastian	I fancy swinging through the trees on those trailing creepers, like Tarzan. That must be like flying.
Annette	Lots of animals live there too.
Jed	Jaguars. Tree frogs. And monkeys.
Cheryl	I think the monkeys would be my favourites.
Sebastian	The big ones, or the little ones?

Cheryl	What do you mean?
Sebastian	Well, there might be big monkeys like gorillas, and little ones. Chimpanzees.
Annette	I think I'd like the little ones best. They make me laugh. The gorillas would frighten me.
Jed	Not as much as the snakes, I bet. Great big pythons and boa constrictors all in the grass. Slithering about. They might kill you.
Teacher	But have you ever thought that they might be killed themselves?
Cheryl	They may kill insects. Butterflies in all the colours you can think of.
Sebastian	And spiders. And lizards.
Jed	I bet there are lots of funny creepy crawlies out there. All huge and furry.
Annette	All making squeaky noises at night. I saw them on the telly.
Sebastian	Ever so exciting. And spooky.
Jed	A rain forest must be a really noisy place. Everything screeching and squawking and flapping about.
Teacher	We can write about the noises of the forest.
Cheryl	All the roaring and growling from the wild animals.
Annette	And chattering.
Jed	Must be a bit like a big city, I should think.
Annette	How do you mean? It's a forest, not a city.
Jed	Well, the city's always full of noise. All the traffic all day. I should think the rain forest is like that, but there's animals there instead of people. And instead of flats, they have great big trees.
Sebastian	I'd love to be an explorer. I'd find new creatures and bring them back home again. I'd keep them safe as pets. I'm going to write about being an explorer and discovering a magic grub. Bright purple and enormous, and it hangs on twigs.

Mr Jones' class

Some 7–8 year olds are doing group activities to learn about the use of scale. They have already done some work on drawing round familiar objects on a piece of paper. Now they encounter things that are too big to fit the paper.

Teacher	We've drawn round lots of different things on our paper. Now, let's have a little problem to solve.
Andrew	What sort of problem?
Teacher	Well, all the objects you've drawn round so far fit on to the paper. Now I want you to draw your desk lid on this piece of paper.
Anne	But we can't, sir.
Joyce	It won't fit on.
Teacher	That's the problem I want you to solve. How can we draw big things on a smaller piece of paper?

Emily	Get a bigger piece of paper – then it would fit on all right.
Teacher	Yes, but what about bigger shapes? Like a frieze board, or a wall.
Joyce	Or an elephant.
Martin	We can't just keep on getting bigger bits of paper.
Andrew	If we wanted to draw the playground, we couldn't find a piece of paper that big.
Teacher	So what are we going to do?
Anne	If we can't make the paper bigger, draw the picture smaller. Then it'll fit on the paper.
Martin	Yes, that should do it.
Andrew	They do that in books, don't they, sir? Lots of book pictures have big things in them.
Teacher	Yes, Andrew, they do. In fact, if you look round the classroom, you'll find that someone has managed to draw the whole world in quite a small way.
Joyce	Where?
Emily	I can't see anything.
Martin	I can – over there. Look.
Andrew	It's a globe. It's got all the countries of the world on, hasn't it, sir?
Teacher	Yes.
Martin	How do they know what size the different countries are?
Andrew	I expect someone goes round and measures them.
Joyce	And then they have to make them small enough to fit on the globe.
Emily	Maps are like pictures, sir. They have sort of pictures of places on, don't they?
Teacher	That's right, Emily. Sometimes they show the whole country, and sometimes they might just show the streets of a town or a city.
Andrew	My dad's got a book with maps in it. It helps him to find his way round when he's driving his lorry.
Martin	How do they know what size to make the streets?
Andrew	Like with globes, I suppose – you have to measure things and then make them smaller . . .
Anne	To fit on the paper.
Emily	I suppose so.
Andrew	My brother's got Concorde in his bedroom.
Anne	He can't have – it wouldn't fit.
Andrew	It's not a real one – he made it out of a kit. It looks just like the real thing.
Emily	Somebody must have measured a real Concorde and then made it like a model.
Martin	So if we want to draw our desk lids, we'll have to measure how long it is . . .
Emily	And how wide it is.

Martin	And then make it smaller. Shorten it.
Andrew	How much by?
Anne	It'll have to be the same on each side, or it won't look right.
Teacher	Why not try to draw it about half its normal size? Measure each side, and then think of what half is.
Martin	Right. You measure how long it is, Andrew. Then we'll see how wide it is.
Anne	And then I'll halve it for you.
Andrew	I'll try and measure the inkwell.
Emily	What for?
Andrew	If we draw the desk smaller than it really is, we'll have to make the inkwell smaller too. If we draw it full size, it will look as big as a dustbin.
Martin	And that won't look right.

These three classroom scenes illustrate situations wherein young learners' complex processes of learning are engaged. Geographical education is taking place within their own familiar environment, and the knowledge, understanding, skills and concepts of geography are developed in the context of pupils' individual potential, prior experience and natural curiosity. The teacher's role, however, is crucial in each situation. He/she acts as facilitator and enabler of this development and as director/provider of tasks which nurture it.

Analysis of the conversation taking place in Mrs Friend's class leaves us with little doubt that the children are building upon the natural experiences and prior knowledge which they bring into the classroom. This experience is reflected by their teacher in specific and relevant tasks in which the children are engaging themselves. While the model is discussed and organised, key concepts and skills of mapwork and graphicacy are reinforced. The buildings are being linked together in physical space and in the children's minds – an important mapwork concept. The learners are familiarising themselves with the idea that a plan (or map) is a representation of space occupied by objects depicted in plan form and of the spatial relationship between them. The interventions by their teacher drawing attention to the 'view from above' are planned to assist this familiarisation. The children are surrounded in this activity by first-hand experiences of the concept of scale – without conscious realisation and discussion of the fact. The teacher uses this opportunity to pose relevant questions – why are these houses smaller than the ones we really live in? – a promotion of valuable geographical discussion, linked to the general development of vocabulary and conversation about everyday things. Without doubt, this simple 'play' activity of reassembling a model is sound early years geographical education, affording practice in recording locations, and development of the vocabulary of graphicacy, including 'opposite', 'in front of', 'by the side of', 'behind', 'next to', 'right' and 'left'. Such vocabulary is linked to an understanding of direction and the more advanced concepts involving grids, co-ordinates and recording specific locations to which the children will progress in their learning. Mrs Friend is successfully allowing natural conversation and experiential learning to take place, while steering the task and its related discussion towards specific elements of geographical education. Knowledge and skills are developed which are entirely appropriate for such young learners' stage of conceptual development.

In Miss Reynolds' classroom, tasks are organised through the topic-work approach – in this example, a topic which clearly has geographical education as a discernible core of content. Conversation illustrates existing subject knowledge which children bring to their task: rain forests are hot and wet, the trees are very tall . . . they need the sun . . . they are home for a wide range of colourful and exciting things – birds, animals, insects and flowers. Snatches of conversation reveal a wealth of existing concepts and ideas, no doubt established as a result of previous work done on the topic and exposure to views of life in rain forests presented by the media, books and conversations with others. The classroom scene certainly illuminates existing subject knowledge. It also demonstrates the erroneous or incomplete nature of this knowledge which exists in the 'world inside children's minds'.

Young pupils' background knowledge of distant environments is an important consideration when planning further work on them, and perhaps the word 'knowledge' is not the most accurate one to use, as Chapter 1 suggests. Children have ever-increasing incidental contact with places around the world – through personal contacts, package holidays, films, television and other media. All these are powerful influences. Inevitably children build up a 'mental map' or image of foreign places which to a large extent may be blurred or false.

As well as factual errors, attention is drawn to the dangers of stereotyping and ethnocentricity that result from media reports. Miss Reynolds' young learners discuss the colourful and exotic aspects of tropical rain forests – large, juicy fruits, colourful parrots, beautiful butterflies and exciting animals. They speculate on swinging through the trees like Tarzan – images probably reinforced by books and films, yet far removed from the realities of a rain forest's destruction, soil erosion and the frequent plight of native peoples. Misinformation and stereotyping can so often arise and be reinforced, perhaps by the teacher's own genuine ignorance of particular facts about a place. A paradoxical argument could be pursued. How important is it for a teacher to build upon a learner's existing knowledge and experiences? Yet to a certain extent these may be incomplete, erroneous or biased. Thus a teacher's task is to establish the pupils' existing knowledge base – to find out what is already known and understood, and also to have some idea of what is not known or partially understood.

In the first two of these classrooms we see evidence of teachers using existing understanding and everyday experiences to enhance future learning tasks. Mrs Friend approached this through everyday 'play' activities, and Miss Reynolds through a structured topic. In Mr Jones' classroom, the children's experience and learning is organised through the subject matter of geography itself. Tasks are planned which will lead to an understanding of scale, a key concept in graphicacy. The teacher sees his role as progressing this understanding, enabling the children's own practical work and spontaneous ideas, while organising certain experiences so that logical connections are made between elements of subject matter. Learning is an organised event – and the teacher provides appropriate ways of introducing the pupils to strategies that will reinforce their discoveries and aid their progressive understanding of the content of geography.

Thus we see three very different examples of approaching learning in geography – one which capitalises on natural or everyday objects and experiences, one which develops prior experience by relying on the integration of subject matter through a cross-curricular topic, and one which introduces specific knowledge in its own right. All result in achievement in learning and represent 'good practice' in geographical education. All three are appropriate methods of developing prior experience into worthwhile learning tasks, and take account of a key issue in planning which is that context is crucial for the facilitation of learning. In each classroom, pupils did not learn arbitrary facts with no relevance to their lives. The goals of learning made sense to the learners, so giving meaning to the learned material.

A number of general conclusions may be drawn from and supported by these examples. First and foremost, a great deal of prior geographical knowledge is brought to a learning situation. Second, young children coming into school are actually good at learning. They make persistent attempts to make sense of their complex world. Third, rather than perceiving children as 'blank slates', a teacher ought to recognise the learners' existing adaptations to their environment. He or she should in some way 'tap into' their predispositions rather than attempt to teach arbitrary associations which are not mapped on to the constraints of experience brought to the classroom.

The task of planning for learning therefore involves designing experiences which build upon children's existing knowledge of the world around them. This can be done in a number of ways, as the classroom scenarios have shown.

If teachers are to pursue this complex task of ascertaining children's prior knowledge and building upon it, two conditions seem essential to the process. First, they must have an adequate understanding of the subject matter of geography: it seems clear that if teachers do not have an adequate grasp of knowledge of a subject it is impossible for them to tease out that subject's underlying principles and intellectual integrity in order to structure learning tasks and progressive activities which take account of these. The teaching task involves identifying clear lines of progression within the subject. Second, they must have the ability to organise suitable learning tasks which children can engage with in the appropriate context and at the appropriate time.

Two general points must be made about learning tasks: they should be both purposeful in the eyes of the learner and relevant to his or her experiences, and should also have the potential for progression or expansion in order to facilitate further learning in geography or a related curriculum area. The teacher's own task involves making judgements about such relevance and potential, perhaps using the following checklist of questions:

Are tasks

- Purposeful?
- Relevant?
- Rigorous?
- Challenging?
- Sequential?

From general characteristics, planning may then take account of more specific analysis of types of task in the context of adequate coverage of the geography curriculum. Task planning should enable pupils to:

- consolidate and practise existing geographical knowledge/skills;
- build upon such existing understanding;
- achieve clearly identified progression within the subject;
- make meaningful intellectual links between geography and other subject areas;
- engage in imaginative thinking and creative problem-solving.

The three geography classroom situations described above provide examples of teaching which aims to take account of setting tasks matched to the learners' ability, experience and interest. Furthermore, they illuminate three possible ways of facilitating further learning. Effective teaching and learning in geography may well incorporate all three of these approaches, extended into the provision of a wide range of appropriate tasks.

PLANNING IN ACTION

Exemplar scheme of work

The Qualifications and Curriculum Authority's exemplar scheme of work for Key Stage 1 (QCA 1998) comprises a set of materials which illustrate how long-term and medium-term plans can be devised for teaching and learning in geography. It shows how geography might be taught to children attaining levels considered to be appropriate for their age. There is no compulsion for schools to engage with this scheme and it is suggested that teachers may find it a useful basis for developing or refining their own schemes of work by adding to or reducing the material it contains, or amending it as appropriate. For readers wishing to investigate the details of this scheme, it shows:

- how a school's work in geography can be divided into units to be taught to different years;
- how units can be sequenced across a key stage;
- how geographical enquiry skills, places and themes can be integrated and taught;
- ways in which units can build on work that has gone before and how they link to other units;
- ways in which units can link with and support English, mathematics, information technology and other curriculum areas (QCA 1998).

The materials use the term 'scheme of work' to describe the overall planned provision of geography in a school, including both key stage plans and units of work. 'Units' are medium-term plans and refer to a coherent set of work, usually designed for a term or less. The 'Key Stage plan' is the long-term planned programme of work for geography for the whole key stage (QCA 1998). Such background and definitions provide useful context for considering the following accounts of policy and planning in action.

Case studies of good practice

A. Cassop Junior and Infant School

Cassop Junior and Infant School is a County Durham village school with 86 children. Class 1 has 19 reception and Year 1 children who work together in the same class. In Class 2 there are 18 children. Cassop is a school greatly influenced by the headteacher's passionate interest in geographical and environmental education. The school is unusual in that it has its own wind turbine that contributes to electricity generation supplied to the National Grid, the school and Cassop village. The turbine was funded by National Grid and Durham County Council, as well as by the school's own fund-raising activities in the local community. The headteacher, Mr McManners, plays a keen role in planning geography, working with other staff to create and implement the school's geography policy and planning documents.

Ethos and approach

The school approach to geographical education heralds practical and first-hand experience as vital in all geographical learning. Worksheets and photocopiable books are rarely used as a geography resource unless they are viewed as an entirely appropriate and interesting means of reinforcing what children have learnt elsewhere. The teachers at Cassop are encouraged to create their own sources and resources for learning based on their own interest, creativity, discussion with other teachers both at home and abroad and children's sparks of interest. Similarly, children's experience of their own school grounds as a basis for work and play is deemed a fundamental aspect of learning. Teachers also make regular efforts to introduce the use of maps and globes to set contexts for many pieces of work; maps and globes then become a key part of everyday classroom work for children of all ages in the school. World events and holidays are marked on world map displays, to provide a geographical context that encourages children to become aware of and interested in maps from an early age.

An important part of teaching geography is the teacher's openness and willingness to be diverted by children's enthusiasms and ideas. Miss Woolley, the Reception and Year 1 class teacher, told us how Cassop teachers do not feel pressured to follow unerringly their plans for the term or half term's work; if a geographical story or topic really catches the children's imagination and interest, then further time is spent on developing activities. An example of such a situation is a 'big book' story telling session about a rain forest which, due to the children's interest, was added into children's topic work on water and water cycles. The headteacher volunteered the use of his own tape-recordings of rain forest bird sounds, and along with a children's painted rain forest display in a classroom corner, headphones and tape-recorder were placed near the rain forest book so that children could immerse themselves in the story and rain forest environment.

Children are always encouraged to talk and explain their geographical ideas and teachers are discouraged from believing that children are unable to cope with complex concepts or new vocabulary. Teaching and learning emphasises the importance of early years learning about distant places. Teachers try to avoid stereotyping places and peoples from other environments and the direct experiences of children, teachers and parents connected with the school are used as a key resource for investigating the wider world.

Geography teaching at Foundation Stage and Key Stage 1 at Cassop School is informed by a series of five planning documents prepared and implemented by all staff. These are reproduced below as follows:

A. Geography Policy
B. Geography Guidelines (including transition from Foundation Stage to Key Stage 1 and to Key Stage 2)
C. Policy for Global Dimension
D. Guidance to all using geography pictures with children
E. Understanding maps in the primary school: a sequence of activities

These documents cover the Foundation Stage, Key Stage 1 and Key Stage 2, therefore showing aspects of how geographical work progresses as the infants move through into the junior classes. Words and phrases which appear within them in bold type indicate aspects which the school emphasises because of their perceived significance. Any commentary on the school's documents appears in italic type.

A. Cassop Junior and Infant School geography policy

I   Introduction

1.1   As with all subject policies the Geography Policy should be read in the context of the school's stated philosophy and general aims.

1.2   Of particular relevance to geography are the aims concerned with:

- teaching and learning of skills in context;
- the importance of first-hand investigation;
- the need to make children's learning relevant and exciting to them;
- the effectiveness of planning to exploit the cross-curricular aspects of topics.

2   Rationale

2.1   The first of our school's general aims is 'to help children to understand themselves and the world in which they live'. Geography has a central role in fulfilling this.

2.2   Geography examines the world and investigates the interaction between the world (its physical make-up, its climate and places) and people within it.

2.3   There are within geography, certain vital skills peculiar to this subject, for example those concerned with the use and understanding of maps. Because of its breadth of content and methodology, geography provides many opportunities to develop and use skills from other areas of the curriculum. Geographical study will often require first-hand observation and investigation and help to promote the exciting approach and development of curiosity highlighted in the school's general aims.

2.4   Geography is concerned with important environmental issues; it can also encourage a better understanding of particular peoples. The school strongly expresses the view that geography can be an important vehicle to counteract ethnocentrism.

2.5   Geographical work will play a major part in developing a **global aware-ness** which we intend to be part of the whole school ethos. Geographical studies will emphasise mutual respect (see Global Dimension within PSHE, National Curriculum PSHE Breadth of Study 5c).

3   Entitlement

3.1   From entering the **Foundation Stage** children are entitled to a range of experiences and activities which form the basis of sound practice in geography. At the Foundation Stage they are entitled to:

- first-hand experience;
- exploration in and outdoors;
- observation;
- prediction;
- problem-solving;
- critical thinking;
- discussion.

3.2 Teaching and learning should be designed to present opportunities to **develop curiosity** (and to satisfy it some of the time!), to **gather information**, to ask questions and to use appropriate language.

Above all, we should be fostering an enthusiastic, outward-looking curious state of mind.

All of these expectations and entitlements are equally appropriate at end of Key Stage 2!

3.3 On entering the National Curriculum phase of education, pupils need to encounter a series of topics and issues which give opportunities to develop **geographical skills**, skills being **one** other key element of the Geography Policy. Pupils will develop these skills through the investigation of the other four elements of the National Curriculum Geography. Work should be in the form of **enquiry** in order to develop understanding and knowledge in four key aspects:

- places;
- patterns and processes;
- environmental change;
- sustainable development.

3.4 Topics need to be presented in a sequence which satisfies the content element of the National Curriculum and provides opportunity for children to work in a progressively more demanding and rigorous way.

3.5 The elements of complex ideas can begin at the earliest stage. At the appropriate level children's work should at all times include the element of **investigation and challenge** central to geography (Why? ... How ...? questions).

3.6 All children will experience **fieldwork and visits**. Years 5 and 6 will be offered a residential field trip and encouraged to go.

3.7 Maps of many kinds will be available in all classrooms. Every classroom will display a world map and a map of Great Britain.

3.8 In addition to knowledge gathered first hand, pupils are entitled to a variety of organised resources including Information Technology from which to access second-hand information.

3.9 There will, within geography, be opportunities to develop specific aspects of PSHE.

3.10   Links with other subject areas should be exploited; concepts and skills in science, history, maths should be involved in a geographical enquiry. Geographical texts and report writing may be employed with literacy and the written aspects of the geography lessons should build upon literacy work.

4   Aims

4.1   The Local Education Authority believes that the geography curriculum offered by institutions should enable pupils and students:

- to extend their interest and appreciation of their own surroundings and those of all the world's peoples **to make their own places and the places of others become interesting to them**;
- to develop positive attitudes of care and responsibility for the variety of human and natural environments and resources in order to help to maintain and enhance their quality;
- to understand the effects that human action has had upon environments and, in turn, how environmental circumstances may influence human behaviour;
- to acquire knowledge about places and locations in Britain and the wider world which will form a framework to set local, national and international events in context;
- to gain knowledge and understanding of the natural world and its physical systems;
- to become competent in the skills and techniques which are required to undertake geographical investigations with primary and secondary data in a variety of forms, and to acquire the understanding necessary to apply and make use of the results of the enquiry;
- to encourage positive attitudes towards the variety of peoples and of human culture and organisation so as to promote tolerance and understanding;
- to understand the significance of location and of distribution patterns in human activities, how places are linked by the movements of people, materials and information;
- to understand the concept behind sustainable development, i.e. to make the most of the present without jeopardising the future;
- to exemplify sustainability by our actions as a school community.

Geography should always be:

- active, thought provoking, a challenge to understanding people and places;
- a celebration of curiosity and a means to satisfy it.

Children should be taught skills and should then use these skills to gather information which will **feed active thinking** towards questions such as:

- What is it really like?
- How did it become as it is?
- How would it feel to be there, to live there?
- How does this connect with me?

Geography should never become:

- a passive collecting of information re-presented without challenge to children's thinking and imagination.

B. Cassop Junior and Infant School – geography guidelines

Introduction

One of our overarching aims is 'to help children make sense of the world in which they live'. In geography this can be taken literally. Geography has some distinct and unique characteristics; it deals with connections, actual spatial connections and connections of cause and effect. Geography **should encourage questions**; geography requires a **curious investigative approach** towards people and places.

In teaching geography it is important to organise activities which lead to the **understanding of important principles or generalisations** by the pupils. Geography must make sense to the pupil not as isolated bits of information but as a network of important ideas which help to explain the character of places; the ways people inter-relate with their environment; the spatial organisation of society and the interdependence of peoples and places.

A note on the planning

The National Curriculum's programmes of study cover three dimensions – Skills, Places, Themes. While any particular unit of work may be based in **one** of these dimensions, we should always involve the other dimensions:

- any work undertaken should involve children in developing and using their geographical skills;
- any thematic study (e.g. rivers, weather, environment, settlement) should be undertaken with reference to actual places;
- any study of a place should involve some themes.

If we take the idea of a 'cube' with three sides of skills, places and themes to represent the programme of study, our units of work can be a vertical or horizontal slice; **it will always involve the three aspects of work.**

Blocked units, continuous strands and skills

Blocked units

For example, Y2 'Where I live' – this will be given a limited block of time (6 hours) in a particular term. The actual time allowed and the pattern of the sessions will be planned medium term (i.e. one term ahead) by the class teacher.

Continuous strands

For example, Y2 'Introducing geographical concepts and vocabulary' – A continuous strand may be visited regularly and often. Again the pattern of time needs to be planned by the class teacher in medium-term plans, e.g. 15 minute sessions two afternoons per week for the 12-week term. The approach and resources will also be planned here, e.g. using the picture bank in groups of three children and occasionally as a class. [*It is worth pointing out that confining geography work to blocked topics is among geography inspectors' key criticisms of geography teaching. Therefore we suggest that continuous strands of geography is good practice.*]

Continuity and progression

The geography work is planned in units in order to manage the delivery of the curriculum. The sequence of the units is planned to encourage continuity and progression. For example, a unit of work on 'Journeys' follows work on 'Where I Live' and is in turn followed by a study of 'A Contrasting Locality'. Therefore, although planned as separate units of work we must constantly help children to make links to their previous experiences and to develop both the geographical network of important ideas and their geographical skills. The geography curriculum involves a considerable amount of revisiting important clusters of concepts. Each visit should attempt to broaden and deepen children's understanding. There are several recurrent elements.

Foundation Stage

The foundations of geography are to be found within the areas of **knowledge and understanding of the world.** At the Foundation Stage we are helping children to '**acquire a range of skills, knowledge and attitudes related to knowledge and understanding of the world in many ways'.**

Children at this age will learn predominantly through **exploration** and by having methods of learning modelled by the adults working alongside them. [*We point out that although Knowledge and Understanding of the World is a key early learning goal through which young children's geography work can be*

*developed, there are countless opportunities for geography teaching and
learning within the other five areas of learning within the Curriculum Guidance
Foundation Stage. It is hoped that, through viewing examples elsewhere in this
book, readers will note where geography work is present within all six areas of
learning.*]

From a geographical point of view we need to place children in situations
where they are **encouraged**:

- to question;
- to observe;
- to gather information, e.g. counting creatures, types of shop, photographs, talk to people;
- to experience surrounding planes;
- to experience the use of equipment – tools, computers, measuring tools,
  maps;
- to express opinions;
- to use experiences, e.g. to make models.

Much of the work will be **practical** and children will be encouraged to **talk**
about the experiences; children will be exposed to the correct and accurate
vocabulary, e.g. road, path, slope, church, chapel, stream, river, etc.

Some of the work will be from secondary sources:

- stories set in different places;
- stories which involve journeys or maps;
- pictures to talk about (or to extend with their own);
- simple maps, carpet maps, models.

Key Stage 1

Through Key Stage 1, pupils will increasingly:

- broaden and deepen their knowledge and understanding of places,
  patterns and processes;
- recognise and describe what places are like using appropriate vocabulary
  concerning landscape, jobs, weather, etc.;
- offer explanations for the characteristics of places;
- identify physical and human processes and describe some of their effect;
- employ geographical ideas learnt in one context to other studies at the
  same scale and at different scales;
- acquire information from a variety of sources, including first-hand
  observation, to investigate aspects of local and more distant and human
  environments;
- develop and use appropriate geographical skills.

Planning for progression

Among the principles which should influence planning for progression in Key Stages 1 and 2 are these:

- teaching should aim to build on pupils' existing knowledge and experience;
- learning tasks should be matched carefully to pupils' capabilities;
- particular attention should be given to those aspects of geography which not only interest pupils at the time of teaching but also provide satisfactory preparation for the next phase of education.

[*We suggest that the same principles are in fact appropriate for planning for progression in the Foundation Stage.*]

Taking account of the requirements of the programmes of study and the level descriptions for geography, it would be reasonable to plan for progression in pupil's learning through Key Stages 1 and 2 in terms of their:

- breadth of geographical knowledge;
- depth of geographical understanding;
- awareness of how places affect people and people affect places;
- development of their own view of people's relationship with the environment;
- development and use of geographical skills, especially in map work and enquiry.

Approach to teaching and learning

More detailed suggestions appear as part of the guidance for actual units of work.

Key issues and principles

- In order to ensure children have opportunities to cover both the **content** elements of the National Curriculum and acquire the **skills,** we will need to take a variety of approaches.
- Where possible, the skills will be introduced and used in context; for example **atlas use and world awareness** could and should be part of any study; sampling techniques and collection and display of information will be introduced and used within the study of locality.
- It is not sufficient to teach these skill as dry exercises; children will be more motivated to learn skills if there is an immediate and interesting use for them**.**
- Some work is planned specifically concerning skills. However (an example being some mapwork in Key Stage 1 or grid references at Key

Stage 2) when this is asked for within our plan it is in order that this skill can be subsequently used in the context of a study.

- In addition to the context (skills and knowledge) we consider it vital to develop positive **attitudes** towards geography (see Aims 4.1 on p. 64). To achieve this, units of work must be presented in a way which:

  a   is relevant to the child (they can see some point in studying it);
  b   links to their experience (start by trawling for what they already know);
  c   encourages curiosity and investigation;
  d   gives the children a sense of ownership of the work (this implies involving children in making decisions – perhaps allowing them to specialise in some aspect);
  e   is interesting.

Unique nature of geography

We must be aware of and encourage values, attitudes and approaches which are unique to geography; for example:

- a love of maps;
- a 'reverence' for the earth and the need to sustain it;
- an appreciation of connections and patterns and cause and effect (how we can trace the factors that result in a place being as it is);
- a respect for the diversity of peoples and their way of life;
- a desire to want to know more about the world.

Questions/problem-solving approach

Certain simple but fundamental geography questions should never be far from any work, questions such as:

What is it like to live there?
How did it get to be as it is?
Why do people live here?
What changes are likely?
What choices are possible?

In addition to the questions we will encourage and pose, children should be encouraged to **begin studies with their own pre-conceptions and generate their own questions** (What do I already know or think? What do I want to know?).

Much of geography should be approached as **problem-solving**. As in all subjects, one of our principle aims must be to encourage children to be **mentally active**; to investigate, consider and evaluate evidence for themselves. Geographical work should never be reduced to arid exercise or the regurgitation of facts. **Thinking skills** work can be developed through geography very efficiently by taking imaginative approaches.

Some of the approaches suggested in our **oracy guidelines** are highly appropriate for geography work.

Exchange work

We intend to develop links and exchange actual work – audio-tape and video-tape – with other schools in Great Britain and abroad. This gives our children a purpose as a focus for their locality work and in exchange, re-receive relevant and useful information. We have a twin school in Kenya and will seek a European partner school.

Development of other aspects of learning through geography

Well-planned Geography topics should yield opportunities for:

Literacy/English work

- a variety of real, purposeful reading and writing tasks: directions, letters to other schools/industry, etc.;
- topics/texts for interrogation, perhaps with literacy lessons.

Mathematics work

- data handling (statistics and data representation);
- co-ordinates;
- estimations (e.g. distance, time);
- data collection, etc.

As with English, mathematics comes alive when children can **use** it to inform their work.

ICT

Opportunities exist for:

- data handling (graphs, charts);
- mapwork;
- sensing (weather recording);
- research, e.g. comparing climate;
- correspondence with others via internet.

The National Curriculum expects ICT to be integrated into geography work.

Personal and social development

Geography should encourage children to reflect upon society and places. It involves making judgement (e.g. what do I like about my village?), considering arguments and points of view (e.g. conflict of quarrying/road building). We can and should take these opportunities to encourage fairness and an ability to see issues from more than one perspective.

Multi-cultural education

Here, the teacher of geography has a great responsibility. We must avoid stereotyping the people of the localities we study. We must encourage empathy and accuracy. We should emphasise the skills, achievement and wisdom of the society studied. We should encourage children to avoid any assumption that our way of life and values are superior. We should, if possible, encourage sufficient details in our studies to allow children to feel that they know actual people such as the Harvey Family, St Lucia or indeed link with actual people, e.g. Marich School, Kenya, Dinard School, France.

C. Policy for global dimension

Rationale

Global links can contribute greatly to children's spiritual, social, moral and cultural development. Global links can provide unique learning opportunities to explore feelings, problems, solutions. Most importantly **they contribute greatly to the major educational aim of helping children to understand and relate positively to the world in which we live.** Working within an area with few ethnic groups we consider it to be particularly important to allow our children opportunities to learn about other cultures.

What will this entail?

Links with communities within other countries, in particular links with specific schools and actual people. We will exchange information, develop work together and exchange work and encourage links of all kinds including visits to and from our linked communities.

Aims

- to better understand the diversity of our world;
- to widen children's perspectives;
- to promote positive attitudes towards people of differing cultures;
- to enable children to make connections with actual people;

- to enrich our learning by sharing ideas;
- to encourage our community to be outward looking;
- to provide real purposes and a real focus for work in many areas of the curriculum.

Progression through the key stages

Over the key stages, pupils' awareness and understanding of global issues might progress as follows:

Key Stage 1

At KS1 pupils begin to develop a sense of their own worth in relation to others. They develop a sense of themselves as part of a wider world and gain awareness of a range of different cultures and places. They learn that all humanity shares the same basic needs but that there are differences in how these needs are met.

Key Stage 2

At KS2 pupils develop their understanding beyond their own experience and build up their knowledge of the wider world and of different societies and cultures. They learn about the similarities and differences between people and places around the world and about disparities in the world. They develop their sense of social justice and moral responsibility and begin to understand that their own choices can affect global issues as well as local ones.

[*Although the Foundation Stage is not mentioned in Cassop's 'Global Dimension' policy documentation, we believe that some awareness of global matters is important in the Foundation Stage. Elsewhere in this book, we highlight research that shows the potential for global awareness exists among children of 4 years. Within the Foundation Stage Curriculum Guidelines there are references towards a global dimension within 3–5 year olds' learning. For example, 'resources from a variety of cultures are expected to be used for children's creative development' (QCA 2001: 116). It is expected that within personal, social and emotional development, early years provision will include 'play and learning opportunities that acknowledge children's particular religious beliefs and cultural backgrounds' (ibid.: 28). Within the knowledge and understanding of the world learning goal, early years practitioners are expected to present 'opportunities that help children to become aware of, explore and question issues of differences in gender, ethnicity, language, religion and culture ...' (ibid.: 82).*]

Eight key concepts

Within this progression through the key stages, the following key concepts form the core of learning about global issues:

Citizenship – gaining the knowledge, skills and understanding necessary to become informed, active, responsible global citizens.

Sustainable development – understanding the need to maintain and improve the quality of life now without damaging the planet for future generations.

Social justice – understanding the importance of social justice as an element in both sustainable development and the improved welfare of all people.

Values and perceptions – developing a critical evaluation of images of the developing world and an appreciation of the effect these have on people's attitudes and values.

Diversity – understanding and respecting differences and relating these to our common humanity.

Interdependence – understanding how people, places and environments are all inextricably inter-related and that events have repercussions on a global scale.

Conflict resolution – understanding how conflicts are a barrier to development and why there is a need for the resolution and the promotion of harmony.

Human rights – knowing about human rights and understanding their breadth and diversity.

School linking

Direct contact with school communities overseas does not simply offer opportunities for research and exchange of knowledge, but can also bring development issues vividly to life. It can also challenge the stereotyped, 'problem-orientated' image of people in less affluent countries and thereby contribute to education in values and attitudes in a multi-cultural global society.

At the time of writing, Cassop has established links with Marich Pass School in Western Pokot, Kenya, and with several Australian schools. The possibility of links with three European schools as part of a Comenius project focusing on environmental issues is being explored. We also have invitations to work with Tanzanian schools through the WWF.

Future developments

• to develop materials of use to Marich School;

- to exchange headteachers with Marich School;
- to make exchange visits to Denmark and France (teachers and possibly pupils).

Staff may also accept invitations to work with schools in Tanzania and in India and to host exchange teachers. Ideally we would like to extend the links to involve the community more actively and perhaps also to involve other schools.

Resources and support

- DfEE guidance 0115/2000, September 2000.
- **Material resources** – The National Grid for Learning (http://www. globaldimension.org.uk) contains a database of good quality materials that can help teachers of all subjects and all key stages bring a global dimension to the teaching (see page 16 of the Guidance for additional organisations that produce and make available their own materials).
- **Organisations** – There are a number of organisations at local and national level which specialise in supporting global perspectives in schools. Their activities include running workshops offering professional development opportunities for teachers, and providing information on school linking, resources and funding (see pages 16 and 17 of the Guidance).
- **Local Education Authority** – Durham LEA has policies relating to the international dimension. There is a designated officer with responsibility for supporting schools developing work in this area.

D. Guidance to all using geography pictures with children – based on the school's library of photographs

The National Curriculum expects children to understand a variety of geographical ideas and to use the correct geographical vocabulary.

As well as their studies of places we plan to use our photograph bank.

Why?

- to encourage curiosity;
- to give children a chance to see lots of examples of geographical features, e.g. coast, mountain;
- to start a conversation so that the proper geographical words can be used – you as teacher use them;
- to help children to think as a geographer – to ask themselves geographical questions.

How?

- small groups with 2–4 children and 2 or 3 pictures – 15 minutes maximum time;
- make the most of each picture, don't skip through;
- look with the children – say very little; **let them talk**;
- encourage speculation. Do it yourself perhaps **but only** after they have plenty of chance to question;
- give full answers if they ask but usually in geography the answers will be 'well I think they could be . . .' thus always encourage other possibilities;
- ask another child what they think of the first child's ideas.

Which words/ideas?

Reception/Year 1	over	land	lake	coast
	under	sea	river	island
	above	wood	stream	mountain
	village	town	weather	
Year 2	volcano	forest	country	climate
	valley	peak	plain	
	cliff	summit	ridge	

Try to encourage conversation which lead to questions such as:

What would it be like to live there? Would I like it?
Why do people live there? What do they do? What spoils it?
What would make it better? How has it become like that?
How is it different from the places I know? How is it similar to places I know?
What can I work out from the picture – e.g. season/climate/rich/poor/quiet/noisy, etc.

Almost any	I WONDER WHY? . . . question
	I WONDER WHAT? . . . question

Information with the picture

This is either in the pack or on the back of the picture; it is only for the teacher's guidance. Don't feel you have to go through it all – this might stop the children talking completely.

Golden rule:

Follow the children's lead then guide that lead towards geographical questions.

E. Understanding maps in the primary school

PERSPECTIVE	Toys on OHP, making literal maps (hand, leaf), floor rubbings (grates, manholes). Guess the object drawn from above.	Make a model village (Lego or boxes) keep on low table & draw from above.	Mapping the desk then classroom. Trace the neighbourhood from aerial photographs.	Draw a plan of house (outside walls).
DIRECTION	Vocabulary of direction, e.g. left, right in relation to classroom objects. Guided walks with older children/ blindfolded. Arrow routes, use of cassette-recorder.	Link directions to sun. Use of shadow stick. Sunrise and sunset. Fix cardinal points in classroom/ grounds. Use of portable direction indicators.	Signpost maps making a toposcope. Link direction to wind (wind rose, vane). Direction of trees (moss, angle of tree).	Use of compass watch / polar star method. Map orientation using grid lines/ north arrows.
LOCATION	Vocabulary of location (e.g. in front of, behind, etc.).	Naming objects on a teacher-prepared map of the classroom. Colour coding prepared classroom/street maps.	Model village. Recording on flat base the places where buildings are located if dismantled. Use grid co-ordinates for accurate recording.	
SCALE/ DISTANCE	Notion of scale via toys, buildings, animal toys, cars.	Draw objects to scale using graph paper.	Draw scaled plan of desk using $2\,cm^2$ graph paper. Draw scaled plans of classroom.	Plan of school grounds using pacing.
SYMBOLISM	Signs and symbols in the street. Features out of the window: invent signs and symbols.	Adventure story. Draw a map of the story with symbols (reverse process).	My ideal place. Draw it with symbols.	Draw a map for somebody else with symbols.
HEIGHT/ SLOPE/ RELIEF	Vocabulary of relief (high, low, up, down). Flow of water in school grounds. Who likes flat places, hilly places.	Use of arrows to indicate slopes in neighbourhood or school grounds.	Pictorial representation of hills and valleys in drawings. Relief games (snakes & ladders).	Layer colouring of school grounds according to high/low land. Use of spirit level.

⇐ LOWER PRIMARY

Figure 3.2 A sequence of mapwork activities (adapted from a table created by Michael McPartland of the University of Durham for Cassop School).

NB Historical maps and town plans have a great wealth of information about the past. Such maps may be used to encourage the skills of comparing and contrasting, of seeking evidence and relating such evidence to present day.

PERSPECTIVE	Journeys to school (cognitive maps), mapping the street.		Planning a place to live for old people; young children.	
DIRECTION	Compass directions, compass bearings. Route finding exercises: verbal mapping, coming to school, what is missing.	Games: Star Wars, Find the Dragon, Let's Go Home, Find the Coin.	Orienteering, compass trails, use of globe/ atlas to reinforce direction.	Route planning exercise, e.g. a new bypass.
LOCATION	Use of alpha numeric grids (A4) for classroom, school grounds. Locate the grid exercises; taxi or police games.	Use of 4 figure grid refs: Eastings, Northings. Relate to the neighbourhood map. Use of street map A–Z index.	Games, e.g. Battleship.	Use of 6 figure grid refs. Relate to features in neighbourhood. Locations on atlas (latitude, longitude) use of atlas index.
SCALE/ DISTANCE	Annotating partially prepared plans of classroom, school grounds, neighbourhood.		Measurement of straight line distances.	Measurement of winding routes (string, paper method).
SYMBOLISM		Games: Domino symbols, Battlefield, Country walk.		Symbols on different scale maps: problem of exaggeration. Describe route – conventional sign use.
HEIGHT/ SLOPE/ RELIEF	Techniques for measurement of height (trees, buildings).		Use of plasticine models to make islands; potato islands, slice and print.	Use of landscape models and use of transects.

UPPER PRIMARY

Figure 3.2 (continued)

B.   *Eglingham Church of England First School, Northumberland*

Eglingham Church of England Aided First School, founded in 1868, serves a north Northumberland rural community that extends well beyond the village of Eglingham itself. The majority of pupils travel to school by car or taxi. The school's 34 pupils are between the ages of 4 and 9 and are taught in two mixed-age classes. Class 1 includes Foundation Stage and Year 1 and Year 2 children of Key Stage 1. Class 2 comprises Year 3 and Year 4 children. The school has been known as a 'Beacon School' since 1998 and benefits from additional government funding to enable teachers to help other schools in the locality.

Acting headteacher Dorothy Douglas explains that the school's approach to geography is thematic and is based on a two-year rolling programme that ensures all relevant aspects of the Foundation Stage and the Programme of Study for Geography are addressed. The school has a highly detailed, comprehensive and flexible set of documents that ensure adequate and appropriate coverage of geography at all levels and at every stage of planning, i.e. long-, medium- and short-term. Available space allows for only a 'snapshot' of this impressive range of documentation relating to policy, planning and implementation.

Policy for curriculum planning

Aims

- To match pupil's performance to their potential.
- To extend and apply skills and knowledge, and to develop concepts and attitudes.
- To ensure agreement, coherence, continuity and progression within the curriculum.

Policy

Planning

The main themes of the curriculum are laid out in a two-year rolling programme of topics and areas of study (referred to as *long-term planning*), applicable to the under 4s and to each key stage. This programme forms the basis of our work. Over a two-year period we intend to provide a balanced, coherent curriculum demonstrating continuity and progression and allowing scope for differentiation. The two-year rolling programme enables comprehensive coverage of many areas through a multi-disciplinary approach, but other areas (or subjects) will require discrete coverage. Time need not be spread uniformly across the week, half-term or whole term, but each year will show a balanced coverage of the curriculum. Those areas not tackled through a topic or thematic approach can be delivered through a continuous strand (such as number work in maths), or through a modular single-subject approach (such as Key Stage 2 music).

At Key Stage 1, a unit analysis is formed for each term (referred to as *mid-term planning*), establishing links where appropriate between curriculum areas. The main focus of work and main opportunities for learning are identified. This is not a detailed analysis of Programmes of Study, but rather a broad view of the overall balance of subject opportunities.

Detailed lesson notes (referred to as *short-term planning*) are then made, outlining stimulus, activity, evaluation and resources. These are differentiated for each year group and curriculum area.

At both Key Stage 1 and Key Stage 2, *mid-term planning* takes the form of unit of work planning sheets for individual subjects, some of which may be linked by a common theme. Programmes of Study, outcomes and Attainment Targets are indicated. *Short-term planning* consists of detailed lesson notes (as described for Key Stage 1); some differentiation by year group or ability group is indicated, and other differentiation may be by outcome or by support from peers and adults.

Daily notebooks are used by teachers to indicate the organisation of the day, classroom management, groupings, and use of additional help (including auxiliary support in Class 1). Comments regarding pupil progress and/or evaluation of work may be included.

Progression

Progression is achieved by the gradual extension of content to develop awareness and understanding. It can be monitored through various forms of assessment, both formal (such as Key Stage 1 SATs) and informal (teacher's ongoing assessment).

Long-term planning at whole-school level

The two-year rolling programme of themes and topics to be covered is set out on clear charts which specify how these address the overall range of curriculum areas to be taught and the school term in which they will be implemented.

The Foundation Stage is taught via termly plans, i.e. three in a year, and incorporates aspects of themes covered within the rolling programme. This comprehensive long-term planning ensures that themes and topics introduced in the Foundation Stage are not repeated in Years 1 and 2.

Key Stage 1 written plans are marked with orange highlights to denote Year 1 and yellow highlights to denote Year 2 work; a system which again avoids repetition within the rolling programme and ensures comprehensive coverage. Within this whole-school rolling programme, geography is taught through sub-topics which are part of overall topics such as 'transport'. Some overall topics lend themselves almost entirely to geography. Sub-topics may last between two and four weeks.

Long-term planning is supported by a series of matrices covering Years 1 and 2 which detail knowledge, skills and understanding and ensure that the full breadth of study is covered. An example of a planning matrix for Key Stage 1 Geography is shown in Figure 3.3. These documents act as a unit of analysis for each topic in the long-term plan.

Medium-term planning

Medium-term planning sheets are prepared for every subject and for every topic which impinges upon it and are colour coded to differentiate between the years. They highlight all aspects of the Programme of Study, targeted learning outcomes and expected levels of attainment for each term's work, as illustrated in the example provided in Figure 3.4.

Medium-term planning is also supported by Topic Webs which address curriculum coverage in diagrammatic form. An example is provided in Figure 3.5.

This web features a topic entitled 'Go Bananas!' The inspiration for this derives from an Oxfam photocopiable resource pack about the journey of a banana from the Caribbean to the UK. The topic is central to the school's work in geography about distant places. We note that the web refers to an initial 'thought shower', which we explain on page 97.

	YEAR A			YEAR B		
	Term 1 Houses, and homes	Term 2 Journey through food	Term 3 Plants	Term 1 People (Harvest, Native Americans)	Term 2 Castles, transport	Term 3 2 habitats (wild/domestic)
Geographical enquiry				✓		
Ask geographical questions				✓		
Observe and record				✓		
Express their own views about people, places and environments						
Communicate in different ways						
Geographical skills						
Use geographical vocabulary	✓	✓				
Use fieldwork skills	✓					
Use globes, maps and plans at a range of scales				✓		
Use secondary sources of information						
Make maps and plans	✓					
Knowledge and understanding of places						
Identify and describe what places are like			✓	✓	✓	
Identify and describe where places are			✓	✓	✓	
Recognise how places have become the way they are and how they are changing			✓	✓	✓	✓
Recognise how places compare with other places			✓	✓	✓	
Recognise how places are linked to other places in the world			✓	✓	✓	
Knowledge and understanding of patterns and processes						
Make observations about where things are, and about other features in the environment		✓				✓
Recognise changes in physical and human features						✓
Knowledge and understanding of environmental change and sustainable development						
Recognise changes in the environment						
Recognise how the environment may be improved and sustained	✓					
Breadth of study						
Locality of the school						
Locality either in the United Kingdom or overseas that has physical and/or human features that contrast with those in the locality of the school						
Study at a local scale						
Carry out fieldwork investigations outside the classroom						

For examples of teaching points, please refer to specific programmes of study.
Main focus of teaching and learning: shade in the appropriate box.
Other teaching points reinforced/revised: tick the appropriate box.

Figure 3.3 Key Stage 1 Geography: Planning matrix: knowledge, skills and understanding.

Unit of Work/Topic: Journey Through Food 'Go Bananas!' Oxfam

Length in weeks: **Time per week:**	**Links to other curriculum areas:** Art, Technology, Music, Literacy, RE, Science, IT, Maths	**Year A/B** **Autumn/Spring/Summer** **First/Second half**
Programme of study	**Examples of learning outcomes**	**ATs**

Geographical enquiry Ask geographical questions Observe and record Express their own views about people, places and environments Communicate in different ways **Geographical skills** Use geographical vocabulary Use fieldwork skills Use globes, maps and plans at a range of scales Use secondary sources of information Make maps and plans	 Links shown on medium-term plans for relevant curriculum areas.	**Level 1** Pupils show their knowledge, skills and understanding in studies at a local scale. They recognise and make observations about physical and human features of localities. They express their views on features of the environment of a locality. They use resources that are given to them, and their own observations, to ask and respond to questions about places and environments.
Knowledge and understanding of places Identify and describe what places are like Identify and describe where places are Recognise how places have become the way they are and how they are changing Recognise how places compare with other places Recognise how places are linked to other places in the world	 Sequencing through photographs from Oxfam pack to show environment and processes.	**Level 2** Pupils show their knowledge, skills and understanding in studies at a local scale. They describe physical and human features of places, and recognise and make observations about those features that give places their character. They show an awareness of places beyond their own locality. They express views on the environment of a locality and recognise how people affect the environment. They carry out simple tasks and select information using resources that are given to them. They use this information and their own observations to help them ask and respond to questions about places and environments. They begin to use appropriate geographical vocabulary.
Knowledge and understanding of patterns and processes Make observations about where things are, and about other features in the environment Recognise changes in physical and human features	Shoe box 'environments'. Tracing distances travelled by bananas to UK. Where do bananas grow?	
Knowledge and understanding of environmental change and sustainable development Recognise changes in the environment Recognise how the environment may be improved and sustained	World Map Jobs Fair Trade	**Level 3** Pupils show their knowledge, skills and understanding in studies at a local scale. They describe and compare the physical and human features of different localities and offer explanations for the locations of some of those features. They are aware that different places may have both similar and different characteristics. They offer reasons for some of their observations and for their views and judgements about places and environments. They recognise how people seek to improve and sustain environments. They use skills and sources of evidence to respond to a range of geographical questions, and begin to use appropriate vocabulary to communicate their findings.
Breadth of study Locality of the school Locality either in the United Kingdom or overseas that has physical and/or human features that contrast with those in the locality of the school Study at a local scale Carry out fieldwork investigations outside the classroom		

Figure 3.4 Eglingham CE First School: Key Stage I: Medium-term planning sheet for geography.

Topic Plan – Key Stage I

Initial 'thought shower' sessions with children to establish prior knowledge of topic, and compare at end of topic as part of assessment process.

ICT
Word processing for labels,
Stories, etc.
Revelation Art Package. Pictures, poster, etc.

Numeracy
Data Handling. Pictograms, Block, Bar. Carroll & Venn diagrams. Subjects: fruit and pirates. Role play: fruit shop – money

Literacy
Topic words.
Banana poems.
Labels for shoe box environments.
Stories from the Caribbean.
Big Book 'A Faraway Place'.
Pirates – fiction and non-fiction.

PSHE
Fair Trade.
Considering statements for an enquiry session.
Caribbean poems and prayers for workshop.

Go Bananas!
Display of banana.
Leaves/boxes/labels, etc.
Caribbean artefacts, including musical instruments, dolls, books, posters.

Geography
Where do bananas grow?
Link to World Map.
The Equator.
Banana growing. Sequence of processes through series of cards provided in 'Go bananas' pack.
Making shoebox environments with plantations, figures, etc., to display sequence from picking to supermarket.

Music
Music from the Caribbean.
Selection of musical instruments.
Dance – using stories, songs, etc. as stimuli 'Banana' songs.

Design and Technology

Food
Banana cake.

Textiles
Tye Dye large fabric samples with definition added with collage, sequins, puff paints, etc.

Art
Mask making.
Line drawing.
Wax relief.
Still life – fruit.
Caribbean painting (donated by parent) to question children 'What do you see?' and to use as stimulus for individual interpretation.

Figure 3.5 Topic plan: Go Bananas!

Short-term planning

Short-term planning at Eglingham School includes lesson plans for each subject and actual methods of tackling activities and intended learning outcomes. Such methods include 'thought showers' and 'putting words in jail' – methods discussed in Chapter 4, page 97. Indeed, the development of 'thinking skills' is perceived as being of fundamental importance in early years geography teaching at Eglingham.

An example of a completed lesson planning sheet, taken from the 'Go Bananas' topic is illustrated in Figure 3.6. Such sheets are supplemented by

	Lesson 1	Lesson 2	Lesson 3	Lesson 4	Lesson 5	Lesson 6
Teacher input/ Stimulus / **Activity**	Visit from Senior Adviser giving talk on chocolate. This will link with 'chocolat crispies', science work and Easter mini unit as well as considering foods from around the world. All Class One.	Whole class introduction to unit. Explain topic. Divide children in pairs older/younger. Distribute banana growing pictures. Read individual short captions. If children recognise their picture they stand in sequenced line with appropriate caption. Discuss. Display.	Recap last lesson. Explain learning outcome sequences. Children working on 4 shoe box environments showing journey of bananas from plant to table. Using modelling clay, cardboard, playmobil figures, etc. to create environments.	Look at large World Atlas. Discuss. In pairs older/younger. Find the UK on outline maps. Y2 mark round trip of ships transporting bananas to the UK (6 days). Discuss. Look at Atlas. Where do bananas grow, what do you notice, why?	Explain outcomes. Provide list of jobs. Discuss. Provide two drawings of banana: Banana costs 10p. Divide into sections. See "Go Bananas pack", p.15.	Warm up game. Explain task. In 2s produce question for group to discuss. E.g. Is it fair for growers to only receive 1p? How hard do they work? Sit in circle. Voting system to choose most popular question, e.g. I vote each. Partners posing winning choice begin. Others join discussion 'I agree/disagree because . . .' End of lesson sum up conclusions. Each child to contribute one sentence if possible but give opportunity to 'pass'.
Learning outcomes		To introduce the idea of a sequence of events. To practise reading and communication skills.	To build understanding of the stages of a 'journey' of a banana' by creating settings.	To give practise in reading and using world maps to help children to appreciate the large distances travelled by bananas. Reading and using maps. Different crops grow in different regions of the world.	Y1 To experience a greater understanding of what the jobs involve. Y2 Introductory discussion. Who gets what? How do growers feel? Is this fair? To help learn about who gets what.	To encourage thinking skills through enquiry process.

Resources
'Go Bananas!' photopack Oxfam.
Artefacts from children.
World Atlas.

Figure 3.6 Geography KSI: Bananas: Lesson planning sheet.

teachers' daily diaries in which they record details of how all activities will be covered at classroom level.

The majority of information and examples provided here are from the school's planning at Key Stage 1. Similarly detailed procedures exist (including long-term plans, weekly plans, topic webs and lesson plans) for the Foundation Stage. The transition from Foundation Stage to Key Stage 1 is a relatively smooth transition because the pupils are mixed within the same classroom. The Foundation Stage children often have the same starting point in lessons as the Key Stage 1 children and they share the same display areas.

The physical layout of Mrs Douglas' Reception and Years 1 and 2 classroom is such that the pupils can readily be grouped. On some occasions the Reception children move into the adjacent school hall and with the support of the two classroom assistants, the three age groups can receive individual attention.

Within the context of this chapter, this case study of excellent practice has necessarily focused on the organisation and documentation of Eglingham School's policy and planning. Further details of the school's work in practice are provided in Chapter 4, page 96.

Chapter 4

Policy into practice

This substantial chapter provides a number of case studies of good practice in early years education, gleaned from various schools and individuals. The purpose of including these examples and illustrative 'vignettes' is to provide practical illumination of some of the theoretical and contextual issues highlighted and addressed throughout the book. The focus of the studies varies in terms of scope and range: some are at the level of whole-school matters; others focus on the specific learning themes of the National Curriculum and approaches to teaching and learning; others on external links and working with partners in the field of geographical education provision. Together they supplement and reinforce issues illustrated by way of practical examples elsewhere in this volume; for example, in Chapter 5 on training and professional development, and in Chapter 6 on resources.

Our case studies are grouped under three broad headings as follows:

Teaching geography

- Teaching geographical enquiry and skills.
- Teaching knowledge and understanding of places.
- Teaching knowledge and understanding of patterns and processes.
- Teaching knowledge and understanding of environmental change and sustainable development.

Making links

- Links across the curriculum.
- Community and parental links.

Assessment and record-keeping

- Progression.
- Collecting, recording and interpreting assessment information.

TEACHING GEOGRAPHY

Teaching geographical skills and enquiry

The presentation of examples of teaching and learning which focus on this particular aspect of the Programme of Study alone is not straightforward: inevitably the examples which follow are extracted from cases of good practice where the highlighting of geographical enquiry and skills is set within the context of broad themes or topics that link with other elements of the breadth of study and with other subjects.

Development of mapwork skills

This topic focuses on inclusion of geographical skills in the curriculum. Every Key Stage 1 child, no matter how young, can be introduced to one or more of the skills of mapwork. Planning for teaching in this area should take account of the basic elements of mapwork (Catling 1988) which provide the skills-based content for any scheme or topic. These are:

1   *Perspective* – presents features in plan form, enables us to see what is hidden from view at ground level.
2   *Position and orientation* – maps show how various features are related to one another in 'space' and where they are located. From them we can give directions. Systems of grid referencing enable us to give accurate locations.
3   *Scale* – maps are scaled-down versions of the real thing. A plan view of a landscape or place is represented on a piece of paper.
4   *Map content* – content varies from map to map. Some emphasise specific features, e.g. streets, buildings, height of land. Content is dependent on the purpose for which the map is intended and, of course, its scale.
5   *Symbols* – are used to indicate what is recorded in the map's content. A key is a related feature, necessary so that the map reader can interpret the symbols.
6   *Additional information* (maps often provide useful information to supplement the content symbols: e.g. names of streets, buildings, towns, etc. types of farmland, shops, age of historic sites).

This content serves to help meet the basic aim of the topic expressed in conceptual terms which is to develop the children's concepts of space and place, both fundamental to geographical education. The content should also be interpreted within the context of the National Curriculum requirements, concerned with skills.

A detailed topic plan can therefore be devised which includes reference to the specific geographical education which forms its central core, expressed in terms of content, concepts and skills. It is then appropriate to consider which other areas of the curriculum will be addressed in implementing this plan so that meaningful links are identified and included in planning documentation.

The basic objectives of a mapwork topic maybe to help children develop the following ideas (stated at the level of adult understanding):

- Maps and plans can be 'read' by understanding basic elements, e.g. symbols, scale, direction.
- Maps and plans tell us about places. They help to locate objects and places in relation to each other.
- Printed maps help to develop our 'mental maps' or images of the world.
- Maps suggest distinct territories in our modern world. Many geographical or environmental issues and concerns do not fall within neat and distinct national boundaries.

Theoretical background

Stages in the development of cognitive mapping may be summarised as follows:

A *Topological (egocentric) stage*. Around 5 years of age. Children will draw 'link-picture' maps. Known places (drawn as pictures) will be connected in some way. Direction, scale, orientation and distance are non-existent.

B *Euclidean (abstract) stage*. Around 10 years of age. Children will draw accurate and detailed maps which demonstrate abstract co-ordination. Scale, direction and symbolic representation will be well developed.

The quasi-egocentric and quasi-projective stages occur between these two. Children will gradually represent their localities and other places as quasi-maps, with increasing attention to detail and continuity of routes. They will show increasing ability to take account of direction, orientation, distance, scale and representation in plan form.

Clearly the first three years in school are the crucial period when pupils should be helped in their transition from topological to Euclidean operations. A wide range of classroom tasks will assist in this progression towards formality and accuracy. Children can be encouraged to draw pictorial, spontaneous maps of such things as 'my house and street', 'my route to school', 'where I go to the shops'. Imaginative picture mapping can also arise from story time – many stories lend themselves to the illustration of journeys or to the reconstruction of places, as discussed in much greater detail in a later case study. This is an excellent cross-curricular link with English through story, discussion and vocabulary.

A key conclusion from research evidence on this topic is that no child in school is too young to be introduced to the appreciation and use of maps. Blades and Spencer (1986) tested the feasibility of teaching nursery age children about map use. Their research involved investigating whether children of this age could be taught how to orientate maps – an essential part of efficient map use. Results indicated that children who had received training in orientation both learned and remembered related skills. Conversely, it was found that a control group was unable to use maps efficiently, performing no better than if its members had been guessing.

Related experiments show that children quickly learn strategies for overcoming problems such as incorrectly orientated maps. This and other research evidence suggest that teachers should introduce mapwork to children much earlier than the traditional age of 7–8 years. It should also be recognised that there is still much research to be done on the abilities required to use maps successfully, and on the development of mapwork skills. The complex mental abilities involved remain unclear. Consequently, there is no strong agreement on the best way of introducing maps to young children, or on the sequencing of mapwork skills. A range of ways of introducing early mapwork into the classroom has been suggested by writers in this field, and they include the use of plan views and aerial photographs. One common area of agreement deriving from research evidence is that geographical concepts are best learned within a particular context. Therefore, the most valuable mapwork activities will probably be those which are meaningful or real to the young learners.

Some of the activities which follow suggest a context (e.g. everyday objects in the classroom, the school playground). Others are presented in more abstract form in the hope that readers will adapt them for use in their own individual situations within the constraints of available resources.

Suggested activities

- Draw plans of everyday objects and use as the basis for comparing plan view with oblique view. Let the children draw around familiar objects on a piece of paper, e.g. key, eraser, pencil, stamp, building brick. Ask them to write a list of the things that remain the same about these objects (size, shape) and things that have changed (details of colour, patterning, texture). Introduce the key idea that plans represent three-dimensional objects in two dimensions. They are the bird's eye view or what we see from above.
- Extend the above activity by dividing children into pairs. One of each pair should provide plan drawings of six objects; the other has to guess which objects have been drawn around. Who can guess the greatest number accurately without needing clues? If necessary, children can provide clues by colouring their objects, adding patterns, details, etc. This underpins a basic understanding of the need to read and interpret plans and maps and the use of keys. It also (without consciously referring to the fact) limits plans at this stage to objects which will fit on to a piece of

paper. The logical progression will be to introduce further activities requiring the use of scale.

- Let the children draw (without accuracy of scale at this stage) plans of other familiar, simple objects for their partners to interpret – perhaps plans of their desk (Figure 4.1). Incorporate keys after partners have made a 'good guess' without them.
- Discuss the key idea that, once plans are drawn, objects are 'fixed' on the paper in relation to each other. If the objects on the desk are rearranged, a new plan must be drawn to represent its accuracy. Stress that this is an important aspect of plans – they show us the fixed location of objects in relation to each other. Larger plans, for example, of rooms, streets and buildings, can therefore help us to find our way from 'object to object'. Explain that we usually use the word 'map' to describe the bird's eye view of larger areas, but maps have similar features to plans and serve the same purpose.

At the simplest level, draw one object in oblique view, e.g. a house (Figure 4.2) and discuss what this would look like when drawn in plan form (Figure 4.3). Ask children to say what a bird would see when flying

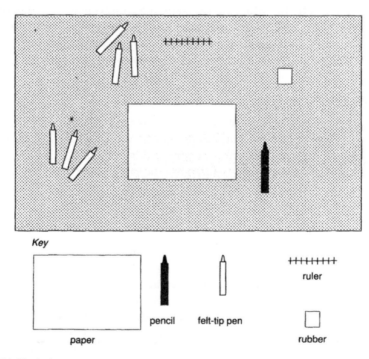

Figure 4.1 My desk.

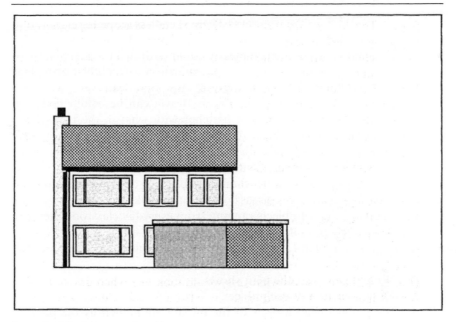

Figure 4.2 Worksheet outline (a).

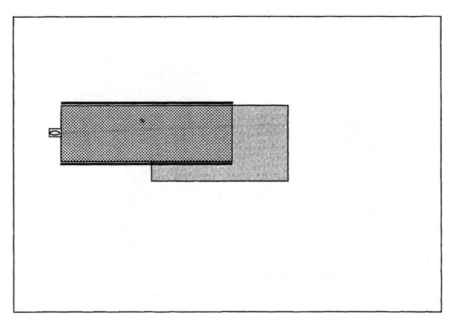

Figure 4.3 Worksheet outline (b).

over it. Would it see the windows? There is endless scope for elaboration of this activity – as scenes become more complex (Figures 4.4 and 4.5).

- Many scenes of increasing complexity could be drawn for the children to 'match' and colour, and they could be asked to construct their own plans from the oblique view. Activities of this kind lead very well into discussion on the use of keys. Objects drawn can be colour coded to show an understanding of what matches with what in the two scenes. Boxes can be drawn below the diagrams to be coloured in as a key. This aspect of work also links with the development of skills of symbolic representation. As already mentioned, young children's natural inclination is to draw pictures rather than symbols. The drawing of plans from oblique views encourages discussion about suitable ways of representing the bird's eye view of objects ranging from everyday classroom items to the wider world of buildings, trees, railway lines, etc.
- Make 'object-in-plan-form' workcards for the children to interpret. Ask them to:
  1 Write down what the plan shows.
  2 Draw a picture of each object.
  3 Write down what aspects of the picture are hidden by the plan.
- Devise games so that the children draw around objects for their friends to try to identify – they can be coloured in and details added to make the drawings look like the real thing. Progress by asking children to imagine

Figure 4.4 Worksheet outline (c).

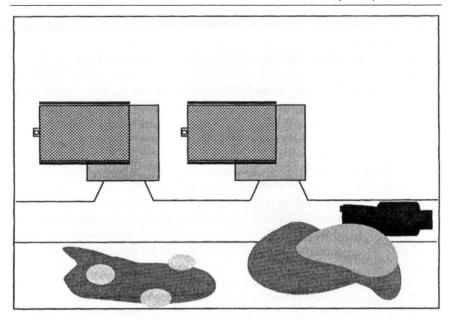

Figure 4.5 Worksheet outline (d).

that a spider has walked onto their sheet of paper and wants to investigate all the objects depicted. Draw a path that the spider takes to visit all the objects. As the drawings are joined in this way, they are linked together in space and in the children's minds. This is an important mapwork concept. Activities like these can extend over several lessons, familiarising children with the idea that a map is a representation of space occupied by objects depicted in plan form, and that the objects are in a fixed location in space.

- As a progression from such activities, children can be asked to construct their own maps (without accurate scale) and devise their own symbols. An important question can then be asked: How do other people interpret your symbols? Again, this links to an understanding of the need for a key, and the idea that many published maps have an agreed pattern of symbols that can easily be recognised. Ideas such as these link skills of map construction with the equally important skills of map reading and interpretation.

- Discuss the use of appropriate symbols for map interpretation. Ask the class to suggest why an agreed set of symbols is useful. What difficulties would arise if everyone's village plan had a different key? Let the children look at a range of similar scale Ordnance Survey maps. While they may not comprehend these in detail, they should be able to appreciate their common key. Point out certain universally agreed symbols, e.g. for rivers, footpaths, phone boxes.

- Take a polaroid or digital camera out into the street. Photograph the view from various angles. Back in the classroom, analyse the content of the photographs. Let the children attempt to draw plans of the same scenes.

Consider:
  - What appears on the photographs that could not be on a plan (e.g. children playing, traffic).
  - What can be shown on a plan that is not revealed by the photographs (e.g. what is behind shops and houses).

- If possible, obtain an aerial photograph of your locality. Compare this with a printed map. Let the children see how many features of the photograph they can identify on the map. What does the map not show?

- Consider the idea of scale. Children in the early years in school are surrounded by experience of this without conscious realisation or discussion of the fact. Use frequent opportunities to raise awareness of scaled-down versions of reality. Questions such as 'Why is the play house in the classroom smaller than a real house?' and 'Why is the dolls' cutlery smaller than that which we use at lunchtime?' will promote valuable geographical discussion, linked to the general development of vocabulary and conversation about everyday things. Introduce the formality of scale by asking how we could represent an object which is bigger than the piece of paper we want to draw it on. (This will lead on naturally from the 'drawing around familiar objects' activities already described as inevitably some children will have selected items that were bigger than their paper.) Initially, concentrate on a scale of half size, done best with pieces of paper or card in the first instance, and then (probably in Year 2) progress to more complex scales and ideas on how we draw such things as our desk, the classroom, the school, the playground. While little formal work can be done in interpreting scales, do introduce children to a variety of published maps, partly as an awareness-raising exercise. They will see that not all maps are of the same scale; we have 'large scale maps' and 'small scale maps'; some maps show the whole world on a piece of paper, others show only the streets of the locality.

- Give practice in locating objects in relation to each other. Plenty of practice can be given in putting models back in the correct place, making sure that apparatus is placed in its correct order, etc. Perhaps a model village could be set out, and then reassembled so buildings and trees are replaced in similar positions. This is sound early years geography, affording practice in recording locations and in simple plan/map construction. Key vocabulary to be introduced includes 'opposite', 'in front of', 'by the side of', 'behind', 'next to'. The progression of these skills in later years will involve an understanding of grids and co-ordinates in order to make specific locations explicit. Such skills are linked to an understanding of direction, which in the early years involves familiarity with the vocabulary of 'right', 'left', 'backwards', 'forwards', etc., and an awareness of rotation of the self in space. Before formal points of the compass are introduced, give plenty of practice in turning through 90 degrees, 180 degrees, 270 degrees and 360 degrees, using terminology of turning to the right or left for a quarter-turn, half-turn, three-quarter turn and a whole turn. Formal elements of direction, the points of the compass, could be introduced at an appropriate stage, beginning with the four cardinal points – north, south, east and west.

- Help children to transfer the skills of understanding of direction to reading published maps. Consult a globe. Explain that north is the direction towards the North Pole from any other location. South is the direction towards the South Pole. East and west can be related to the rising and setting of the sun. If the time of year is appropriate encourage the children to observe the sunrise and sunset, noting thereby which rooms in their home face east and which west. Study published maps and note how direction is indicated.

- Much scope exists for linking PE activities with understanding of direction. Divide children into groups in the school hall or playground and play games where they are asked to follow instructions relating to movement through 90-degree angles. Five children in a group provide an ideal number, one in the centre and four at the cardinal compass points. Children can take it in turns to be in the centre and make appropriate movements. After each turn, the centre child must state who he or she is facing, who is behind, who is to the right and who to the left, thus reinforcing related vocabulary.

A final element of mapwork, that of relief, or height of land, is perhaps the most difficult of all to introduce at a formal level. How difficult it is even for adults to appreciate the abstract idea that a certain place is so many metres above the level of the sea and represented by contour lines. In the infant school, it is perfectly appropriate to reinforce basic vocabulary of relief, such as 'high up', 'low', 'hills', 'steep' and 'gentle', and to show maps which indicate that some land is higher than others. The relief of the locality can be discussed; perhaps some children have to walk up or down hills to get to school or to the shops, and some may visit hilly or mountainous areas, which can be described in terms of their being 'high up', with views 'over' other land which is 'lower'.

The above activities are specific to the development of understanding of the basic elements of mapwork. While pursuing these, have a good range of maps on display for children to observe. Even if the formality is beyond their conceptual capacity, young children will gain a great deal from awareness that various forms of map exist. It is perfectly appropriate to display as many forms of map-style representation as possible, including maps of the world, large-scale maps of the locality and school environment, street plans of your town or village, A–Z type maps and Ordnance Survey maps. Add to these regular displays of the children's own maps and maps of imaginary places.

This topic can be augmented by some valuable and more general cross-curricular interpretations of the theme. For example:

- Explore the origins of map-making. Thousands of years ago the very first 'maps' were mere scratches in soil or sand. Prehistoric people used symbols of this kind to help them find food, water and their way back home from a hunting expedition. Draw pictures of cave people carving a sign for water in the earth.
- Ask the children to make a list or talk about the variety of information we can obtain from world maps, e.g. locations of countries, oceans, names of major cities, rivers. Look at a variety of maps of one country (an ideal opportunity to demonstrate the use of atlases) and point out that maps can be devised to provide a wide range of information.
- Tell the story of Christopher Columbus, who sailed west in 1492 in search of the Indian Spice Islands. His famous voyage led to the discovery of two previously unmapped continents – North America and South America. Thus the world was seen by mapmakers to be a very different place.
- Read stories that tell of journeys across land and sea, both real and imaginary. Let the children draw spontaneous maps of fictional journeys and trace the route of factual ones on printed maps.

This case study on developing mapwork skills has been included for two reasons. First, to give a number of practical ideas which will be of use to anyone planning topics on this subject. Second, to demonstrate that mapping is an example of education which is specifically geographical, and therefore needs to be addressed in its own right as a discernible and critical area of learning; it can be linked in a meaningful way to other areas of the curriculum. Furthermore, to a large extent, it arises spontaneously out of traditional good practice in the early years classroom. It is an excellent example of how the skills of geography (in this case graphicacy) can contribute to the general intellectual development of children in the first three years in school.

Developing thinking skills at Eglingham Church of England Aided First School, Northumberland

Mrs Douglas' class at Eglingham School (see also page 76) engages with a wide range of geographical themes and topics. Pupils are systematically encouraged to develop enquiry and thinking skills which are recognised as being of fundamental importance to geographical education. The class contains up to five different age groups or cohorts of children: Foundation Stage children, including some Reception children from the previous year, a

January intake of nursery children and an Easter intake as well as Key Stage 1 children in Year 1 and Year 2. It is a challenging teaching context that requires careful thought about how to tackle skills among children of all ages and abilities. Some of the activities which Dorothy Douglas finds work very well are described here.

An '**Enquiry**' activity commences with a 'warm up' game, which focuses thinking and aids concentration. An example of such a game is when children sit on chairs in a circular formation, then attempt to stand up individually saying 1, 2, 3, etc. The aim is to have all children on their feet. If two or more children even attempt to stand together the game reverts to No. 1. The main activity then involves dividing the class into groups, each with two or three children. Groups are encouraged to pose a question concerned with any aspect of a geography topic being studied at the time. An example might be: 'Why don't we grow bananas in England?' The class then vote on the one question they would most like to address, choosing their own method of voting. This gives rise to a whole-class discussion, beginning with comments and ideas from the children who posed the initial question. This activity encourages children to think up a whole range of questions and then proceed to focus on particular ideas and enquiries in an orderly way. Children develop skills such as speaking up and waiting their turn, but do not have to contribute unless they wish to. Children also learn to practise the use of geographical vocabulary. At the end of the enquiry the class agrees on a short statement to sum up the discussion. Each child has the opportunity to add to this summary which sets out to answer the original question.

Sometimes, children in Mrs Douglas' class are not quite sure that they understand a word or skill so individual children, groups of children and the whole class have the opportunity to put a word or a concept or skill into **jail**. This means that some aspect of learning that is a bit difficult can be put aside and explored further in order to really grasp it and reach a clear under-standing. Mapping exercises, work on scale and attempts at graph inter-pretation have all been into jail for a time because they involve difficult concepts and are hard to put into practice for some children. Such an approach means that children do not have to worry if they 'can't do it' or 'don't understand it' until further lessons have unlocked what a certain word or skill means.

Often, Mrs Douglas conducts **'thought showers'**. Such brainstorming events take place with the children at the start of a topic in order to establish prior knowledge and to enable comparison of this with end-of-topic knowledge as part of the assessment process. The 'shower' conversations thus start off with the children being encouraged to say everything they know or have heard about something or some particular place. These initial ideas are revisited at the end of the topic or set of lessons when children are invited to change their minds in the light of their learning and reflect on the new things they have discovered. Children are encouraged to know that it is acceptable to change their minds and that learning is a process which sometimes involves removing original ideas and replacing them with new ones; also that it can be a process of building on and developing what is known already.

Another much enjoyed and highly successful thinking and problem-solving activity at Eglingham School employs a drama technique known as the **'1, 2, 3, freeze'** method. It is a splendid way of consolidating skills and assessing knowledge of, for example, patterns and processes. It is also an example of good cross-curricular work – linking geographical knowledge with drama; and can furthermore be used as a basis for assessment. Mrs Douglas explains: 'I accessed this method many years ago through an early years drama course and have expanded and changed it so that it can include the entire age range from Foundation Stage pupils to Year 2 taking part in the same session. The activity works well with two adults taking lead roles, e.g. teacher and classroom assistant, but can be equally successful if an adult and a child lead it. One of the leaders acts as a central figure in the drama. He or she begins the activity by sitting on a chair looking extremely "worried". The other person leads the children in the unfolding process that then takes place. The children begin by sitting on the floor in front of the worried central figure. They chant "1, 2, 3, unfreeze" and the figure comes to "life" and explains what the problem is. An example of such a problem could be that "it is Easter and I have never eaten a chocolate egg in my life." The idea of the activity is that the children then set about solving the problem. They chant "1, 2, 3, freeze" to the leader, who then becomes "invisible" while they discuss the problem. The leader of the problem-solving needs to be inventive and help take the drama forward through constantly moving and changing scenes as ideas evolve. For example, the children may say "let's go to the shop and buy her one" (an egg) – at which point the leader may suggest "no, let's make it a very special egg" and point to some cacao trees "growing in the corner of the room that are ready to be cut down". Through such unfolding ideas and drama the children explore the process from growth of ingredients to manufacture of the finished chocolate egg – always pausing and keep the figure with the problem informed of progress. They engage with this person by chanting "1, 2, 3, unfreeze" at appropriate points and explain, for example, "we are doing such and such ... we have cut down beans ..." etc. etc. ... reinforcing the process in their own minds. There will also be constant referral to the chair for clarification of points, or gathering of further relevant information, always done by "unfreezing" and then "freezing" the figure once again until the solution to the problem is found. In the example of the chocolate egg, the conclusion of the activity could be the presentation of "the egg" to the person in the chair, who then shares it with the whole group.

'I have found that "the sky is the limit" with drama activities. You can do anything and journey anywhere in the world through them in order to help with geographical learning. Good activities will be child centred, with the teacher always prepared to "seize the moment" and lead the thinking and action forward.'

Practising geographical enquiry and skills in Ebchester School Grounds

For some schools, one of the best environments for encouraging young children to talk and ask questions is the school garden. Richard Coombes, who is headteacher at Ebchester Church of England Primary School in County Durham, believes that: 'While out in the garden and school grounds, the children talk and ask about everything ... things they'd never say in the classroom.' The school garden and the school grounds form a beautiful place for learning, just walking around outside is enough to inspire any number of questions.

At the time of writing Ebchester School has 92 pupils, 5.5 staff and 3 support staff. The school's geography policy has a section that addresses the teaching and learning of geography skills; asking questions forms a part of

Plate 4(i)   A tiled map of the school grounds is one of the imaginative features of the outdoor environment.

Plate 4(ii) Looking over the pond to the stone wall and the end of the school field.

this programme of study within the policy document which states that children's geographical skills should develop during the Foundation Stage and Key Stage 1 with:

Use of appropriate vocabulary

E.g. use of everyday words to describe geographical features, e.g. hill, river.

Asking geographical questions

E.g. beginning to ask and respond to everyday questions about places.

Undertaking fieldwork

E.g. making observations about a place.

Making maps and plans

E.g. drawing a plan of a familiar place.

Using and interpreting maps and globes

E.g. understanding that a map is a picture of a place.

Using secondary sources

E.g. using resources provided to answer questions about a place.

Collecting and recording evidence

E.g. drawing a picture to record a building.

Communicating knowledge

E.g. recounting a walk around the school grounds.

Children in Year 1 and Year 2 classes at Ebchester undertake five geography topics, all based on QCA units that are explored during a two-year rolling programme. Each topic engages children in enquiry and skills development.

For the '**Around our school**' topic, teachers address the programmes of study: 1b, 1d, 2a, 2b, 2c and 2d. Children in Year 1 draw simple maps of their routes to school; they write instructions for someone else to follow the routes; they label a whole class plan of the school; children orally describe the route to school from their own maps and try to order or place in sequence buildings or places of interest that are passed on the way. Surveys are made to investigate how all the children travel to school and basic bar graphs are made. The class teacher Nicola Woolley uses relevant websites to show children maps of the local area, helping children to locate the school and their homes. Local photos are collected and a digital camera is used by the teacher and children to make a 'virtual tour' of the village or the local town nearby.

The topic '**How can we make our area safer?**' is Geography Unit 2 within the QCA scheme of work. Year 1 children work on programmes of study 1a, 1b, 1c, 1d, 2a and 2b. Children are invited to engage with questions about roads and traffic; they conduct a survey among themselves and their families, they express their opinions about safe transport and parking and they suggest solutions; children recount and record the findings of a traffic-observation walk around the local area; the class sends emails to the local council about safety in the local area and children use digital cameras to record elements of traffic on local roads.

At Ebchester, '**An island home**' addresses 2c, 2d and 2e from the skills and enquiry programmes of study. Children in Year 2 learn how to use dictionaries and glossaries to find definitions and learn new words such as 'jetty', 'headland', 'mountainside'. Nicola Woolley uses the popular stories about *Katie Morag*, written by *Mairi Hedderwick*, to familiarise children with Scottish island environments. Although, the island setting of Struay in the stories is fictional, maps and atlases are used to locate other Scottish islands and children follow a route on a map from their home area to the main Scottish islands. CD ROMS depicting pictures of Scottish islands are used with taped stories and videos as secondary sources of information.

Programmes of study 1d, 2a, 2c, 2d and 2e are addressed in the Year 2 topic **'Going to the seaside'**. Photos, websites and holiday programmes recorded from television provide children with appropriate secondary sources for this topic. Where possible, a travel agent comes into the school to talk with the children about their experience of seaside locations. Children relate their knowledge and understanding of their own locality to another (seaside) area and maps are used to identify the coasts and seaside resorts. Simple sketch maps are created when children obtain information from a seaside photograph and children write a non-chronological report or travel guide based on a real or imaginary seaside trip. As an alternative means of communication, the children create simple computer-generated pictures of seaside places with a graphics package.

'Where in the world is Barnaby Bear?' uses the well-known and popular Barnaby Bear® resources created by Elaine Jackson and the Geographical Association. The Barnaby Bear official website can be found at: http://www.barnabybear.co.uk/ and the Durham LEA site that provides resources for studying unit 5 can be found at: http://www.durhamlea.org.uk/barnaby/. These websites provide helpful secondary sources for geographical learning and asking questions in particular. Skills-related programmes of study used for this topic at Ebchester are 1d, 2a and 2d; the children sort, classify and represent information about Barnaby's travels in a block graph or pictogram; they identify on the map a variety of places around the world where Barnaby can sometimes be found. The children often take their own bears or school bear abroad and record the bear's adventures on film. Children develop a sense of distance associated with travel, by identifying the nearest and furthest places that Barnaby or the school bear visits.

Reception children at Ebchester have no official scheme of work for geography but much of their work acts as preparation for what they will cover in Year 1. For example, children will be familiar with the travels of Barnaby and their own school bear. In particular, activities for Reception children lead into the 'Around our school' topic and work towards the National Curriculum Breadth of Study 6a and 6b.

Every Wednesday – come rain or shine – Debbie Dickson, the classroom assistant, takes Reception children out into the school grounds between one o'clock and twenty past two. After about ten minutes break, the children return inside for the last half hour of the school day. The outdoor learning sessions are planned and supervised by Debbie, who is full of imagination and with bags of enthusiasm; she clearly loves being outdoors herself.

Some activities carried out with Ebchester's Reception children are listed here; they all address some of the Foundation Stage stepping stones associated with the 'Knowledge and Understanding of the World' early learning goal and they can help the children progress towards Key Stage 1 geographical skills and enquiry development. Children are involved in:

- asking questions about the bat boxes in the school grounds: why are they there, when the bats go there and whether any other animals use them;
- making observations about squirrels' visits to the bat boxes and recording and counting how many squirrels they see;
- visiting the school pond and drawing what they see;
- collecting bits and pieces of the woodland environment to compile a 'temporary' picture while outdoors. No glue is used, instead, children take photographs of their pictures and then return the leaves, twigs, nuts, shells, grasses back to the wood to be recycled or used again for a mini beast habitat;
- using books about bats and squirrels back in the classroom;
- noticing patterns and changes in the environment according to the daily weather and the seasons;
- using directional language as they move about the woodland area, going left right, backwards and forwards, up and down and through the woods;
- doing shape and colour activities: finding objects of particular shapes outdoors; using smell, sound and touch to observe features of the school outdoor environment.

Specific 'Knowledge and Understanding of the World' Foundation Stage stepping stones addressed in this work include where the children:

Show curiosity, observe and manipulate objects

Find out about, and identify, some features of living things, objects and events that they observe

Talk about what is seen and what is happening

Notice and comment on patterns

Show an awareness of change

Ask questions about why things happen and why things work

Construct with a purpose in mind using a variety of resources

Comment and ask questions about where they live and the natural word

Notice differences between features of the local environment.

TEACHING KNOWLEDGE AND UNDERSTANDING OF PLACES

Thinking about homes

Background

'Homes' is one of the most frequently studied topics in early years classrooms. The subject is an excellent focus for cross-curricular interpretation, and lends itself splendidly to the coverage of geographical attainment targets. This particular case study describes some activities appropriate for interpretation of this theme with Year 1 or Year 2 children, which successfully allow for coverage of ideas relating to the locality and more distant environments, and which cover a range of geographical content. Unlike many topics on the theme, this particular example of good practice places emphasis on thinking and reflection – hence the heading 'Thinking about homes'. Thus the children are actively involved in thinking and making judgements about a range of homes, including their own. Because of this reflective focus, learning links naturally with elements of environmental education. It has to do with thinking about the quality of environments, as well as scientific and geographical accuracy.

Activities

Encourage reflection on the basic idea that all living things, including animal, plant and human life, need a home. Ask the children to sit quietly and close their eyes. Guide them to some imaginary scenes of homes. The following scenarios will be useful, although one would presumably focus on only one at a time:

A

You are a flower. You have beautiful red petals facing the sunshine. Your leaves are bright green and you have a stem reaching down into the ground. The soil is your home. Your roots hold you firmly in place. You do not move from your home. You have everything that you need there. Think about what it feels like to be a flower. How does the ground around you feel? Are there other plants living nearby? Do animals and insects come to visit you? How do you get your water and food?

After this scenario has been read while the children are quiet and have their eyes closed, ask them to talk about their reflections – each could describe their flowery neighbours, imaginary visitors, and what it may feel like to derive water and food from the soil.

B

Imagine you are a worm. Try to think what it feels like to be a worm. You are slippery and slimy and wriggle your way across the ground and through the soil. You like your home to be dark and damp. You like to wriggle your way to the top (surface) of the soil when it has been raining. You do not have arms and legs. You do not have fur and feathers.

Think about what you might like to eat. Leaves have fallen on to your home from the trees. Do you like your home? Who do you share it with? Do you have enemies who share your home?

This scenario can obviously be adapted to a wide range of animals and bird life. Follow up the quiet reflective period with time for discussion on what it may feel like to be a worm, or whatever, in a home which is totally different from ours, yet which provides all life's basic needs – food, shelter, etc. There is clearly tremendous scope for elaboration of this concept into discussion about what a range of life needs are expected from a home.

C

Now imagine that you are going into your own home. ... You have just got home from school. Imagine your front door and you are now going inside. Think about what you can see as you go through the door. What does it feel like to be home?

Now imagine that you are hungry in your home. Would you go and find some food? Would you ask someone for some food? What might you have?

Now imagine that you are thirsty ... think about where you find a drink. ...

Now think about where you go to sleep in your home. Think of your bed and imagine you are climbing into it. ... What does your bed feel like? What can you see in the room you sleep in? What do you like best about your home? Would you change anything if you could?

This scenario should lead to a great deal of discussion in which the children are helped to realise that they depend very much on their homes for food, warmth, comfort and shelter. (Note that this activity should be treated with sensitivity if there are children in the class from unhappy or problematic homes.)

Having considered a number of scenarios about homes of different kinds, discuss similarities and differences that occur in plant, animal and human homes. Emphasise the fact that every living thing needs food, water, shelter and space in its home. Everything needs a home. This could well lead to the production of a wall display, showing homes of different kinds (animal, plant, human) and in different places – both near and distant. To assist this, make a collection of pictures of homes in different places, and discuss their similarities and differences. Suggest that the children draw pictures of where they live to display alongside your 'homes with a difference'. Ask them to show things that they need to live in their drawings. Key questions to discuss as the display is being prepared and assembled include the following:

- Why do people need homes?
- What do homes provide for us?
- Why do animals need homes?
- What do homes provide for animals?
- Why do plants need homes?
- What do homes provide for plants?
- What do homes protect us from?
- Why do people's homes often look different in other lands?
- What makes a 'good' home (for animals, plants, people)?

Extension ideas

Clearly there is tremendous scope for elaboration of these basic ideas into a whole range of geographical and scientific studies. Many will be obvious. The following suggestions provide a useful extension to the 'thinking about homes' basic concept:

- Habitat surveys (trees, woodlands, ponds, hedgerows, walls, etc.).
- Study of your neighbourhood – setting homes in the general context of living in a community. Perhaps this could focus on 'living places' (homes), 'working places', 'playing places' and 'special places'.
- Dwellings – focus on living places of humans in the locality and further afield, considering building materials, size, layout and function. This provides clear links into studies of distant lands. After suitable research and stories, perhaps children can talk or write about a day in the life of a child from another culture, describing how this person lives in his or her home. Focus on range and size of dwellings in our world, as well as differences in building materials, layout and function. Consider, for example, the simple tepee, consisting of skins, poles, pegs, door flap and smoke flap; also the mansion home of some children of Western cultures, complete with as many bathrooms as bedrooms, swimming pool and games room. Ask the children which they would prefer to live in and why; consider whether size is always an advantage. Do they think that a complex home is always better than a simple one?
- Space to live – suggest to the children that every living thing needs a certain amount of space in order to live. Ask them what it would feel like if two classes had to share their classroom; if another ten people moved into their house. This extension will help children to begin to appreciate a number of important concepts; for example, that a habitat can only sustain a certain number of living things; that overcrowding leads to a decrease in the quality of a human environment; and that increase in the human population leads to problems in our world. This activity could

lead to discussion about (and action on) organising your classroom so that space is used in the best possible way for all its occupants, and about the children's 'personal' space which they have in their own homes. Take a walk into the neighbourhood. Ask the children to look out for examples of how families use their space. Do they have gardens? If so, how do they use them? Do they have fences? If so, why? What can we find out about people by looking at their homes and how their space is used? Last, but not least, consider the space of the school environment. Can the children think of ways of improving the use of school space? (For example, plant flowers in dull areas of the grounds; provide more litter bins to keep open spaces clean.) This extension helps to encourage a focus on values and quality of 'home' space – both personal and communal.

Learning from fieldwork

Steve Ashton is the Education Officer for Tees Valley Wildlife Trust. With the help of an assistant and two project officers, he provides a set of environmentally focused activities for children at Key Stage 1 and Foundation Stage. Approximately 50 schools and nurseries in the local area are informed about early years activities via a termly newsletter. Aspects of one popular and well-established activity for early years education are illustrated here. Steve provides a set of teaching sessions and a resource pack based on a river area called **Lustrum Beck,** located on the western edge of Stockton on Tees town centre.

Selected sheets from the Key Stage 1 part of Steve's Lustrum Beck pack (adapted from Enviroscope – RSNC, 1993) are included within the next few pages (information on the whole pack can be found in the resources section at the end of this book). The aim of the pack is to provide teachers, early years practitioners and pupils with activities highlighting biodiversity in their local areas. The work is part of a wider Lustrum Beck Corridors project, which intends to encourage local people (adults and children) to get outside, learn about the wildlife close to their homes, engage in new skills and become involved in physical projects to improve local green spaces.

The activities and pack are not entirely geography focused; they include a great deal of science work. There are science-based objectives concerning various habitats, species of animals and plants in the area as well as heavy emphasis on aspects of the citizenship curriculum. In terms of geography, the Lustrum Beck resource pack specifically provides ideas for local Teesside teachers addressing Unit 1 'Our School, the Local Area' within the QCA geography scheme of work. The pack could also be used by teachers addressing Unit 6 'Investigating Our Local Area' or Unit 14 'Investigating Rivers'. The Lustrum Beck work is a good example of a place study for Key Stage 1, whichever QCA unit it might be linked with. Place, as an aspect of the Geography National Curriculum, is studied as the children are involved in:

2a Identifying and describing what places are like (e.g. during the 'Creature Features' activity, observing and describing the features which may be good for some wildlife such as a thick healthy hedge, birds or bat boxes, nuts and berries in the autumn).

2b Identifying and describing where places are (e.g. recognising where the beck is located within the local Stockton area, what other known places are near by).

2c Recognising how places have become the way they are and how they are changing (e.g. knowing about how past shipping shaped the marsh and river areas; knowing about changes that occur as wildflowers are sown in the meadows around the beck).

Examples of teachers' notes from a nature trail activity and worksheet from an environmental report and 'creature features' activity follow (Figures 4.6 and 4.7).

Although the activities based around the beck, the parkland and the marsh clearly form an example of a place study, many other aspects of the Key Stage 1 National Curriculum Geography Programme of Study are addressed in the Lustrum Beck work. For example:

- *Geographical enquiry and skills*
    1a asking geographical questions (e.g. where does this railway go? what things here have been made by people?)
    1b observing and recording (children recording what they can feel, hear, smell ...)
    1c expressing views about people, places and environments (e.g. what is the best part of the Lustrum Beck park area?)
    2a using geographical vocabulary (e.g. 'upstream', 'downstream')
    2b using fieldwork skills (e.g. sketching the stream area)
    2e making maps and plans (children draw simple maps or pictorial representations of their routes).

- *Knowledge and understanding of patterns and processes*
    4a making observations about where things are located (e.g. where are bird boxes located and why?; where is the children's playground equipment located and why?)
    4b recognising changes in human features (e.g. noticing and talking about the planting of the herb garden to attract insect life).

- *Knowledge and understanding of environmental change and sustainable development*
    5a recognising changes in the environment (e.g. noticing human impact on the area, dog mess, vandalism, attractive artwork, seating for visitors)

Title: Great North Park Nature Trail				
Year Group		Duration: 2 Hours		
Aim: Introduction to Great North Park and the habitats and some of the species found there.		Objectives: To know about the various habitats found in the area and about some of the species of animals and plants found.		
National Curriculum links: That there are different kinds of plants and animals in the immediate environment, that there are differences between local habitats, to describe the features of the local environment, to express views on the features.				
Lesson Content				
Time	Activity	Pupils Activity	Teacher Activity	Resources
10 mins	Introduction – safety Walk to site	Listen	Talk	
5 mins	Start of walk manmade natural	Look, listen Collect leaves	Discuss	
10 mins	Leaves	Looking Sketch	Different shapes = different species	
10 mins	Stream		dip	dipping equipment
15 mins	meadow	walk and observation Collecting	Discuss meadows	
15 mins	walk back palette activity			
Differentiation				
Homework Use frame to write about visit Design leaflet Draw map				
Equipment Pond dipping		Health and safety Initial talk – stream danger		Links Works in local area

Figure 4.6 Great North Park Nature Trail: Teacher's Notes.

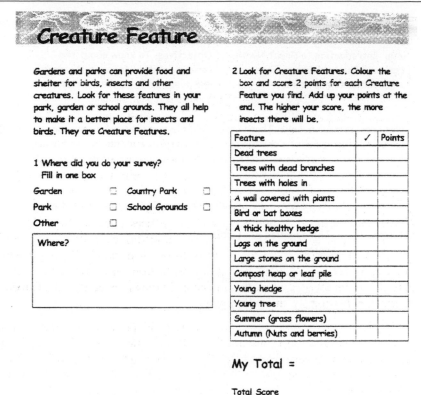

Creature Feature

Gardens and parks can provide food and shelter for birds, insects and other creatures. Look for these features in your park, garden or school grounds. They all help to make it a better place for insects and birds. They are Creature Features.

1 Where did you do your survey?
  Fill in one box

Garden	☐	Country Park	☐
Park	☐	School Grounds	☐
Other	☐		

Where?

2 Look for Creature Features. Colour the box and score 2 points for each Creature Feature you find. Add up your points at the end. The higher your score, the more insects there will be.

Feature	✓	Points
Dead trees		
Trees with dead branches		
Trees with holes in		
A wall covered with plants		
Bird or bat boxes		
A thick healthy hedge		
Logs on the ground		
Large stones on the ground		
Compost heap or leaf pile		
Young hedge		
Young tree		
Summer (grass flowers)		
Autumn (Nuts and berries)		

My Total =

Total Score

More than 24	Heaving with Creepies
21-23	Insect City
15-20	Not bad for bugs

3. Have you got any ideas on how the area can be improved for wildlife?

Figure 4.7 Creature Feature: Pupil worksheet.

5b recognising how the environment may be improved and sustained (e.g. activity considering improvements for area and their consequences).

- *Breadth of study*
  7a studying at a local scale
  7b carrying out field work investigations outside the classroom.

The Lustrum Beck activities are especially helpful for teachers who may not have the confidence to carry out fieldwork-based geography and/or develop science skills. Steve feels that this kind of work suits teachers; it involves carrying out the activities they would like to be able to carry out but with the guidance of people they consider to be 'the experts'. Schools don't always have easy access to the resources that Steve uses such as hand lenses, binoculars, disposable cameras for children, a resource bank of ideas (and people!) that are specifically suited to developing geography fieldwork with young children. Teachers also like to take inspiration for particular activities back to their own schools, while feeling secure in the knowledge that a fun day out addresses National Curriculum work.

Note: Tees Valley Wildlife Trust is one of 47 local Trusts that comprise the UK environmental Non-Governmental Organisation (NGO) collectively called The Wildlife Trusts. Examples of good practice from some of the other local Trusts are included within this book. Further information about the Trusts can be found on website http://www.wildlifetrusts.org.

Beyond the locality: teaching through a topic on invertebrates

This geographical topic on invertebrates from exotic, faraway places followed on from a previous scientifically focused topic on mini-beasts found in the school grounds. It was conducted with a mixed-ability Year 2 class for half a term. It should be noted, however, that the invertebrates used, being natives of other countries, were acquired for the purpose of this topic and it was accepted that they became 'long-term' residents of the classroom. They could hardly be returned to the wild at the termination of the work in hand. This clearly was no disadvantage, as the children gained a great deal in terms of learning how to take care of these fascinating forms of life. Practical details of culture and rearing of suitable species are included at the end of the discussion of this topic, for the benefit of those readers wishing to pursue this theme. The emphasis which follows is on discussion of the topic and its appropriateness in terms of addressing some of the key issues relating to distant lands teaching, rather than on a lengthy description of practical classroom tasks.

As a whole, the topic forms a superb example of worthwhile geographical education linked with the core area of science. From the geographical perspective, a major aim was to help the children develop a sense of 'place', that essential element of geographical education concerned with the reciprocal relationship between people and their environment. This was achieved through the development of activities, as described below, which were based on real objects from distant places, thus creating the all-important concrete link between the learners and environments of which they had no personal experience. Emphasis throughout was on first-hand, investigatory tasks. Motivation for the topic was no challenge for the teacher concerned. The young learners were totally captivated by the fascinating appearance and, indeed, the sheer size of the creatures in question. One of the earliest questions to be investigated as giant hissing cockroaches, giant African land snails and giant millepedes ambled their way across squared paper, was how their sizes compared to the UK relatives of these species. Discussion and imaginative writing generated a wide range of relevant vocabulary, creative thinking and spontaneous suggestions for further investigations. Detailed observation paralleled measuring, experimentation, illustration and recording tasks. Movement, feeding, breathing, reproduction, lifecycles and habits were observed, investigated and recorded in appropriate ways, covering a wide range of scientific, mathematical and cross-curricular skills (including observation, problem-solving and communication). From the immediate and the observable, the teaching skilfully steered questioning and investigation into the area of the native background of these creatures.

'Why don't we have millepedes this size in our country?'
'In which countries would you find such creatures in the wild?'
'What do they eat? . . . where do they live?'
'What is the weather like in their native lands?'
'Do they live in forests, or open lands?', etc.

Many questions were generated by the children as were answers, some of which were far more accurate than others. Gradually the topic evolved into twin sub-themes of 'Invertebrates of the Tropical Forest' and 'Invertebrates of the Desert'. A rather exciting and successful series of lessons ensued in which geographical/environmental knowledge and understanding emerged as a discernible and worthwhile core. Planning and organisation ensured that this focus covered a range of specific issues, incorporating knowledge, understanding and skills from the curriculum areas of both geography and environmental education.

Issues of conservation were at the forefront of discussion. Young as these learners were, they demonstrated genuine concern for the need to preserve the world's timber resources and appreciation of the different ways of life of rain forest communities, and the problems of desertification and living in an arid zone.

This topic illuminates many of the theoretical points and issues raised in Chapter 1. Research into children's knowledge, and awareness of distant lands in the early years reported there, showed that children have a range of basic understandings, alongside inevitable gaps in or erroneous knowledge, and perhaps biased or stereotypical knowledge. The teacher in this case study appreciated at the outset the need to find out as much as possible about the children's existing background knowledge of the distant lands which were to be studied, so that this could be built upon and indeed challenged constructively. She was aware of the children's incidental contact with places throughout the world, as a result of media contact, holidays, stories and personal contacts, and talked with them extensively about their ideas of forest and desert lands. She attempted to find out about the resultant 'mental maps' or images of these places held in the children's minds; the perhaps blurred 'world inside their heads'. She was also well aware of the issues of stereotyping and bias, and took positive steps to ensure that accurate, up-to-date images of rain forests and desert communities were presented to the class, bearing in mind the suggestion that children absorb, from the media and social discourse, attitudes and prejudices about other nations and peoples well before they learn accurate factual information about them.

The class teacher avoided possible pitfalls associated with teaching about distant places such as portraying out-dated or stereotyped images of places and people, giving a limited view of a country and using biased resource material.

Another key issue accepted by this teacher was the need to relate distant lands learning to reference points in the children's own lives. If tasks are in some way linked to the pupils' own locality or personal experiences, first, they will identify far more easily with the topic, place or people under consideration; and, second, they will be helped to develop an understanding of the interdependence of the modern world. Relevance may also help in the elimination of bias and stereotyping. If learners can feel a part of the 'total world' and appreciate the importance of links between nations, they may be less likely to view distant people as alien or remote from present-day reality and world issues. The distant lands dimension developed out of suitable reference points in the children's own lives, in this case, invertebrate animals which could be compared with their native counterparts.

To consider this point in general, there can be no better starting point than that which is 'real' and exciting to young children. Animals, plants, food, weather and homes are perhaps five of the most highly motivating and worthwhile connections between nations of the world which can be developed. The first three at least provide tremendous scope for using real objects as the point of contact between the children and the land of their origin. One single object, e.g. the snail, rubber plant or pineapple, could stimulate considerable motivation and generate a complete sub-topic on its natural environment. Alternatively, a collection of artefacts/souvenirs, maps, photographs, etc. could be established about the land to be studied.

A final, general issue to be picked up at this point concerns how decisions are made in a school about which places in the world are to be studied. The teacher in the case study described here focused upon two global environments – tropical rain forests and desert lands – and thus the approach was from a 'habitat' point of view rather than from the selection of one specific foreign town, state or country to study. Her decision was guided by the invertebrates available; in other words, the focus of the study or the links with the children's own lives dictated the areas of the globe that came under close scrutiny. That was a perfectly reasonable and acceptable method of selecting places. There are, however, other approaches to this task, and so a number of general points will be made.

Selection of places cannot be divorced from a more general discussion on planning the curriculum, so that a good range of places are studied across the Key Stage 1 (with appropriate 'bridges' into Key Stage 2). It is perhaps sensible to select places which:

- provide a balanced spread of knowledge of places around the world;
- cover a range of scales – local, regional, national and international;
- provide opportunities for adequate coverage of elements of content.

It seems sensible for schools, when working out curriculum plans and topics, to make a list of criteria for selection of places so that a balance is achieved. Such criteria might well include:

- Study of places of which teachers have personal experience. Thus they can talk knowledgeably about distant lands, having travelled there, lived and eaten there, viewed the scenery and talked with indigenous people. Objects, souvenirs and photographs in a personal collection will be valuable teaching aids.
- Study of places of which the children, their parents and friends have personal experience. Once again, souvenirs and photographs will be readily available, as will stories of 'real life' in the land. A class is far more likely to be motivated by the study of somewhere that one of its members can speak of than somewhere selected at random.
- Study of places where school contacts and links can be developed. It would be extremely useful if, for example, the children could exchange letters, photographs, writing, weather statistics and news stories with children who live in the distant place. Contacts could be made in both foreign and distant UK locations. A school in London, for example, could 'twin' with one in the highlands of Scotland. An ongoing school link will be much more productive than a short-term exchange set up for the duration of a single topic.

- Study of 'topical' places – that is, ones which are receiving plenty of media coverage that can be a source of information, cuttings, photographs and discussion. Such places range from those enduring disasters to those hosting current events, e.g. the Olympic Games.
- Study of places from which interesting objects, plants or animals are available, this being the criterion used by the school referred to in the case study topic.

By implementing the above suggested set of valid criteria for selection of places to study, it is likely that a good range will be achieved, and that there will be a balance between places studied by the school regularly (with a wide range of resources built up for the purpose) and those studied on a one-off basis for some good reason. Whatever criteria are used, it should be emphasised that teaching and learning must aim to help children identify with the place or 'foreign' people under consideration. If they can feel a part of this world, and have a developing understanding of the interdependence of modern nations and societies, they may be less likely to view distant lands as totally alien, exotic or remote from their own reality.

TEACHING KNOWLEDGE AND UNDERSTANDING OF PATTERNS AND PROCESSES

Patterns and processes in the Gloucester area

The first short selection of activities suitable for Key Stage 1 pupils presented here and relating to the study of patterns and processes are adapted from planning booklets and worksheets created by Margaret Westmore, Sarah Rowlatt and their education team who are based at Robinswood Hill Country Park, two miles from Gloucester – the home of Gloucester Wildlife Trust. The second set of activities derives from play-work practised by Lily Horseman at Herefordshire Wildlife Trust.

Look at the view!

For this activity, children are presented with three basic sketch maps showing different views from the top of Robinswood Hill Country Park. For each of the three maps, children are asked questions that enable them to see different aspects of physical and human environments, depending upon where they look.

Can you point to these things in the view on your picture? (using a sketch map of the view from the top of Robinswood):

In the park: a bushy tree quite close to us
two tall thin trees

a picnic table and barbecue
a log and tree stump
bushes
short grass
long grass
a stony path

In Gloucester (using sketch map 2):
the hospital (a big building with a small chimney)
the cathedral (a big old building with a tall tower)
houses
the railway line
a playing field

Far away (using sketch map 3):
the Malvern hills (they are big and pointy)
A hill called May Hill (it has a clump of trees on top)
some fields
a road (look for cars and lorries moving along).

Look at the city!

For this activity children are given word sheets that help develop their literacy skills while they work on observing where things are located as well as patterns and process of transport.

What can you see? Draw circles around the words (given to children on a sheet). *How many ways can you see people travelling around?*

by car   on foot   by train
by plane   by truck   can you see any other way?

Can you see where people work?

factories   offices   shops
schools   farms   a hospital

Can you see more places where people work? Where are they?
Can you see places where people live?
Point to some housing estates that you can see.

Rock Day

The activities and games that take place on Rock Day at the Robinswood Hill Park are particularly good at addressing patterns and processes, encouraging children to observe features of the environment and begin to understand changes in those physical and human features. Foundation Stage and Key

Stage 1 children are able to learn the names of different types of rocks and examine their texture, their colours, and practise new geographical vocabulary. Words that might be used on the day might include:

smooth shiny rough matt particles bumpy pebbles crumbly limestone sandstone quartz.

Children distinguish patterns among the rocks perhaps by simply identifying differences between the rocks' colours for example:

White and cream;
Grey and brown;
Yellow, orange and red.

Using large layers of coloured paper held by two children, it can be demonstrated how the land folds and some rocks are made in this way. At the end of the Rock Day, all children thoroughly enjoy 'making' their own rocks complete with fossils to take back to school.

An activity that can provide a really fun introduction to rocks, for children of any age, has been introduced to us by the Geographical Association's Field Studies Working Group. It involves children looking at a plate of different kinds of biscuits before they look at the rocks. By asking children to try to sort the biscuits (may be five different varieties) into groups, children will probably sort them by shape, colour and texture. Children will no doubt want to sort them by taste, but this should be left until the end of the activity! Next, different types of rocks are presented to children and again they are asked to do some sorting. The sorting of the rocks can take place according to similar criteria as the biscuits. The Geography Programme of Study that requires children to be taught to observe features in the environment does not have to be limited to study of large-scale features; some rock study that examines the little details can help progression and enjoyment in understanding changes in physical environments.

Geographical play in Herefordshire

Lily Horseman works with Foundation Stage children in pre-school groups, play groups and nurseries. As 'Wildplay' Officer for Herefordshire Wildlife Trust, with the help of her local Early Years Development and Childcare Partnership (EYDCP), Lily provides a whole range of outdoor activities that enable geography learning experiences among 3–5 year olds. One goal of 'Wildplay' is building confidence among early years providers who then develop their own outdoor activities that act as building blocks for children to gain fieldwork experience and develop environmental awareness. Here we illustrate with activities that help Foundation Stage children meet the Early Years Learning Goals, prepare for Key Stage 1 learning about patterns and processes, while linking with National Curriculum Science:

- For each activity, children are given a 'ticket of entry' which is a leaf that children convert into a badge to wear. This ticket and badge becomes a sign of commitment towards looking after the environment and it acts as reminder to be aware of the environment where they are playing and learning.
- Children learn about processes of plant growth and patterns in the seasons through gardening clubs. Gardening activities have been used successfully with traveller children to help them gain knowledge and understanding of their own world and to learn about the special patterns and processes of their local temporary environment.
- Even the youngest of children can record weather patterns by keeping a colourful weekly weather chart. A piece of card is marked out by an adult so that it has 8 squares across the top, 8 down the side (a total of 64). Children draw and paint different weather symbols across the top then paint the 8 squares down the side in rainbow colours marking the days of the week over the top. Every day, children can draw the appropriate weather symbol in the appropriate square.
- Children play 'shadow-tag' in an open space on a sunny day. One player tries to catch or tag another by stepping on his or her shadow. No one is allowed to hide in the shade. The player who is caught then becomes the next one who is 'it'.
- A 'fireworks' display is created without any fire or noise. On a sunny day children hold colanders above the ground so that they cast shadows and dots of lights created from the colander holes which can be seen as 'fireworks'. Instead of colanders, thick paper can be used with tiny holes cut into it.
- For an understanding of why some clothes or places are warmer than others in the sun, children place sheets of different-coloured paper on the ground outside. At least one sheet is black and another white. Children feel the different pieces of paper once they have heated up in the sun and this gives rise to discussions about such things as people's choice of clothes in hot countries, why dark coloured seats in cars make the car hot.
- An understanding of the sun's warmth can be followed up with children making a solar oven from a cone of black card which is covered with silver foil on the inside. Fruit is placed inside clear bowls covered with clear plastic film and then 'cooked' in the solar oven for about an hour.
- Notions of 'journey', and changing environment are beautifully recorded through the 'Mapstick' activity described in Gordon MacLellan's book *Talking to the Earth* (1995: 58–9). Lily uses this activity with children of all ages. Children begin with a stick – either a stick is held individually by each child or one stick can be shared by a group. Different items are attached to the stick as children take a walk or journey across a landscape. For instance, blue wool attached to the stick can signify passing by water; grasses and leaves can be tied the stick; feathers can be

collected and small pieces of weaving, twigs, pine cones and shells can be attached. The teacher needs a small collection of materials that can help the tying process or represent colours and textures of environmental features that cannot be captured. The important part of the activity is encouraging children to use their imagination to collect their own natural objects that should be attached in sequence to create a visual, three-dimensional 'map' and create a story of the journey and environment.

Lily's inspiration for these activities has come from a variety of sources including the Scottish Environmental Education Council (SEEC 1997), Derbyshire environmental educator Gordon MacLellan (http:// www.creepingtoad.org.uk/toadhall.html) and Forest Schools (http:// www. foresteducation.org.uk/index.asp).

TEACHING KNOWLEDGE AND UNDERSTANDING OF ENVIRONMENTAL CHANGE AND SUSTAINABLE DEVELOPMENT

Violet Lane Infant School, Staffordshire

Violet Lane Infant School lies on the hill of Stapenhill which is located at the edge of Burton-on-Trent. Staff and children have a marvellous view of the local environment: industrial areas, residential areas and woodland. The school is set within the national forest and has its own area of woodland while being situated on the edge of a busy and urban area. There are many reasons why this school has become one that encourages environmental learning among its young pupils. Above all, the enthusiastic headteacher and the staff have learnt how to make the most of a network of local people and organisations, and to investigate useful sources of funding and assistance from national and local bodies. The result is that environmental education and sustainable development is part of the school's ethos and daily practice.

Violet Lane is the largest infant school in Staffordshire with approximately 400 children aged between 3 and 7. There is a total of 54 staff, including all the auxiliary staff, and there are 11 classes: three Year 2, two Year 1, one mixed Year 1 and Year 2, one mixed Reception and Year 1 and three Reception classes. The school also operates two nursery classes.

The environmental ethos

Dr Diane Barker is the headteacher of Violet Lane Infant School and Mrs Carol Dyche is the geography co-ordinator as well as a Reception class teacher and 'Eco co-ordinator'. This means that Mrs Dyche co-ordinates the school's continual working towards an Eco-School status (http://www.eco-schools. org/). 'Eco-Schools', established in 1994, is an international programme of environmental education and means of managing schools according to sustainable development principles. Violet Lane's recent achievement of its second Green Flag Award as an Eco-School motivates both staff and pupils to continue engaging in environmental activities regularly, which develops a sound basis for environmental behaviour outside school, as well as a sense of reward and pride for the school's efforts.

Dr Barker also encourages the school to enter local borough competitions and initiatives that have a gardening and environmental focus. By doing this, she finds opportunities for the school to build links with bodies that provide prizes, funding and people who come into school and help out with environmental activities, PSHE, art and aspects of the geography curriculum.

Currently, a link with a local horticultural centre and garden centre provides opportunities for a gardening expert to engage children in planting flowers and vegetables during school time and during after school gardening club. The link with the next door secondary school has enabled older children to come and decorate Violet Lane school grounds with colourful paintings near the nursery wall. Sometimes, as is the case with many school grounds, vandalism and destruction of the shared woodland area is a problem; it is a negative aspect arising from the close proximity to the secondary school. At Violet Lane, the problems are not dwelt upon and the teachers focus upon the importance of preparing the young children to enter primary and secondary school with a strong bond with their local environment and a positive outlook that involves resolving the litter problems that local older children and adults may create nearby the school.

A caring attitude towards all living things is considered to be a part of education for sustainable development education at Violet Lane. Examples of this are evident in the whole school's involvement in collecting clothes to recycle for re-use in Eastern Europe; recycling and re-using by sending unwanted items in shoe boxes to less privileged families; the sponsorship of a donkey called Charlie C. Charlie C is kept in a park in Sutton Coldfield and the children of Violet Lane infants continually raise money for his welfare. Recently children with special needs took a school trip to visit the donkey. It is clear from a visit to Violet Lane, from the displays and literature around the school and from children's conversations, just how important Charlie C is to all the children. They are developing a sense of care for other living things that complements an understanding of environmental change and sustainable development.

Environmental education has developed through the engagement of all teaching staff into the planning process. Every subject co-ordinator has identified links between individual subjects and geography – in particular environmental aspects. After a trial period of specifically Eco-centred subject lessons for each class within the school, the staff at Violet Lane decided that this method of planning was unsatisfactory. Instead a more holistic approach

Plate 4(iii) Eco-Schools Corner: Noticeboard and can crusher bin.

Plate 4(iv)   Violet Lane nursery garden and wall, painted by adjacent secondary school pupils.

for integrating environmental geography was adopted to meet the needs of the National Curriculum and run Violet Lane Infants as an Eco-School.

As a reminder for readers, we reiterate that the National Curriculum for Key Stage 1 pupils requires that children are taught to be aware of changes in the environment and recognise how the environment may be improved and sustained (Geography Programme of Study 5a and 5b). The Foundation Stage area of learning enables children to develop a basis for environmental understanding as children are expected to:

- examine objects and living things to find out more about them;
- notice and comment on patterns;
- show an awareness of change;
- comment and ask about where they live and the natural world; notice differences between features of the local environment;
- gain an awareness of the cultures and beliefs of others.

Effective learning for the Knowledge and Understanding of the World area of early learning includes practitioners making effective use of the outdoors and the local neighbourhood.

The following list of activities demonstrates the school's approach to teaching for understanding of environmental change and sustainable development:

- Each teacher highlights within his/her weekly plan where environmental learning is addressed (this way, as the plan is visible to all staff in the school, a whole-school scale of monitoring geography takes place).
- A can crusher, composting bins and colourful litter bins have been purchased from money raised and are used daily around the school.
- Hymns are chosen for school assemblies which particularly reflect the school ethos of caring for the earth.
- Twice a year, Year 1 and Year 2 children are consecutively involved in six once-a-week after school gardening clubs. The gardening club acts as a means for all children to become involved in noticing environmental change and improving the school grounds: the benefits of the sessions available for Year 1 and Year 2 are then transferred to children at Reception and Nursery stage, who also become involved in gardening during curriculum time.
- Outdoor learning and environmental geography are items upon the agenda at every staff meeting, thus enabling all staff to get fully involved.
- Violet Lane has a sensory garden with herbs planted, wind chimes, different texture stones, rocks, plants that rustle in the wind and mirrors to reflect light. A pond is being developed nearby with a wild area to encourage frogs and minibeasts to the area.
- The school woodland, shared with the nearby secondary school for curriculum use, has been cleared by Violet Lane parents, and money has recently been raised to develop proper paths.
- A walk-to-school campaign has resulted in a 'walking bus' whereby children who can feasibly walk from home to school are accompanied by adults to help counteract the negative safety, pollution and health impacts of so many cars being used for children's home-to-school journeys.
- Two events take place each year within the school that have a specifically environmental focus: firstly an environment day during which the school's woodlands are used for lessons and the Reception classes have a seaside environment re-created in their school grounds. Sand is delivered to the school to generate a beach and so the youngest children enjoy a complete change of their environment – no doubt viewed as an exciting, albeit temporary improvement! Sand castle competitions are held, tents are put up, paddling pools are filled and a Punch and Judy show helps create a seaside atmosphere. Environmental themes are a part of the week's beach use, and stories such as Sam (the dog) Hurts his Paw (Tidy Britain Group 1994) are used to encourage children to think of the dangers of littering and pollution of seaside areas.

- A second event during the school year which has an environmental focus is the whole-school book week. Children's reading is steered towards factual and fictional books that have an ecological or sustainable development message. Geographical skills and connections with the natural world are also built up via children's literacy topics using the stories of *Goldilocks* (Reception Class), *Little Red Riding Hood* (Year 1) and *Hansel and Gretel* (Year 2) for fairytale trails around the school's woodland. Other examples of environmentally themed books can be found in the resources section at the back of this book.
- Every week, one child from each class from Reception through to Year 2 meets up with Mrs Dyche to have an Eco-Committee meeting. The children in the Eco-Committee carry out the school recycling each week, organising can recycling and collecting individual classes' waste paper for a central bin. The children in the committee are selected by teachers for their creative thinking and their ability to remember to do the recycling and report back to classes with messages or instructions for environmental action to take place in each class.

In every classroom throughout the school a sign is displayed, written by the Eco-Committee children themselves:

Smoking: please do not smoke near our school. Cigarettes can burn us. They make lots of litter.

Recycling: Recycle paper and cans. Send your old clothes to our school.

Saving energy: Remember to shut doors and windows. Switch off taps and heaters.

Our world: Always recycle rubbish. Shut the doors. Don't throw things out of car windows. Keep in the warm heat.

Litter: Don't throw litter on the floor. Pick it up and put it in the bin or take it home.

Charlie C: We are going to look after Charlie C and raise money to buy him food and shelter.

Dogs: Please leave your dogs at home or keep them on a lead.

Our School Grounds: To help the environment, try to stop standing on the lovely plants, the sludgy mud and on the nice fresh green grass that some animals eat.

An Eco-Committee meeting

During our visit to the school, Eleanor, George, Luke, Matthew, Megan, Melissa, Mitchell, Rosie and Thomas met in a brightly decorated nursery classroom for their Thursday afternoon Eco-Committee meeting. The children began by carrying in the recyclable magazines and paper from their classrooms, which they sorted carefully, checking to see if there were any other materials accidentally included but that could not be recycled. During the sorting exercise, Thomas found shiny silver foil type plastic that had been used to wrap promotional material for magazines. Mrs Dyche asked what could be done with it. Thomas replied: '*Ah, I've got the hang of it, we could use it on our Winter display ... it takes the light and reflects it.*'

While the children were sorting their paper and sharing the heavy bins between them, Mrs Dyche continued to ask them questions, such as: '*So who is in charge of looking after the environment in the school?*' As might be expected, children replied: '*You*', '*Dr Barker*', '*the teachers*', until Mitchell said '*it's us*'. Mrs Dyche replied that it was indeed all the children's job in the school and especially those in the Eco-Committee to look after the environment. Matthew responded: '*First time I heard about Eco, I thought yeah I want to do that, because I like helping!*' Mrs Dyche continued to ask the children questions while we walked to the large yellow paper recycling bin, outside in the school grounds. '*How do the others in the school know what the Eco-Committee are thinking about?*' The children replied with conversation:

Eleanor	... because we put litter in the bin, we did those signs.
Thomas	When I was walking up to the school, I saw cans, crisp packets ... they are not throwing the rubbish in the bins ... it's everywhere.
Luke	We could make some more signs to put up at the side of the hill or a bin ... near the school gates.
Thomas	It's not us its ... Paulet (the secondary school nearby).
Mrs Dyche	Well, we think that if you are looking after the environment now and not throwing litter, you won't be throwing litter when you go to the big school.
Thomas	My mummy recycles paper.
Mrs Dyche	Grown ups sometimes need to be taught to recycle and look after the world, we can help do that can't we?

Mrs Dyche went on to talk about how the recently collected cans weighed 10 kilograms and the can recycling company had given the school £4 in exchange for the cans. She said: '*That's enough to buy some bulbs to plant in the garden or a book on recycling or perhaps a new bin or some new signs for the woodland area.*' The children were told that the school had been given some bluebell bulbs and the Eco-Committee talked for a while about which part of the school would be nice for some bluebells, '*... instead of litter*', commented one child, '*we could put them all around the bottom of the trees*'.

The Eco-Committee children chatted about ideas for the Christmas Fayre to raise money for Charlie C, the adopted donkey. The group discussed how the school litter picking was going and where most litter was found. For the next week, the Eco-Committee planned to report back to their classes, and come to the next meeting with ideas for the school Eco Action Plan. One of the children suggested an idea that should be included: '... *the lights ... the light out there in the corridor is always left on, all day and all night. We've got to turn it off.*'

Experience-based activities

The children at Violet Lane learn about sustainable development and environmental issues primarily through a focus on looking after their own environment, and through first-hand experiences. Each class in each year group takes walks around the school, the local park and allotments noticing the 'good' and 'bad' aspects of the environments as well as possibilities for improvement. The repetition of this activity during the time each child spends at Violet Lane infants, means that it becomes quite natural for children to develop an aptitude for recognising and reflecting upon environmental change as well as extend their geographical language and present teachers with opportunities to assess children as they reach levels 1, 2 and 3 of the Geography Attainment Target, with an environmental emphasis:

Level 1:   Children recognise and make observations abut the features of places. They express their views on features of the environment of a locality.

Level 2:   They express views on the environment of a locality and recognise how people affect the environment

Level 3:   They offer reasons for some of their observations and for their views and judgements about places and environments. They recognise how people seek to improve and sustain environments.

   To give a flavour of the environmental and sustainable development themes that are studied throughout the children's time at Violet Lane infants, some of the titles of areas of study (which are then taught via a subject-based approach) are listed in Figure 4.8 alongside examples of activities. The repetition of theme is a deliberate part of planning.

Repeated experiences

One of the most successful aspects of Violet Lane Infant School's approach to environmental and sustainable development education is the infiltration of such matters into the everyday lives of children. Although there are indeed special 'events' that focus on environmental matters, such events are by no means 'one-off'. They occur regularly throughout a child's time at the school and the whole-school events act as celebrations for what goes on day-to-day, week-to-week and at classroom level. This approach is linked with the fact

Class	Area of study/ theme	Activity example
Foundation/ Nursery	The very hungry caterpillar	Think about places where caterpillars might live. Use the woodland and sensory garden to smell, look closely, listen carefully and have a feel of leafy environments
Reception	Appreciation of our world Animals in the environment	Using the pictures that link to the tale of Sam Hurts his Paw (Tidy Britain Group 1994), put the pictures in correct order and re-tell the tale discussing what people having the picnic could do to prevent the dog from hurting his paw on the glass and other litter.
Year 1	Trees as homes Litter Appreciation of our world Saving water Looking after our environment Local fieldwork	Design of 4 signs using no words to give meaning to the messages: – recycle glass – bicycles only – environmentally reusable – litter bin
Year 2	Appreciation of our world Reclaimed materials Pollution	Use the story Peter's Place by Sally Grindley and Michael Foreman as starting point. Think of ways to clean up a polluted beach area; mark on pictures areas where pollution is happening.

Figure 4.8 Planning: Areas of study and activities.

that learning experiences are *repeated* and built upon, so that a Reception child's woodland experience, noticing different features of trees will be repeated at Year 1 and Year 2, progressing to attainment of knowledge about the names of Elder, Rowan, Alder, and identification of the leaf shapes and the changes in these trees from season to season. The regular and repeated activities – whether they involve contributing to the school woodland flower diaries or the re-use of paper that has been used on one side only – enable children at Violet Lane to develop a kind of habitual response and natural interest in environmental change and sustainable development.

MAKING LINKS

Links across the curriculum: Derby High School Kindergarten

Derby High School Kindergarten provides us with an example of an early years approach to teaching and learning geography that links with other curriculum areas.

During one whole summer term, a multi-cultural class of Year 1 children study a topic entitled 'Our Local Environment'. It is a geography-focused topic that links with other subjects, in particular: ICT, Maths, English, PSHE and Art. The topic covers more than one Programme of Study. It offers opportunities for children to gain and practise geographical enquiry and skills, knowledge and understanding of places, knowledge and understanding of patterns and processes, and knowledge and understanding of environmental change and sustainable development. The topic's links with PSHE are made through the use of a Caribbean story that enables children's learning to cover the geography curriculum Breadth of Study requirement 6b that calls for children to be taught about an overseas locality.

Background

The kindergarten, which is part of Derby High School's junior department, provides geography according to four documents relevant to Foundation Stage and Key Stage 1:

- the National Curriculum;
- the kindergarten's geography policy;
- an aims and objectives document, drawn up with the support of Key Stage 2 and Key Stage 3 staff within the wider school;
- a scheme of work used in the kindergarten.

The examples presented in this case study of links across the curriculum are for children in Year 1, working at Key Stage 1. However, it is worth noting here a little of the background behind the Year 1 children's learning. The kindergarten's scheme of work for geography at Foundation Stage states that:

> For the 3–5 age group geography is included in the Early Learning Goal of 'Knowledge and Understanding of the World'. During the early stages of learning, the children are encouraged to develop curiosity about their world and to make sense of what they find out. First-hand experiences and activities are used to encourage exploration, observation, problem-solving, prediction, decision-making and discussion over a wide range of topic areas.

Mrs Brebner, a Reception class teacher, emphasised to us that Foundation Stage geography work, like all other work, must be very flexible and reactive. Sometimes an area of discussion will develop from children's own interests, thereby necessarily 'interrupting' the teacher's plans. An example is one 4-year-old boy's fascinating question that gave rise to some discussion on environmental matters of waste and recycling: 'Are cigarettes biodegradable?'

asked Kayten Girn. Indeed, some 4 year olds will enter Key Stage 1 quite capable of asking demanding and interesting questions that demonstrate an environmental awareness, a developed geographical vocabulary and a need for a teaching approach that integrates geographical, scientific and moral thinking.

Key Stage I – Year I planning

Returning to the Year 1 case study, the Geography Programme of Study for Key Stage 1 is covered within the two years of Key Stage 1. Geography work is not spread evenly throughout the years but is taught in topic format with topics lasting between two and six weeks. The kindergarten scheme of work states how the 'Our Local Environment Topic' fits in with the Geography Programme of Study requirements that are addressed in Year 1 (see Chapter 2 for requirements indicated in parentheses here):

- Throughout the year, this class will study the following areas in a topic-based way; the seasons and their effects on weather, crops, animals and birds (4b, 5a).
- Senses – implications for the environment and adaptations required to help people who are blind, deaf or disabled (5a, 5b).
- **Our local environment** – the school environment – layout, plans, favourite places, playground design (3c, 5b), journey to school, street features and furniture, the houses and homes we live in, including names and purposes of rooms, types of houses and different locations (7a, b), people who help us in our local environment and local amenities (1a, b, c, d) (2a, b, e) (3a, b, d, e) (4a, b), compare local environment with another community in the Caribbean (1a, 1c, 3a, b, d, e, 4a, 6b).
- Use of atlas and globe to locate UK in relation to holiday destinations (2c, d, e).
- Identification of basic features on maps and use of a simple key (2a, c, d, e), using co-ordinates on simple plans and directional work with left and right (2c, d, e).

Cross-curricular activities

Below we detail some of the activities undertaken by Miss Buckley's Year 1 class that link with other National Curriculum subjects.

Individual children compile a graph to show how the class travel to school (linking with the **Maths** Programme of Study concerned with processing, representing and interpreting data). This activity follows whole class discussion of the home to school journey. In addition, children write about what they have noticed about the journey: length, mode of transport and places and things they pass on the way. This activity is a particularly worthwhile class discussion and subject for class display work because children travel to their school from many different directions and the distances vary. Owing to the fact that many children take a long car journey to school, a mapping task would be difficult for many Year 1 children, so an imaginative writing task is more appropriate and links the activity with the **English** curriculum. The writing activity allows children to imagine that they are late for school and either using their own experiences of what they see on their school journey or through use of the picture on the worksheet, children use geographical vocabulary to describe their journeys between home and school.

Miss Buckley's Year 1 children are encouraged to think about their own homes and houses within their local environment topic. Basic computer word processing skills (**ICT**: Programme of Study: Developing ideas and making things happen Programme of Study 2a; also Breadth of Study 5b) are expected from Year 1 children as they state who is in their household and write their own address. The sub-topic of houses within the overall Year 1 Our Local Environment topic enables children to understand processes of home-building, materials used as well as the names of parts of houses and types of houses such as terraced, semi-detached, bungalow. A computer activity using a programme from a Dorling Kindersley CD ROM 'Learning Ladder – preschool' gives each child in the class opportunities to learn about maps and plans. The **ICT** activity (addressing Developing ideas and making things happen 2b, 2d; Breadth of Study 5b) involves a plan of a bedroom, from the computer software, with which a child works independently to identify individual objects then click and drag the plan drawings of various bedroom furniture, such as bed, desk, lamp, teddy bear, onto a new blank bedroom plan. The Year 1 children had already begun a little plan work, drawing several desk items from above, during their work in the reception class. Children practise their plan drawing and interpreting skills by walking around the school grounds and drawing simple plans of objects in play ground areas. Through walks around school children become familiar with kindergarten and junior school outdoor and indoor areas. In the classroom, children are encouraged to express preferences about favourite areas in the school, drawing on writing skills (**English** En3 Writing) to write a short piece entitled 'my favourite place in school' (Figure 4.9).

Another connection is made between **ICT,** geography and **English** when children use the programme called 'Lessonmaker' (http://www. edutechsystems.co.uk/) which involves selecting words from a word bank, entering text, loading the word bank, learning about responding to instructions, becoming more familiar with directional language such as left and right as well as practising new-found knowledge about the process of house-building (Geography 1d, 3c, 4b, ICT Finding things out 1a, 1b, 1c; English En2 Reading). English resources from the 'Essentials for English' and 'Nelson English Foundation Skills' photocopiable worksheets are found to be useful for an assessment exercise in which Miss Buckley checks children's

TIME TO TALK

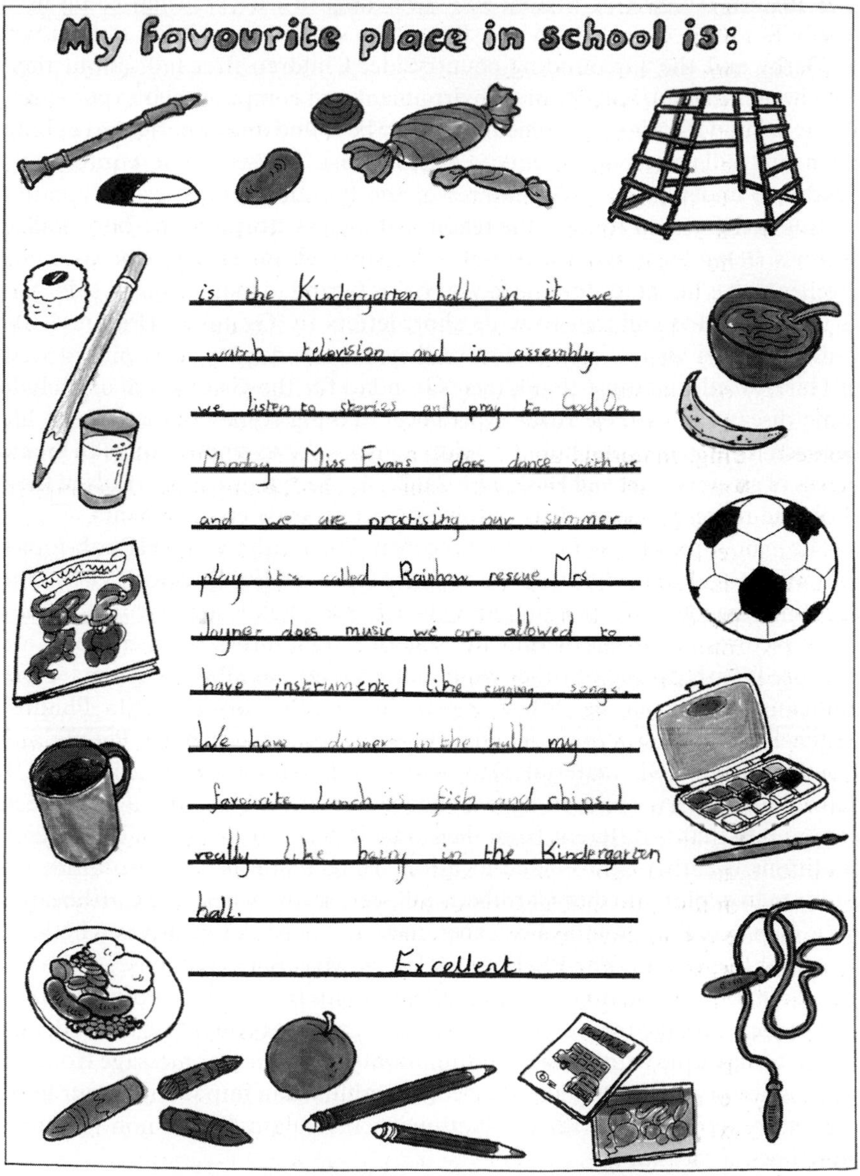

My favourite place in school is:

is the Kindergarten hall in it we watch television and in assembly we listen to stories and pray to God. On Monday Miss Evans does dance with us and we are practising our summer play it's called Rainbow rescue. Mrs Joyner does music we are allowed to have instruments. I like singing songs. We have dinner in the hall my favourite lunch is fish and chips. I really like being in the Kindergarten hall.

Excellent.

Figure 4.9 My favourite place in school.

progress with the geography work about houses, streets and use of directions (relating to the geography enquiry and skills Programme of Study).

A further example of writing activities (**English** En3 Writing) being used within this topic is one which investigates the school's proximity to the town of Derby and the surrounding countryside. Children first talk about their own houses in an urban or rural environment and compare their experiences. While acknowledging that some things may be found and experienced in both town and village environments, a writing task is used to test informally children's understanding of features of the two different areas. A creative writing activity then follows the reading of a class story/picture book called *Harry's Home* by Lawrence Anholt. The story about Harry, who as a city dweller makes an unaccompanied visit to his Grandad in the countryside, acts as a stimulus for children to write short letters to 'Grandad' (Figure 4.10). Children either write as themselves or they use the identity and point of view of Harry. Children must thank their Grandad for the visit as well as include some discussion of their rural experience, making some comparison of life between rural and urban living. Children also work in small groups to create pieces of artwork (**Art and Design** 1a, 2a, 2c, 4a, 5a, 5c) using materials of their choice to represent their ideas of town or countryside environments.

The main topic of Our Local Environment links with two **PSHE** sub-topics that are also addressed during the summer term in Miss Buckley's class. The first links the local school community which Year 1 children experience (they draw pictures of people within the school community and their roles are discussed) with people of other communities overseas (PSHE non-statutory guidelines 2f, 2h, 4a, 4c, 5f). The stimulus for this work is Rita Phillips-Mitchell's book *Hue Boy* and the Hopscotch photocopiable 'People and Communities' KS1 material (Hopscotch Educational Publishing 2003). Through the story, children have a chance to learn a bit about a Caribbean community that is different from their own in terms of overall lifestyle, diet, traditions, weather and village location. Here there are opportunities for children to explore further Caribbean villages, seeing where the Caribbean is on a map, recalling holidays or experiences of friends or relatives who have visited or lived there. The PSHE work led by Miss Buckley focuses upon the story's character Hue Boy, who is smaller than his friends. His mother worries and so seeks to take measures to help him to grow – through use of food, and a variety of people within the local community. A particular message from the story is how a community and the people within it can impact upon our lives. This story work links with the National Curriculum PSHE non-statutory guidelines 2f, 4c, 4d, 5a.

The second **PSHE** link with the 'Our Local Environment' topic is also sourced in story. Within Year 1's PSHE scheme for the summer term is a Caring for the Environment theme; this fits well with the overall term's work on the local environment and links with PSHE non-statutory guidelines 2a, 2e, 3d, 4c, 4d, 5b and 5c. The book by Nicola Moon called *Billy's Sunflower* is

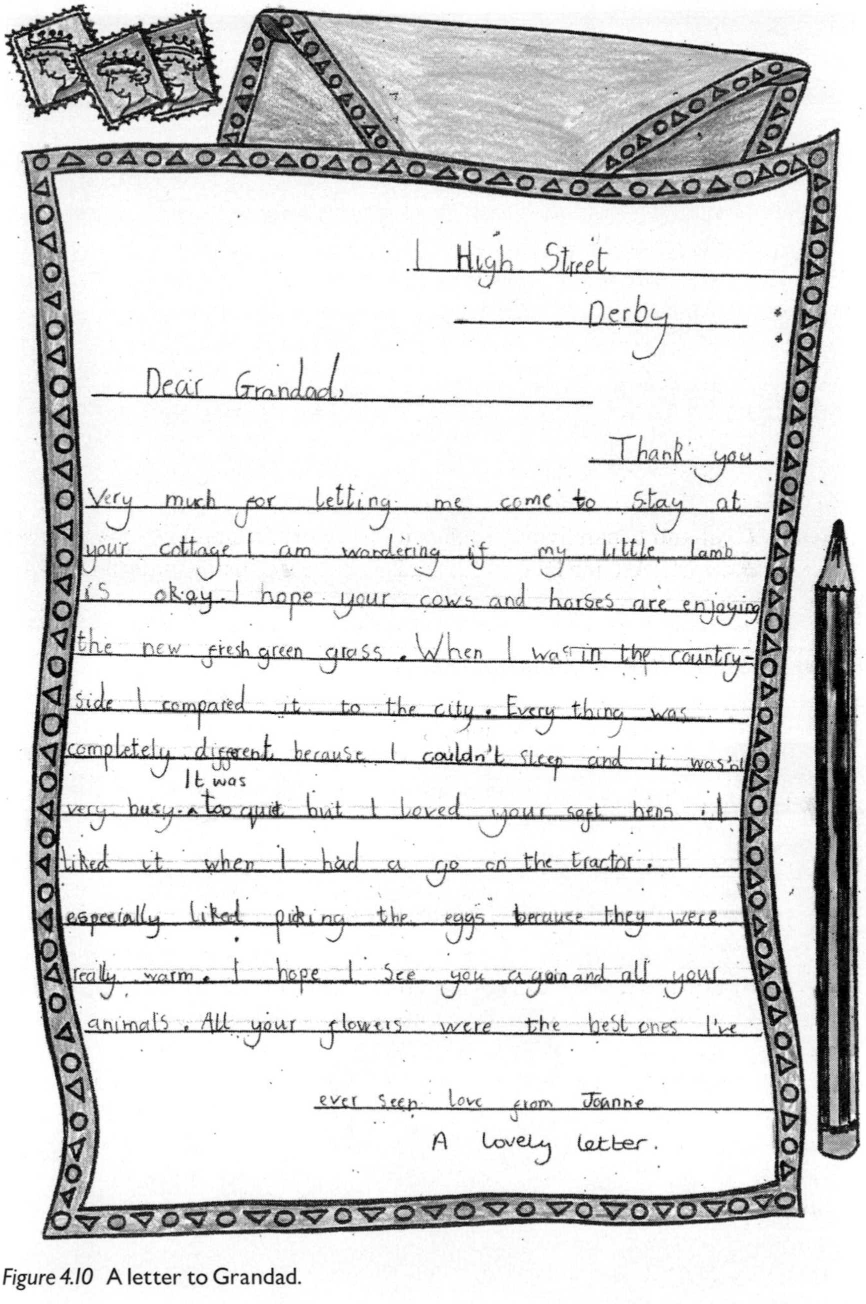

1 High Street
Derby

Dear Grandad,

                    Thank you
Very much for letting me come to stay at
your cottage I am wandering if my little lamb
is okay. I hope your cows and horses are enjoying
the new fresh green grass. When I was in the countryside I compared it to the city. Every thing was
completely different because I couldn't sleep and it was'nt
                    It was
very busy. too quiet but I loved your soft hens. I
liked it when I had a go on the tractor. I
especially liked picking the eggs because they were
really warm. I hope I see you again and all your
animals. All your flowers were the best ones I've

ever seen love from Joanne
          A lovely letter.

Figure 4.10 A letter to Grandad.

Plate 4(v)   Collage artwork of a town environment.

Plate 4(vi)   Collage artwork of a countryside environment.

about a young boy's efforts to grow a sunflower from seed. It grows and grows until it begins to die and shed its seeds. The strong emotions Billy feels while caring for this plant, eventually collecting its seeds for the birds and for growing new plants the following year while learning to understand the cycle of life and death, address the significance of nature and things of beauty. Miss Buckley's class uses the story to re-consider the children's own local environment. Children identify activities that harm and that help nature. They practise the process of paper recycling and learn about what happens to paper when it is recycled as opposed to being thrown away. Children are encouraged to think carefully about the connections between the sunflower in the story and the school natural environment and trees, which can be affected by children's own actions of using paper and recycling it. These activities link with Geography's Programme of Study themes of understanding patterns and processes and environmental change and sustainable development.

An interesting aspect of this Year 1 topic is that study of local environment does not have to remain inflexibly close to the literal home and school environment. Local environment can mean school *and* home, even if children's homes are a considerable distance from the school location. Local environment can also include the local environment of other people, fictional and real – in distant environments. Teachers of Foundation Stage and Key Stage 1 children sometimes express concern that a local environment topic – a statutory aspect of the school locality Programme of Study 6a – can become stale, dull and rather limited if the subject of study is unimaginatively limited to the immediate environment. This case study has demonstrated that linking the topic with other aspects of the curriculum not only serves a practical purpose, but enables the school locality study to provide opportunity for and draw upon exploration of other skills and concepts within the Geography Programme of Study and beyond.

The use of story

This study shows how a single story, commonly found in early years classrooms, can form the basis for exciting and worthwhile geographical education. The teacher in question took as a starting point the story entitled *Red Fox* by H. Giffard (Frances Lincoln, ISBN 0–7112-0747-X). Preparation involved an analysis of the story in terms of its potential for geographical work, identified page by page throughout the book, and recorded as a list of geographical language that could be developed, links with Programmes of Study and levels of attainment, and the potential of illustrations. This analysis is summarised below.

The story was then read to the children and the geographical potential as outlined was developed through discussion of text and illustrations, and related tasks. One key task, for example, involved the children in drawing their own spontaneous maps of the journey of the fox.

Analysis of story: its potential for geographical education

Red Fox

Briefly, this story describes the journey of a fox setting off in search of his food. The story is initially set in the countryside, starting at the fox's den in woodlands; however, as the fox searches further afield for his food he ends up in a town. In the story, therefore, children are introduced to the contrast between rural and urban areas. Furthermore, the fox's journey passes a variety of different places, and is a good starting point for developing children's mapping skills, encouraging children to remember all the different places that the fox has passed.

Let us now turn to an analysis of the book's geographical content in terms of its language and pictures. The analysis has been carried out page by page, in the following manner:

Page 1
1   *Language*
     'over the faraway hills' = direction/distance vocabulary.
     'hills' = geographical features.
     'den'.

Page 2
1   *Language*
     'stay here' = locational language.
     'I'll find something to eat' = setting the scene for the journey.
2   *Picture* – countryside scene
     woods
     hills – reinforcing the children's understanding of these.
     den = geographical feature.

Page 3
1   *Language*
     'headed for' = directional language.
     'farm' = geographical feature – recognising that different buildings have different purposes.
     'farmer' = indicating that adults do different kinds of work.
2   *Picture*
     woodland/hills/yard/buildings for different purposes – reinforcing understanding and geographical features.

Page 5 – 'red fox ran off towards the pond...'
1   *Language*
     'off towards' = directional language.

'pond' = geographical feature – recognising the different ways in which water occurs in the environment.
2   *Picture*
see the farm buildings near to the pond.

Page 7 – 'He heard a faint rustling in the corn field nearby.'
1   *Language*
'corn field' = geographical feature.
'nearby' = locational language.
2   *Picture*
wheat field with a woodland in the background, therefore helps to rein-force children's understanding of different land uses.

Page 10
1   *Language*
'behind the glowing moon' = locational language.
'Then he heard a scuffling at the edge of the wood'
'edge' = locational language.
'wood' = geographical feature.
'he sprang towards the noise' = directional language.
'across' = directional language.
'field' = geographical feature.
'Red fox chased him down to the railway line'
'down to' = directional language.
'the railway line' geographical feature – illustrating different modes of transport.
2   *Picture*
woods/hill field = reinforcing the geographical features introduced in the text.

Page 11
1   *Language*
'a fast train came round the bend'
'round the bend' – directional language.
2   *Picture*
fields with cows grazing = illustrating another land use in the country-side.

Page 12
1   *Language*
'up the bank' = directional language.
'bank' = geographical feature.
2   *Picture*
railway track and train.

steep bank with sheep grazing.
woods – recognising different relief in land.

Page 13

1   *Language*
'Red fox went to the river'
'went to' = directional language.
'the river' = geographical feature – illustrating another term in which
water occurs in the environment.
'reflections from a nearby town'
'nearby' = locational language.
'town' = geographical feature.
2   *Picture*
hill, river, town at edge of picture, thus indicating its 'nearby' position.

Page 15

1   *Language*
'The huge buildings' = reinforcing the idea that different buildings have
different purposes.
'the streets' = geographical feature.
2   *Picture*
showing a typical town scene, therefore is quite a contrast to the earlier
scene of the countryside.

Page 17

1   *Language*
'turned a corner' = directional language.
'narrow street' = geographical feature.
'across a yard' = directional language.
2   *Picture*
Urban setting outside a home, again showing a contrast with the fox's
home at the beginning of the story.

Page 19

1   *Language*
'home' = geographical feature.
'across' = directional language.
'the fields' = geographical feature.
2   *Picture*
Fox leaving the town and re-entering the countryside, therefore a direct
contrast between the two places is seen.

It is evident that this story book introduces many geographical features,
reinforced in the pictures, which should enable the children to understand the

geographical terms more fully and, perhaps more important, it provides a more meaningful content.

Teacher's evaluation

The work carried out with this book involved Year 1 children. I felt that the children enjoyed the story as they were enthusiastic when discussing it. Similarly, I felt that they enjoyed focusing on the illustrations as they picked out the geographical features they had heard about in the text and pointed them out. This showed that the children had a good understanding of these terms, e.g. wood, field, pond, river and farm. Indeed, children seem to gain a much better understanding of things when they see them in pictures; undoubtedly, it helps them to put things into more meaningful contexts. Thus, these children demonstrated that they could use geographical vocabulary to talk about places and furthermore were able to identify these features in the pictures.

The book was especially helpful in stimulating discussion about the countryside. The children contrasted the countryside and the town. One child, for example, described the countryside as 'green and quiet', whereas she said the town was 'grey and smoky and busy'. It was interesting to hear what the children thought about these two contrasting places. As all the children lived in a town, they found it easy to describe towns through their own personal experiences. However, they all seemed to have a good understanding of the countryside, especially since quite a few of them had never had any direct experience. It seemed that they had picked up most of their ideas from what they had seen or heard from a variety of sources, and this demonstrates how important and influential these indirect experiences of the world are for children, enabling them to develop and widen their understanding of the world generally.

When we talked about the places that the fox visited, the children seemed to remember nearly all the places that he had passed and, more important, they were able to sequence them. In our discussions, it was evident that the children had picked up the locational language introduced in the story. For example, when they were sequencing the fox's journey, one boy, Duane, picked up on the term 'nearby' and said confidently that he could remember that 'the pond was nearby the farm'.

This demonstrated that he had a good understanding of this term. Indeed, I was surprised by just how much detail the children remembered about Red Fox's journey. This was the first book where I had gathered the children's response, and I had previously anticipated that I would have to help the children more. However, when asked which places he had passed, together they covered every feature, showing that they had taken in all these places when they listened to it for the first time.

Having established that the children had a good understanding of all the places visited, I introduced the idea of making a representation of Red Fox's journey. However, before I did this, I had to ensure that the children had a good understanding of the term map. I was surprised to find that the children were all quite familiar with this, and furthermore they described a map as 'something which shows you where things are'. On further questioning, it seemed that they had come across maps in everyday life; for example, they had seen them in towns and in some shops.

Before they started to make their own representations, we briefly discussed what sort of things should be included on the maps. The children realised that they needed to include all the places that the fox had passed. I was also pleased to find that they wanted to distinguish between the countryside and the town.

The maps produced were extremely pleasing (see Figures 4.11, 4.12 and 4.13). It is interesting to note that the maps show all the features in the correct sequence, and that the children have shown these in more symbolic form. It has been suggested that young children's maps are likely to be pictorial and that houses are likely to be drawn as 'stereotyped houses'. In these maps, however, the children have moved on from pictorial representation. Additionally, the children have also used colour effectively, green to denote country areas and black for the town areas. This further illustrates that the children distinguish between the two contrasting areas.

I was pleased with the way that the book stimulated the mapwork, and it helped to foster a greater understanding of the countryside as well as promote other geographical knowledge.

In general, findings suggest that children's literature is an effective way of introducing young children to geographical skills, concepts and vocabulary, and, what is more, is an enjoyable way.

Sheffield Hallam University's School of Education with School Partners

The following extracts from Sheffield Hallam University's handbook for school-based mentors and students illustrate how geography supports learning in the following areas: literacy, numeracy, citizenship, sustainable development and ICT.

GEOGRAPHY SUPPORTING LITERACY AND NUMERACY

Geography lessons should aim to develop children's geographical knowledge, understanding and skills. Geography, however, can also provide a real world context particularly for the development and practise of literacy and numeracy skills.

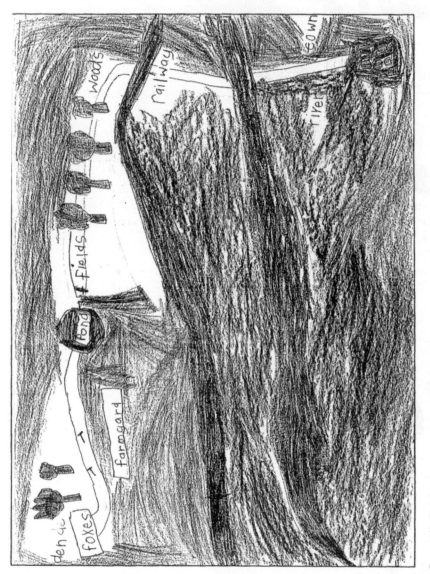

Figure 4.11 Children's mapwork from *Red Fox* (a) Atif.

Figure 4.12 Children's mapwork from *Red Fox* (b) Louis.

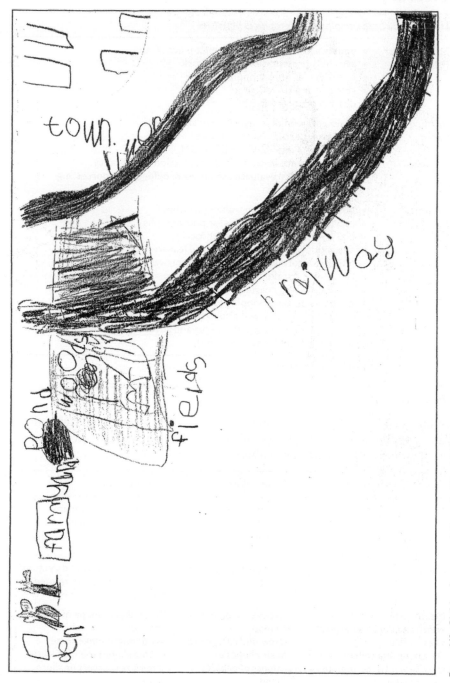

Figure 4.13 Children's mapwork from *Red Fox* (c) Chloe.

Literacy

Literacy	Examples of geographical activities
Speaking and listening	• debate about the use of a derelict piece of land • assembly presentation on fieldwork • interviewing for a shopping survey • role play in a travel agents • describing the weather
Reading	• fiction or poems to develop a sense of place • newspaper article on a local issue • information on WWW or CD-ROM • using reference books to find information on a locality • research skills – evaluate usefulness of different resources, e.g. holiday brochures
Writing	• poster campaigning on walking to school • captions or speech bubbles for photographs • diary of a child's life in another locality • description of a human or physical feature • letter to local council suggesting improvement to local park • list of what to take on holiday • poem following coastal fieldwork • questionnaire on shopping habits geographical enquiry will also extend children's vocabulary (nouns – physical and human features; verbs and adverbs, e.g. when describing processes; prepositions – location)

Numeracy

While some of Sheffield Hallam's suggestions for numeracy development through geography work are also suited to children working at Key Stage 2, we have inserted in italics some alternatives for younger children:

Collect and record data	Present data	Interpret data
Traffic survey – tally chart	Pictogram of different types of vehicles	Why are there so many lorries on the road?
Measuring temperature – chart	Graph to show temperature over 2 weeks	How is the temperature related to the wind direction? *How is temperature related to the seasons?*
Measuring river channel width and depth at several sites – table *Observing and collecting river pebbles according to colour and shape*	Cross-section linked to map *Draw and categorise basic shapes or colours of pebbles found*	What affects shape of river channel *What might make some pebble shapes rounded while some have corners or sharp edges?*

Preferred holiday destination – questionnaire	Tally chart	Why do we prefer certain places?
Land use survey – map *Simple map of school or classrooms showing area used by different people (teachers, older children, younger children, cooks)*	Graph to show different land uses *Colour blocks on map to represent different areas*	What is the main land use? *What do different people need from different spaces in school?*

Children can also interpret data obtained from a variety of other sources such as:

- travel brochures/WWW – data on weather/climate, costs of holidays and flights;
- timetables;
- road atlases.

Children can investigate numbers and shape in the local environment. Mathematical skills can also be developed in the context of mapwork, for example through work on co-ordinates, grid references, distance, direction and scale.

GEOGRAPHY AND THE WHOLE CURRICULUM

Geography provides a wealth of opportunities to contribute to children's social, moral, spiritual and cultural development. It can bring a European and global dimension to their understanding of the world as well as enrich and reinforce cross-curricular elements of the curriculum such as citizenship and sustainability.

Citizenship

Education for Citizenship is seen as having three distinct but interconnected strands which will prepare young people for adult life: social and moral responsibility, community involvement and political literacy. Geography provides opportunities for children to acquire skills, understanding and attitudes which will contribute to their development as global citizens.

- using an enquiry based, participatory approach which involves critical thinking;
- developing ideas about fairness and the nature of responsibilities;
- recognising their own values and attitudes;
- sharing opinions, discussing and analysing relevant issues;
- recognising other people's perspectives;

- working in groups;
- developing a sense of place and sense of community;
- carrying out fieldwork in the community (a survey on the effects of environmental change on different people; proposing changes to improve the local park);
- learning how decisions are made at a local scale (role playing a public meeting; writing to the local council about parking issues);
- identifying how local and global events and issues are connected and interact;
- identifying similarities and differences between people and places, on a local to global scale, valuing diversity and developing positive attitudes (linking with children nationally and internationally by email);
- inviting members of the local community into school;
- investigating how people use local facilities;
- understanding events in the news, locally and globally.

Students should not avoid addressing controversial issues in their teaching but they need to think through their approach carefully. Children need to be aware of different perspectives on an issue; students need to avoid indoctrination.

Sustainability

Geography provides opportunities for children to investigate relevant environmental and development issues. As with citizenship, this involves looking at issues from a local to global scale and identifying how they are connected and interact. This again necessitates a practical approach and the use and development of skills such as enquiry and critical thinking.

Geography promotes environmental awareness and responsibility while at the same time making children aware that solutions to environmental issues are not always easy to find and agree on.

Children can address sustainability through activities such as:

- learning about physical processes;
- learning about the needs of society;
- investigating the impact of traffic and how it can be managed more effectively;
- investigating how a derelict piece of land might be used to be of benefit to the community;
- investigating the impact of tourism on a locality and how it could be managed more sustainably.

(Sheffield Hallam University 1999/2000: 25–7).

ICT

There are numerous ways in which teachers can evaluate the success of the connections they make between geography and ICT, for example by considering:

- methods using ICT for effective teaching and assessment of geography;
- pro-actively planning for ICT to enhance geography learning;
- the most effective organisation of classroom ICT resources for meeting learning objectives in geography;
- the specific contribution that ICT can make to teaching pupils with special needs.

Teachers are encouraged to use ICT effectively in association with geography-related objectives by:

- ensuring ICT-based work focuses on well-defined geographical questions;
- ensuring ICT-based work develops children's skills or knowledge of places, patterns, processes, environmental issues and sustainable development themes;
- ensuring ICT is the best way of meeting teaching objectives, e.g. using a paper atlas (not CD-ROM) would be the best tool to introduce older Key Stage 1 children to using contents and index pages to find places;
- ensure that children are aware of how ICT is helping them learn in geography, e.g. using web-cam images to see what other places look like at any point in time;
- ensure that children are aware of the role played by ICT in geographical aspects of everyday life, e.g. weather forecasting and communicating with friends and family in distant places.

(Adapted from Sheffield Hallam University 1999/2000: 44–6)

The examples of cross-curricular links between geography and other subjects that are detailed in this chapter represent a tiny proportion of the links that can exist across the whole curriculum and that do exist in real teaching and learning situations. As early years practitioners will know, boundaries created between subjects can sometimes be illusory or unnecessary. Very young children respond well to educational and play experiences that connect concepts and styles of learning. Such experiences also provide excellent potential for community and parental links; to which we now turn.

Community and parental links

Ebchester School, County Durham

Reception class children at Ebchester School, who spend much of their time learning outdoors in their school woodlands, tackle early stages of numeracy in a fun way that also enables their development in relation to the Knowledge and Understanding of the World early learning goal; the children's environmental awareness is almost certainly developed too. The classroom assistant hides among the leaves some numbers that are sticky or made from Velcro. Once children go off into the leafy woodland, they spend valuable time familiarising themselves with their local woodland environment while searching for particular numbers which they collect and stick onto their clothing. Ebchester School clearly experiences the benefits of involving the parents of school children and people in the local community. The school grounds are a wonderful example of the wider school community's contribution to children's outdoor and geography learning environment. The first things to strike a visitor at Ebchester School are the grassy amphitheatre, the sculptures and pieces of natural-world inspired artwork. The school has attracted funding for parents and local artists to create willow structures including a large willow cat (Plate 4(vii)) and willow cone shapes rather like tepees. The creation of the 'book of herbs' – a wicker soil-and-plant-filled structure shaped like a book – was inspired by a local myth about the 'Ebchester witch' who grew herbs (Plate 4(viii)). A story-telling seat in the school grounds is another lovely feature of the outdoor classroom. It was created by the children and local parents, many of whom are artists themselves. Such structures are used and enjoyed daily and add to the children's delight and willingness to learn in the outdoor environment. A tiled map, a quiet garden dedicated to the memory of one of the school's little girls, the den, the living sculpture, the bat boxes and school woodland adjoining the playing field are all aspects of the school grounds where community members and visitors have helped and continue to create a very special place.

Parents are further involved in Ebchester through a gardening club that runs one day a week. Parents have set up an after-school club for themselves and the children to work in the school garden. Other schools also use Ebchester's school grounds as a learning resource. Networking with other schools will be further enhanced when a sports and arts community centre will be built in the school grounds, funded by money from a lottery grant. Mr Coombes, the headteacher, believes that one of the benefits of being a small school in a small community is the potential for adapting to change and the needs of that community. Mr Coombes suggests that the school is blessed with a set of local parents who are a really talented set of 'movers and shakers' in the community.

Every year, Ebchester parents engage in the creation of a felt picture connected to harvest time. As in many schools, the seasons are greatly celebrated in Ebchester and children gain a sense of the changing seasons, landscape and weather as well as an understanding of the resources that come from the land. During harvest time, children make a list of the names of local elderly people, place their names in a hat and then pick out a name so that each child takes a harvest gift to one of the elderly people in the village.

Plate 4(vii) The Willow Cat.

Connections to the wider community are developed through walking the paths to the local convent. A bridge that is crossed on the way is 'dressed'. Another regularly used path nearby the school takes children to a farm which every child visits once a year via a sponsored walk. All these links to nearby people and places, and the use of local paths and connections are helpful in

Plate 4(viii) The Book of Herbs.

contributing to the children's sense of place, their understanding of scale, and their feelings of belonging within a local community.

Examples from elsewhere

It is of course, not only in small schools such as Ebchester where splendid work can be done linking with parents and the wider community. Other examples of good practice we are aware of in early years learning contexts include:

- Parents help out on school trips, both local fieldwork and excursions beyond the school environment.
- Parents and members of the community come into schools to offer talks and activities based on their work or skills, thus broadening children's knowledge and understanding of the wider world.
- Local people who have visited distant places for work or holiday can be a helpful addition for geography learning. First-hand experiences can be talked about and photographs and artefacts can be shared.

- Elderly people in the local area can come into school to talk about how places have changed over the years, to help children learn about concepts of change, development and degradation of an area. The potential for 'elders' of the community to enhance children's geographical and environmental education through regular contact with schools and school visits is demonstrated in the United States (EASI 2003).
- Those working in recycling, waste industries or environmental programmes help out with projects on rubbish disposal and environmental improvement. Schools and teachers can be assisted to set up and maintain successful recycling programmes as a result.
- Artists, writers and performers can be funded using a variety of outside sources to work with children for a week or half term project to explore particular geography topics. In particular, environmental and outdoor themes provide inspiration for creative work concerning landscape, environment and story (see for example: http://www.creepingtoad. org.uk/toadhall.html).
- Environmental organisations and conservation groups provide play and learning experiences that focus on particular aspects of the geography curriculum or Foundation Stage early learning goals, often offering fieldwork experiences and the chance to visit both urban and rural locations rich in wildlife and interesting habitats.

The Great Outdoors Project – a partnership between Sheffield Wildlife Trust and the Learning through Landscapes Early Years Team

Katherine, Linda and Jan are working together to provide environmental education for children between 3 and 5 years in the Sheffield and Rotherham area. Katherine is Education Manager for Sheffield Wildlife Trust. Linda has just been appointed the project officer for The Great Outdoors Project funded by Onyx, a company providing sustainable waste management and recycling service for Sheffield. Jan is employed by 'Learning through Landscapes', an environmental group that primarily works with schools promoting school grounds as sources of enjoyable learning and play for children (see http:// www.ltl.org.uk/). Jan is one of Learning through Landscape's first Early Years Officers whose role is to assist practitioners of Foundation Stage and other adults who care for children aged between 3 and 5.

The three key staff run The Great Outdoors Project at Magna Science and Adventure Centre in Rotherham, South Yorkshire. A 15-minute walk from the centre takes visitors to a nature reserve which is intended as the physical location for children and their accompanied adults to experience the project's activities. The nature reserve then acts as a starting point and inspiration for outdoor experiences to be carried out elsewhere – for children in nurseries, in childminders' care, in reception classes and via parents. The Great Outdoors

Project is an example of a newly developing case of provision of outdoor learning.

The project will operate closely connected with the guidelines for the National Curriculum Foundation Stage. The team working on the project understand that early years practitioners are keen to use and learn about ways to embrace National Curriculum requirements and guidance.

The goals of the Foundation Stage by no means overshadow the goals of meeting local community needs and encouraging a sense of place among children and adults who use the project. Addressing local needs is an important objective for the project particularly because of the geographical location of the communities nearby the reserve. The proximity of major roads and dual carriageways, as well as local people's sense of boundary between the locations of Sheffield and Rotherham mean that local people can often feel separated from each other and they can feel severed from safe outdoor play areas. For the push-chair user, major roads and dual carriageways can seriously inhibit use of local outdoor areas and create divisions between neighbours. People in the local community who would receive access to safe outdoor places would be targeted first to become beneficiaries of the organised activities based upon the nature reserve, and it is hoped that the local community would then be able to experience a breakdown of artificial and human-induced boundaries and barriers.

The needs of the local early years education providers will be explored by Linda through a period of consultation and piloting of activities. The requirements of children and groups with special needs will inform the design of sessions, specific activities and spaces on the nature reserves; already the reserve is equipped with wheelchair access. The requirements, interests and worries (such as transport, access, mealtime arrangements, costs, safety) expressed by the adults involved with the project will be taken on board and fed into further project development. From the education team's previous experience it is clear that many early years practitioners will need to be convinced of the education and play value of outdoor learning and they must feel comfortable with the practicalities related to working with very young children outside (clothing, timing, bathroom arrangements).

The Great Outdoors activities will be relevant for adults not so much as a training opportunity but as a 'seeing is believing' experience where the positive processes and outcome of outdoor play are witnessed and act as a means of encouraging adults to try similar activities in other settings. Parents and providers who bring children to the reserve will be encouraged to observe *how* children's learning is happening and it is thought that use of a digital or disposable camera (with photograph permission) will enable both children and adults to later reflect upon their experiences – how they learnt and what they learnt. There is an aim to infuse the early years providers something of a 'research practitioner' mentality whereby providers become more involved and interested in observing the processes and the benefits of learning outdoors. This in turn may lead to providers continually re-assessing and planning for what children need and gain from outdoor learning experiences.

Although the reserve and a sensory trail will be the key resource used in activities, one of the aims of the project is to ensure that childcare providers are able to repeat or design similar experiences outdoors in their own settings. For this reason, many natural resources that are easily adapted, transferable and affordable such as leaves, stones and everyday items will be used as resources for learning. Resource boxes, set up by Linda, will include objects and story books that can be borrowed by practitioners and easily used in other settings. Katherine, Linda and Jan are convinced that resources and items used in children's play should not be 'fancy' or so unusual that other early years practitioners would not be able to repeat activities. The team intend that children should learn using predominantly natural objects, which have the double advantage of encouraging children's imagination and creativity to flourish while being adaptable and transferable for use in different situations. The four seasons theme of the project will strongly guide selection of the activities and resources boxes; such a theme will help children understand and enjoy the different scales of changes that occur outdoors over time. Children will be able to experience the special elements of seasons that can affect the world and people's senses including mood. The focus upon seasons and consequently weather will enable early years practitioners use the weather more as a resource rather than viewing it as a barrier to outdoor learning.

This example demonstrates that institutions other than schools and nurseries are developing outdoors-based geographical type activities, working closely with parents and the local community and providing guidance for the early years age group and associated carers and practitioners. Where practitioners are not trained or are not yet familiar with use of 'the outdoor classroom' as a starting point for geography and other areas of learning, the help of an outdoor-learning provider and 'expert' can be invaluable.

ASSESSMENT AND RECORD-KEEPING

Progression

There is no statutory requirement in the National Curriculum for Schools to assess geography through the use of Standard Assessment Tasks. Teachers are free to engage with their own forms of assessment and with pupil self-assessment as they see fit. Assessment serves as both a basis for planning further work and also as a means of monitoring and recording pupil progress.

It should incorporate ongoing formative assessment as well as summarise assessment which provides details of achievement at a particular point in time.

Assessment then, is linked to features of progression, which, according to the QCA are characterised by:

- an increase in breadth of studies: the gradual extension of contents – places, themes and environments – to be considered;
- an increasing depth of study: the gradual development of general ideas and concepts and deeper understanding of increasingly complex and abstract processes, patterns and relationships;
- an increase in the spatial scale of study: the shift in emphasis from local, smaller-scale studies to more distant, regional, national, continental and global scales;
- a continuing development of skills: to include the use of specific geographical skills such as mapwork and more general skills of enquiry matched to children's developing cognitive abilities;
- increasing opportunities for children to examine social, economic, political and environmental issues: the chance to develop greater appreciation and understanding of the influence of people's beliefs, attitudes and values on alternative courses of action relating to people, places and environments.

(QCA 1998)

An example of thinking on early years geography assessment which focuses on progression comes from Sheffield Hallam University School of Education (1999/2000: 25). Assessment and recording of children's work should ideally include a range of styles and formats for children's work such as:

- **writing** – report, diary, story, questionnaire, letter, newspaper article, poem, list, description;
- **visual work** – painting, poster, diagram, cross-section, video, photograph, graph, table, printout, map, three-dimensional work such as model, artefact or weather equipment use and creation;
- **oral work** – presentation, role play, debate, interview, description, discussion.

Figure 4.14 suggests how practitioners might judge children's progression through each of the four aspects of the Geography Programme of Study. The first row in italics lists what the practitioner could do to aid the progression. The subsequent four rows provide interpretation of the National Curriculum Attainment Target that Key Stage 1 children could meet (level 4 is more appropriate for Key Stage 2 children or particularly gifted children at Key Stage 1).

Level	Enquiry and skills	Knowledge and understanding of places	Knowledge and understanding of patterns and processes	Knowledge and understanding of environmental change and sustainable development
DO*	• talk about observations, sometimes recording them • talk about experiences • ask questions to gain information • use language to describe position	• talk about where they live & their environment • awareness of purposes of some features in the area in which they live • show respect for people of other cultures • look closely at similarities & differences	• look closely at patterns & processes	• treat their environment with care & concern • show a range of feelings such as wonder in response to their experience of the world
1	• make observations • express their views • use resources provided and own observations to respond to questions	• recognise & make observations about human & physical features of places	• recognise & make observations about human & physical features	• express views on features of the environment of a locality they find attractive or unattractive
2	• describe features • express views • select information from sources provided • use information provided to ask & respond to questions • begin to use appropriate vocabulary	• describe physical & human features of places • recognise features that give places their character • show awareness of places beyond their own locality	• describe physical & human features • begin to use appropriate vocabulary	• express views on attractive & unattractive features of the environment of a locality
3	• describe and make comparisons • use skills & sources of evidence to respond to a range of geographical questions	• show awareness that different places may have both similar & different characteristics • offer reasons for some of their observations & judgements about places	• describe & make comparisons between human & physical features in different localities • offer explanations for location of some of these features	• make comparisons between physical & human features of different localities • offer reasons for some of their observations & judgements about places
4	• describe patterns • suggest suitable questions for geographical study • use a range of geographical skills & evidence to investigate places & themes • communicate findings using appropriate vocabulary	• appreciate importance of location in understanding places • show understanding of how physical & human processes can change features of place & how changes can affect lives & activities of people living there	• begin to describe geographical patterns & to appreciate importance of location • recognise & describe physical & human processes • show understanding of how processes can change features of places	• describe how people can both improve & damage environment • show understanding of how processes can change features of places

*Do these activities at stages of early learning and attainment before level 1.

Figure 4.14 Progression in National Curriculum Geography through Programmes of Study and level descriptions (Sheffield Hallam 1999/2000:35–6).

Collecting, recording and interpreting assessment information

The remainder of the chapter focuses upon the all-important tasks of collecting, recording and interpreting assessment information, which are clearly transferable to a focus either on geographical or on environmental content. Precise documentation and methods of recording will of course vary from school to school. Pupil records, which provide a profile of geographical education and related environmental experiences and attainments across the curriculum, need to be maintained by the class teacher or subject co-ordinator. Complete documentation may comprise a wide range of written material, including pupil profile sheets, class and individual records, samples of children's work, overall schemes and specific learning plans.

Success in the collection of relevant assessment information is dependent upon crucial teacher skills, notably observing, listening, testing (in the formal or informal sense), interacting with pupils (conversation, questions and feedback), and scrutinising recorded outcomes of learning tasks. The essence of assessment in geography is thus communication between teacher and learner – communication which helps the learner to appreciate what has been learned, and the teacher to plan tasks and first-hand experiences that will promote future learning of concepts and skills or development of attitudes/ concern. In early years classrooms this will necessarily involve time for watching, listening and questioning individual pupils and groups as well as interpretation of children's work.

Attention is now focused on the teacher skills of observation, listening and questioning, which are of critical importance to geographical education because of its emphasis on experiential and investigatory learning.

Observation should be approached as a skilled and strategic task, given that classroom observations may either be planned or spontaneous. Spontaneous observations are an important aspect of all classroom situations, perhaps particularly so when pupils go about their learning tasks in an independent way, knowing what their investigations involve and the availability of the resources necessary to perform them. Obviously no teacher can possibly record what is happening in a classroom all the time. It is far better to focus on specific features or interactions, and to record significant events in a variety of contexts than to watch a class without a focus. Suitable contexts may include:

- individual tasks, e.g. selecting appropriate equipment to measure a desk, drawing a simple plan or map;
- group work, e.g. building a model village according to a predetermined plan, involving the collecting together of the necessary elements of the model, discussion, allocating tasks, listening to the views of others and collaborating to produce results.

A cautionary note about spontaneous observations is that early years teachers generally have 'eyes in the back of their heads' and a tremendous capacity to notice many events all at the same time. This in many respects is a great asset – but can be a weakness in assessment. Partial information may be acquired in this way, which may be inadequate for making judgements on learning. Whenever possible, spontaneous observations should be recorded carefully to 'back up' or assist the planned schedules.

Planned observations will have a clear objective; for example, to assess whether a pupil understands that a knowledge of direction can help in the location of objects in space or whether he or she can successfully reduce a 30 cm line to the scale of a half. Such observations and their results will be informative and help with future planning, confirming progress made in teaching and learning. When planning observations, it is necessary to decide exactly what will be looked for, ways in which it will be tested or checked, and whether the task will involve interaction with the learner or simply seeing what is taking place. Decisions must also be made about whether the interchange will be used to extend the learner's thinking at that time, and how the outcomes of the observations will be recorded.

Checklist for planned observations

- Decide what/who you are going to observe and why.
- Decide whether you intend to test or check the observation in another way or at another time.
- Decide whether you will be unobtrusive or whether you wish to interact with the teaching during the observation process.
- Arrange the individual group or class so that the observations can take place in a 'natural' way (without abnormal behaviour or complete rearrangement of furniture).
- Concentrate on the task in hand.
- Take detailed notes of what you see – perhaps recorded on a pre-planned form.
- Make time to read and interpret notes while the observations are fresh in the mind.
- Decide how they will relate to other assessment data.
- Decide how results will assist overall assessment procedures and the design of further appropriate learning tasks.

Listening is such a crucial skill in the assessment process that perhaps a separate recording sheet should be designed and filled in at appropriate times. Comments made above about observations also apply to listening strategies. Many early years teachers are outstandingly good at listening to six conversations at once and extracting their essence, but is this enough to illuminate children's learning? Sessions for listening need careful planning if results are to be valid and useful. Some sessions may involve a teacher in listening while all children are busily engaged in tasks. At other times, children and teacher may listen together; for example, when an individual is reading a story out loud or the class is having a discussion. Matters to consider when planning listening include:

- Decide what/who the focus of attention will be. Is it to be on what the children say to each other or to you?
- Decide whether you intend to test or check outcomes by asking pupils to repeat what they have said or explain it further.
- Decide whether you will be unobtrusive, or whether you wish to engage in conversation while also listening.
- Arrange the pupil(s) in such a way that listening can take place 'naturally'.
- Take notes of what you hear – perhaps recorded on a pre-planned form such as Figure 4.15.
- Decide how these will relate to other assessment data.
- Decide whether you wish to talk more (or hear more) about the conversation you have recorded.
- Decide how results will assist overall assessment procedures and the design of further appropriate learning tasks.

Figure 4.15 provides a suggested design for a planned listening recording sheet.

The use of a tape-recorder can be valuable, particularly where several children are engaged in discussion and when it is difficult to take adequate notes. Be aware, however, that tape-recorders pick up unwelcome background noise, and that tapes take a long time to listen to, and even longer to transcribe.

The skills of questioning play a crucial role in the assessment process, alongside observation, listening and testing. The range and quality of questions posed by a teacher will reveal not only ways in which the learner is thinking, but also the kind of thinking being encouraged and expected. Thus questioning results in important two-way communication in the learning process.

Questions can be posed at a variety of levels, ranging from simple 'closed' questions of fact, requiring little more than 'yes' or 'no' answers, through to sophisticated questions of analysis, synthesis and evaluation, such as: 'What do you think would happen if . . . ?', 'Can you think of ways in which . . .?'

Each category of question produces a response that initiates a specific kind of thought process. By employing questions at a variety of levels or categories, learners will engage in a variety of cognitive processes. Lower-order thinking involves retrieval of facts or information from memory. Questions involving thinking of this kind often begin with the words: What? Where? When? Who? The knowledge recalled will probably be in the same

Name(s) of pupils observed		
Year Group	Date of observation	Time
Ongoing work relating to Programme of Study (✓)		
Enquiry and skills ☐	Places ☐	Patterns and processes ☐
Environment and sustainable development ☐		
Specific task(s) pupil(s) engaged in		
What was said		Who said it
Notes on responses/difficulties made apparent		
Any further comments/recommendations		Was the conversation recorded? ☐ Yes ☐ No
Related assessment details		Recorder

Figure 4.15 Recording listening: suggested format.

form as it was learnt and will not go beyond that basic information with which the learner is familiar. Higher-order thinking requires a change in the form of existing knowledge, perhaps to compare or contrast, to apply it or extend it, explain or analyse, reorganise or evaluate, synthesise or solve problems. In other words, learned material must be recalled and then used or applied to provide an outcome or answer of a higher cognitive level. Both levels of questioning are essential for effective progression in geographical education. Lower-order questioning will encourage memorisation of facts and rote learning; higher-order questioning is essential for promoting more complex thinking processes associated with issues and the promotion of concern for the world.

Figure 4.16 gives examples of questions in various categories, and the required thinking related to them, derived from appropriate elements of

Category	Teacher question	Response
Knowledge	Recall of facts and basic understandings or observations	1 How wide was the playground? 2 What is the name of the river we saw? 3 What animals does the farmer have?
Comprehension	Comparing, contrasting, describing, explaining	1 Can you explain why farmers grow food? 2 Which is higher – the river bank or the house on the hillside?
Application	Applying knowledge to solve problems, classifying, selecting, using	1 Can you follow this plan to put the model village back in the right place? 2 Do all the world's people live in houses like ours?
Analysis	Drawing conclusions, making inferences, finding causes, determining and using evidence	1 Why do you think people in the Arctic eat a lot of fish? 2 Why is water running down the side of the hill?
Synthesis	Solving problems, making predictions, proposing	What do you think would happen if the world got warmer and all the snow melted?
Evaluation	Judging, evaluating, deciding, appraising	Do you think it is a good idea to cut down trees in rain forests?

Figure 4.16 Summary of teacher's questions and cognitive processes related to Key Stage I geography.

curriculum content. Readers are encouraged to interpret their own classroom and fieldwork situations in a similar way, thus providing analysis of children's thinking which could contribute to an overall profile of assessment in geography. Figure 4.17 provides a sample recording sheet for this purpose. The middle and right-hand columns are left blank so that the sheet can be filled in for an individual child. The right-hand column should be used to

Name of pupil		
Topic		
Category	Teacher question	Response
Knowledge		
Comprehension		
Application		
Analysis		
Synthesis		
Evaluation		

Figure 4.17 Questioning: individual recording sheet.

record examples of answers provided by the pupil alongside the questions asked by the teacher at the appropriate level of required thinking; that is, the sheet is used to record responses to planned questions posed by the teacher. It provides an 'at a glance' guide to the level of questioning that a pupil is capable of responding to in a consistent and successful way. Questioning should not be left to chance. The effective teacher will plan for questioning in geography with the same rigour as for any other aspect of the early years teaching role.

In summary, the use of questioning alongside observation and listening helps a teacher to ascertain:

- whether the pupil has learned the intended outcomes of specific tasks and activities;
- the success (or failure) of specific teaching strategies;
- how the pupil is performing relative to others of a similar age;
- whether the pupil is ready for the next stage in a particular progression of learning;
- the nature of particular difficulties (if any) that the pupil is experiencing.

Together with interpretation of pupils' written work, these skills form the basis for successful recording and assessment procedures, and make a substantial contribution to planning and evaluation of tasks, schemes and programmes of work in geographical education.

Chapter 5 contains several examples of activities suitable for staff discussion and inset sessions which focus on assessment tasks.

Record sheets

We have no wish to add to the proliferation of simple recording sheets available. It is assumed that staff are well used to filling in written records relating to Programme of Study coverage. A focus has therefore been placed above on augmentation of such records by teacher assessment skills, which can make a significant contribution to individual children's profiles.

That said, no chapter on record-keeping and assessment would be complete without reference to sheets suitable for children to make their own recordings when undertaking first-hand investigatory work or field studies.

Figures 4.18 and 4.19 are suggestions for sheets suitable for recording children's experiences and feelings while undertaking tasks in what might be termed 'environmental geography'. Clearly such sheets could be adapted for other areas of the Programme of Study.

What do you think of the street? Place a tick in one of the boxes below:

I think the High Street is:

Beautiful	☐	☐	Ugly
Quiet	☐	☐	Noisy
Tidy	☐	☐	Untidy
Deserted	☐	☐	Crowded
Open	☐	☐	Cramped
Safe	☐	☐	Dangerous
Windy	☐	☐	Calm
Warm	☐	☐	Cold
Exciting	☐	☐	Boring
Good for old people	☐	☐	Bad for old people
Old	☐	☐	New
Dirty	☐	☐	Clean
Friendly	☐	☐	Unfriendly
Good for children	☐	☐	Bad for children
Sleepy	☐	☐	Lively

Figure 4.18 Thinking about the street.

Where did you go?	What were you reminded of?
	What was your funniest thought?
	What was your strangest thought?

What did you taste?	What did you smell?

What did you hear?	What did you feel

?	What words did you encounter? (spoken, written)

What did you see? (graphic answers only)

Figure 4.19 Questions to ask on a trail.

Chapter 5

Training and professional development

This chapter provides examples of professional training and continuing development related to two essential contexts for these matters – the school itself, and in partnership with external bodies. It outlines a number of activities which could be adopted in schools for staff discussion meetings or more formal continuing development sessions. They are appropriate for use by a gathering the size of an average school staff. Each of the suggested activities is freestanding, and aims to enhance thinking or practice on some aspect of geographical education or education for sustainable development. Case studies of good school practice are also included. All are intended to be thought-provoking, useful, relevant to every staff member, and indeed fun to take part in. They aim to provide practical reflection on a number of theoretical issues raised in this book. Following on from the in-school materials, we focus on training and professional development in association with partners. Examples of good practice are provided which focus on schools' links with initial teacher training establishments, and with local education authorities.

IN-SCHOOL ACTIVITIES AND CASE STUDIES

First, we outline a number of activities which could be adopted for staff discussion meetings or more formal in-service training sessions. They are appropriate for use by a gathering the size of an average school staff. Each is freestanding, and aims to enhance thinking or practice on some aspect of geographical education or environmental geography. Thus the activities are not in any particular order, nor are they intended to follow on from each other in a planned sequence. They are intended to be thought-provoking, useful, relevant to every staff member, and indeed fun to take part in. They aim to provide practical reflection on a number of theoretical issues raised in this book.

Activity 1   Back from the holidays

Aims and organisation

This activity is designed to help staff reflect upon their own travels, their potential for contributing to geographical education in the school, and on the accuracy of knowledge gleaned in this way. It is ideal for an autumn term 'one-off' staff meeting, when summer holidays are fresh in people's minds. You will need a large empty notice board, some paper, felt pens and drawing pins. Ask each staff member to bring along one photograph or poster relating to his or her holiday travels – of a location abroad or in the UK.

Procedure

Go round the assembled staff and ask each person to put up his or her chosen photograph on the board and talk for a few moments about the place visited – the things they enjoyed best about it, anything they did not enjoy, and to comment on perceived differences between this place and the home area. At the end of each short talk, let other members of the staff jot down questions or comments on a piece of paper (one can be scribe for the group); for example, anything they particularly wanted to know about the place that the speaker didn't mention, anything they can add to what the speaker mentioned because of their own personal knowledge, anything they disagree with. Pin the sheets by the photographs, and discuss the results. They should provide information on the collective knowledge of the staff, which should be helpful in selecting places for study in future topics; give an idea of photographs and other resources available about places visited; and, above all, give insight into teachers' own gaps in knowledge or even stereotypical knowledge about places gained as a result of reading or a brief visit to a destination. This overview should be helpful when developing topics that provide accurate, up-to-date information about distant lands, and help to raise awareness of possible pitfalls to be subsequently avoided in the classroom. End the session by making lists of available resources, including objects and artefacts from the places discussed.

Activity 2   Refining a topic web

Aims and organisation

This activity may well be familiar to many schools, but it is included to emphasise the need for planned refining of topic webs. These frequently do not go beyond a brainstorming session in any systematic way at whole-school level. You will need several large (poster-size) sheets of paper and felt pens.

Procedure

Decide on the geographical topic to be planned and elect a scribe for the occasion. Construct a topic web through a brainstorming session:

- Write the topic title in the centre of a large sheet of paper.
- Invite staff members to call out possible activities, thoughts and ideas relating to the topic as quickly as possible. The scribe should write these around the topic title, in no particular order or sequence.
- Photocopy the end product, and give a copy to smaller teams (e.g. two members of staff or even an individual) representing specific subject areas. Make sure that teams cover each core and foundation subject and cross-curricular links.

Each sub-team should then refine the web by identifying the activities and suggestions which can be linked in a meaningful way to the subject area being considered. Geography should, of course, be considered by a sub-team, even though it is the focus of the whole topic.

Reassemble as a whole staff and redraw a refined web with the topic title in the centre, surrounded by subject-headed listings provided by the sub-teams. It could well be that some subjects dominate the web, while others have little documentation. This is a healthy state of affairs, reinforcing a key principle of good topic work which is that some areas link meaningfully through certain topics, and no topic should 'drag in every subject' for the sake of it. Acknowledge the key areas linking with geography on this particular occasion, and make notes for future reference of areas not covered or marginally related, so that these may warrant attention by other means or at other times.

Reconvene the sub-teams and let each now add specifics of the Programme of Study that may be covered for their area (if relevant) and a breakdown of the suggested activities into those which aim to teach skills, those aimed at developing concepts, and those which promote learning of values and attitudes. Feed this information back for incorporation on to the master plan. Figure 5.1 provides a diagrammatic representation of the stages involved in topic refining.

Activity 3   An ear for geography

Aims and organisation

This activity aims to give practice in developing the skills of listening in order to review, monitor and assess children's geographical learning. Throughout this book it has been emphasised that oral work in the first three years in school is of the utmost importance; therefore, a teacher's listening skills are critical. Prepare for this session by asking one teacher from each year group (Reception, Y1, Y2) to make a short tape-recording of a pair of children or

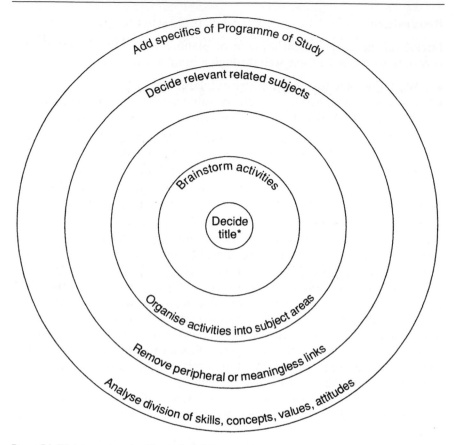

Figure 5.1 The stages involved in topic refining.

small group undertaking tasks in geography, and perhaps interacting with the teacher while performing their allocated tasks. (This itself is a skill worthy of practice, as discussed in Chapter 4.)

Procedure

Listen to the tapes, either as a whole staff or in groups (i.e. exchange each other's) and discuss them. Consider evidence of learning or understanding relating to any aspect of the Programme of Study for geography (or areas of learning in environmental education) and any obvious gaps or mistakes in the children's learning. Consider the role of the teacher, if applicable, as heard on the recording. People's interpretation of the recordings could be written on sheets designed for the purpose, such as the pro forma for listening suggested in Chapter 4 (see Figure 4.15). No attempt should be made to transcribe the tapes, as this is a time-consuming task which cannot be done as a matter of routine when assessing children's geographical work. Discuss the place of recorded evidence in your overall school plans for assessment of geographical learning.

Activity 4   Analysing children's work

Aims and organisation

This activity stimulates discussion on examples of children's written work in geography, and leads to some understanding of difficulties involved in using children's work for assessment purposes. It should reveal the extent to which there is agreement among staff about children's levels of performance, as indicated by their writing and drawings. You will need the examples of work provided in Figures 5.2, 5.3, 5.4 and 5.5.

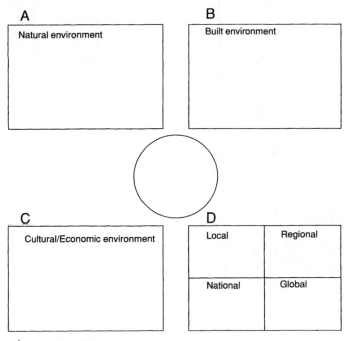

A

Natural environment

B

Built environment

C

Cultural/Economic environment

D

| Local | Regional |
| National | Global |

How to use this sheet

- Write the topic title in the centre circle
- Place ticks as follows in boxes A, B and C to indicate emphasis.

   ✓ ✓ ✓ ✓ major emphasis
   ✓ ✓ ✓   some emphasis
   ✓ ✓   little emphasis
   ✗   no emphasis

- Place one or more ticks in the appropriate sections of box D to show the emphasis of the study in terms of geographical location(s).

Figure 5.2 Example (a) of children's work which might be used for assessment purposes.

a Plan oF our table

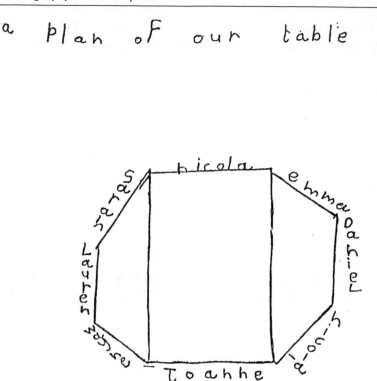

Figure 5.3 Example (b) of children's work which might be used for assessment purposes.

Procedures

The examples of work provided deliberately do not indicate the ages of the children responsible for them. Neither do they suggest whether they are 'good', 'poor' or 'average' in terms of performance at any given level of attainment. Suggest that the staff study them carefully, bearing in mind the Programme of Study and levels of attainment for geography, and try to write a set of criteria which could be used when making judgements about levels at which the children are working. Differences in opinion will be inevitable. These can be discussed and attempts made to reconcile them as far as possible so that a consensus of opinion is arrived at which will be helpful when looking at future examples of work.

A follow-up activity could involve staff undertaking to provide examples of work from their own classrooms, selected because they meet the agreed criteria for the various levels of attainment. These new examples can then be shared with the staff as a whole, and further discussion can ensue about the application of assessment criteria.

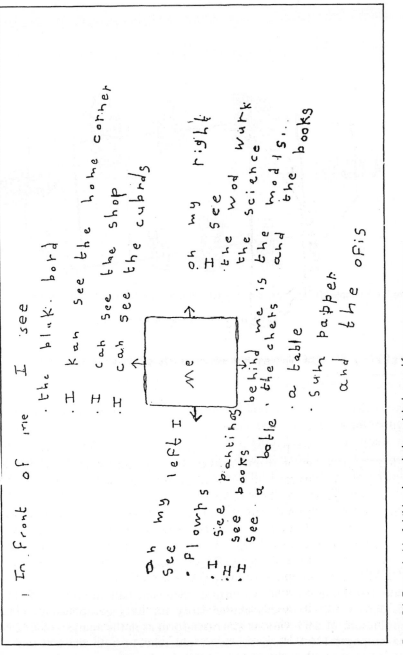

i In front of am I see
. the bluk. bord

. I kan see the home corner

. I cah see the shop

. I cah see the cubrds

Oh my left I
see
. Plowhs
. I see pantings behind me is the
. I see books
. I see a botle . the chets and
. a table
. sum papper
  and the ofis

oh my right
I see
the wod wurk
the science mod1s...
and the books

Me

Figure 5.4 Example (c) of children's work that might be used for assessment purposes.

This is where we sit in red group

Figure 5.5 Example (d) of children's work that might be used for assessment purposes.

Activity 5 Geography through story

Aims and organisation

This activity aims to give practice in the analysis and development of the potential for geographical education in children's stories. It is based on the case study 'The use of story', in Chapter 4. One or more story books considered to have geographical potential will be required for this activity, perhaps selected from the list provided on pages 196–9. The number of stories required will clearly depend on the number of staff at the meeting, but it is suggested that groups of two to three people analyse one story.

Procedure

Divide staff into groups of two or three. Set aside half an hour for them to read, discuss and analyse a chosen story for its geographical potential. Record results of deliberations in written form as in the analysis of *Red Fox* given on pages 136–9. Suggestions should refer to both the text and the illustrations in terms of their potential for developing geographical vocabulary and linking with Programme of Study.

Reconvene as a whole staff group and discuss the potential of all the stories analysed. Type up suggestions, and agree to trial them in classrooms, leading to the production of written evaluations.

At a subsequent staff meeting, circulate and consider each of the evaluations. Make decisions on the appropriateness and potential of the trialled stories. File the assessments of potential together with evaluations, comments and perhaps examples of children's work deriving from the stories in your collection of school resources.

WORKING WITH PARTNERS

Initial teacher training and partnership schools

Sheffield Hallam University is one of a small number of teacher training institutions that enable students to link early years specialism with geography specialism. Most initial teacher training institutions now require students to choose to be subject specialists in the core subjects Maths, English and Science, reflecting their emphasis in the National Curriculum. Other institutions that do enable early years specialists to focus upon geography include: Roehampton at the University of Surrey, St Martin's College, Ambleside campus and the University of the West of England, Bristol. The Graduate Teacher Training Registry supplies information on courses where geography may be studied within teaching courses (http:// www.gttr.ac.uk/).

Initial teacher training at Sheffield Hallam University

At Sheffield Hallam School of Education, Alison Ryan and David Owen are responsible for geography within the BA (Hons) Programme for Education with Qualified Teacher Status (QTS). Alison admits that the course emphasises the early years specialism more than the geography specialism, but this emphasis necessarily reflects the schools' contexts in which students will later work.

Geography within early years teacher training

The BA course for students specialising in teaching 3–7 year old olds is three years long and each year is split into two semesters. A 'taster' session of geography as a Foundation Subject is provided for all students and this introduction has recently increased from 6 to 8 hours. However, 8 hours of geography can provide very little preparation for infant and primary teachers who specialise in other subjects. This means that the role of a geography curriculum co-ordinator is still very relevant; the training of geography specialists is vitally important as they will often be needed to support geography teaching and learning across the whole school in which they will work after training. Sheffield Hallam enables students to be well-equipped for such a leadership role in geography.

Modules in which early years geography students focus on their subject specialism and develop their pedagogical knowledge include the following: three modules concerning learning and teaching Foundation Subjects; two modules concerning a geography-based enquiry or piece of research; one module on co-ordinating the curriculum. Additionally there are three geography subject knowledge modules: Geography and the local environment, Geography and the global dimension, and Contemporary ideas and concepts in geography.

What are geography student teachers expected to know and do?

Throughout the course, early years geography students must collect evidence of their progress and achievement in their professional and academic skills; this is demonstrated within the students' Professional Standards Portfolios that are assessed at the end of each year. One of the 12 sections of the portfolio is based upon a student's progress with his/her geography specialism. Within the portfolio, students must demonstrate via a variety of tasks and evidence that they:

    a have a detailed knowledge and understanding of the Geography National Curriculum programme of study and level descriptions across the primary age range;

    b can cope securely with geographical questions which pupils raise;

    c understand the progression from QCA's Early Learning Goals to KS1, the progression from KS1 to KS2, and from KS2 to KS3;

    d are aware of and know how to access recent inspection evidence and classroom relevant research on teaching primary pupils in geography, and know how to use this to inform and improve their teaching;

    e know pupils' most common misconceptions and mistakes in geography;

    f have a secure knowledge and understanding of the content specified in the ITT National Curriculum for ICT in geography teaching;

    g are familiar with geography-specific health and safety requirements, where relevant, and plans to avoid specific hazards;

    h have a secure knowledge to at least a standard approximating to GCE Advanced Level geography in those aspects taught at KS1 and KS2.

(Sheffield Hallam 1999–2000: 47–8)

As well as the portfolio assessment exercises, there are other more innovative assessment tasks given to students. Alison believes that a particularly enjoyable and useful exercise for students is their creation of a teaching pack that focuses on the study of a local area. The pack must be designed to be used with teachers of children between 3 and 7, as geography-based work. The local area chosen by the student can be any area that they know really well, or it could be a particular example of school grounds. The packs are used in practice rather than just left on the shelf as pieces of assessment. Another exercise carried out by students has produced some relevant and original pieces of research into geography work at early years level. From time to time, students' work is appropriate for development into a piece of research suitable for publication. Examples of titles and short abstracts from students' work include:

Teaching about Mexico: an evaluation

The aim of this enquiry is to gain a better understanding of how KS1 children learn about distant localities and the perceptions they have. It also considers the contribution that photo packs and ICT have in developing children's understanding of distant places. The results show that children can have preconceived ideas about distant localities and that through the teaching of a unit of work these perceptions can change. Photo packs appear to be a more powerful teaching resource than ICT when teaching and learning about distant localities.

(Homaira Ibrahim)

KS1 children's understanding of geographical vocabulary

This research investigates the perceptions and understanding of certain geographical terms held by Y1 children. These represent some of the physical features that teachers are required to teach at this age. The findings indicate that children of this age have problems with some terms and even familiar features present difficulties. The research provides an insight into children's perceptions of geographical features, language they use to define them and whether children can apply their language and understanding to identify features in photographs.

(Elizabeth Hill)

Owing to the wealth of published research that seeks merely to investigate children's geographical understandings, interests and abilities, a recent alteration to early years geography provision at Sheffield Hallam is the geography team's emphasis upon students engaging in action research. For example, students design a web page outline that would be useful for a geography curriculum co-ordinator and which can be used and developed in schools. Additionally, students have in the past undertaken other ICT-related pieces of action research: creating and reviewing web pages or web quest activities, which schools can use for teaching and learning about distant localities. The web pages and activities are designed for use by teachers who are not geography specialists.

Links with partner schools – Initial Teacher Training (ITT) within the school

The Sheffield Hallam BA early years course meets the minimum legal requirement for teaching practice; students spend at least 24 weeks of their degree in school and every semester students spend time in schools working with school-based mentors. This amounts to students spending over 25 per cent of the degree course on school placement. Alison and David try to match up their geography students with teacher mentors in schools which have a specialism or particular interest in geography. This cannot always be achieved because so few early years teachers are geography specialists themselves, yet this potentially disheartening situation can be beneficial to students who can assist schools with a desire to improve or revitalise their geography work. The challenge can profit both students and schools where the profile and practice of geography can be improved.

Teachers who become mentors to education students can train to become moderators, assessing students' progress and development. Mentors can also receive credits towards their own degrees or further degrees, so in a sense the mentors/moderators can develop a research-practitioner approach to their own teaching.

In and around Sheffield, teacher-mentors who take geography students on placement are given a wealth of guidance from Sheffield Hallam School of Education. Mentors receive a 50-page handbook, parts of which are reproduced here to demonstrate the kind of positive and reflective relationships that should develop between teachers and students training to be effective providers of geography for young children.

THE ROLE OF THE GEOGRAPHY MENTOR

(Through this booklet the term geography mentor will be used. This person could be the geography co-ordinator or student mentor, or interested class teacher. Good practice would involve a dialogue between the student and teachers in all three roles.)

The role of the geography mentor

- Recruitment and admissions
- Interviewing potential geography students for admission to the course

Y1 foundation and block school experience
- Support geography specialist students in completion of geography school based tasks
- Support geography specialist students in teaching part or all of a geography unit of work if school timetable permits

Y2 ICT and block school experience
- Support geography specialist students in completion of geography and ICT school based task
- Support geography specialist students in teaching part or all of a geography unit of work if school timetable permits

Y3 Assessment, block school experience and co-ordinator practice
- Support geography specialist students in assessment and resources audit tasks
- Support geography specialist students in planning geography unit of work
- Ensure geography specialist students teach, assess and evaluate a geography unit of work
- Induct students into role of geography co-ordinator
- Support students undertaking geographical research

The geography mentor as teacher educator
- The current partnership pattern gives the opportunity for class teachers, mentors and co-ordinators to **use their experience and teach** the students to teach. A geography mentor would also fulfil this role when working with geography students.

Geography mentoring strategies

Normally mentoring sessions will follow on from an observed teaching session. The mentoring session will have a focus that can be negotiated with the student in advance, or have come from the observation of the lesson. The list below gives some guidance as to appropriate foci; however your professional judgement will determine what is relevant and useful to the student:

- Appropriate use of geography subject knowledge when answering children's questions
- Use of the enquiry approach
- Student's own subject knowledge in relation to children's misconceptions
- Development of children's mapping skills
- Lesson planning, e.g. focus of learning objectives or differentiation strategies
- Reviewing the student's use of ICT
- Assessing and recording different aspects of geography
- Health and safety issues

It is a good idea to start the mentoring sessions with open questions that encourage reflection:

> *How did you feel about how you introduced the local environmental enquiry?*
> *What progress are you making in answering children's geographical questions?*
> *What were the children learning when they used the CD-ROM atlas or Roamers?*
> *How are you using your assessment from previous sessions to inform your planning today?*

What kind of mentor do you want to be?
One classification provides four stereotypes of school mentors:
Experienced realists
Facilitators
Protective friends
Experts

Experienced realists believe students must learn from tough classroom experience and on the advice of experienced teachers on whom they can model themselves. Experienced realists are not very keen on theory and prefer the practical. They also see confidence as the key, but they choose to expose students to harsh realities rather than protecting them.

Facilitators accept that there are different ways of being successful. They think that teachers and students can learn from each other. Their main strategy is to make the students reflect on their teaching and only offer suggestions when requested. Students are regarded as hard working and professional.

Protective friends also have a very positive view of students, but they give less emphasis to critical reflection and are more inclined to be protective. They give a lot of personal attention and emotional support, and the blurring of the line between professionalism and friendship can be a problem. Protective friends have some uncertainty about their own teaching, and some can remember lacking in confidence in their own early days of teaching.

Experts have the skills for teaching and are confident that these can be passed on to the students through advice and copying. They make little attempt to allow the students to identify their own agenda for development. Experts may enjoy having students, but do not feel that they learn from them.

Based on work by Brian Ellis (1997)

Which stereotype would you want to identify with?

We also reproduce here another part of the handbook that informs mentors about how they should review students' progress as geography teachers. The purpose of the section that follows is not only to present a picture of excellent teacher training that exists for geography early years students, but also to provide examples for teachers so that they might check if they themselves are demonstrating 'best practice' in geography teaching and learning. Furthermore, the section can be used as a basis for professional development. In the examples that follow, 'Jaimie's' approach at Grade 1 could be considered to represent where things are working well, whereas Grade 4 teachers like 'Gwyn' in the example are in need of a good deal of help and improvement.

Grading using pen pictures for specialist geography students in Years 2 and 3

Grade 1

Jaimie visited the school and audited the potential of the local area for geographical learning. She had negotiated with her geography mentor to create a challenging and well-planned unit of work based on appropriate opportunities shown in the school's geography scheme of work. She ensured that she used the enquiry approach across the whole unit of work and also in individual lessons. She provided a variety of resources to complement resources provided by the school.

Her medium term planning gave excellent opportunities for the children in her class to develop their understanding of the four aspects of geography while experiencing a wide range of teaching and learning strategies. Her geographical enquiry exploited links to literacy, numeracy and the children's social, moral, spiritual and cultural development. This was clearly indicated in her planning. She utilised the school and University ICT resources to their full effect in her geography teaching and developed the children's use of ICT in geography.

She made full use of fieldwork opportunities and planned an excellent local visit in which all safety aspects were planned for as part of a thorough risk assessment. Co-operation with other adults was exemplary. (*Similar evidence could be collected if student used a visitor to aid children's geographical learning.*)

Her short-term planning was excellent; lesson objectives were focused and based on previous assessment data to ensure progression. She enthused the children through her teaching leading to high quality work from the class. This work formed instructive interactive displays and some children were given the opportunity to report the results of their work to other members of the school community. Her subject knowledge was excellent; this was evidenced in her asking and answering of geographical questions in the class.

She used a variety of assessment strategies to ensure that all children in the class were challenged and given the opportunity to progress. Records were comprehensive, useful and well maintained. She negotiated with the school's SENCO and her class teacher to provide meaningful geographical experiences for three children with mild learning difficulties.

She set focused and achievable targets for herself and achieved them in consultation with other teachers and members of the school community.

Grade 4

Gwyn was unsure of local geographical opportunities for teaching. Consequently the unit of work that she planned lacked a local context and failed to motivate and interest the children on many occasions. Her medium-term planning did not reflect good practice as exemplified by the school, university or QCA geography planning. Her approach across the unit of work was often didactic and focused on place knowledge development or skills development in isolation. When questioned, she had little understanding of the enquiry approach to geographical learning, or the structure of the geography curriculum.

Her medium-term planning provided opportunities for the children in her class to experience activities that were designed to occupy them rather than develop their geographical learning. Gwyn often had difficulty answering children's geographical questions and revealed many gaps in her subject knowledge.

Her geography lessons often did not develop children's geographical capabilities. The purposes of some lessons were difficult to define, as her learning objectives were often indistinct. She sometimes utilised some of the school's ICT resources in her geography teaching but was not confident with the hardware or software.

A 'cause for concern' form was issued in week two of the practice and a university moderator consulted with the geography mentor and the student at the midpoint review. Achievable targets were agreed upon based on:

> Planning lessons with focused geographical objectives
> Planning learning activities that developed the children's learning rather than occupying them colouring in maps or worksheets.

She did not make use of existing fieldwork opportunities. (*Similar evidence could be collected if students used a visitor to aid children's geographical learning.*)

Her short-term planning was inadequate; lesson objectives were not clear and did not clearly link to the appropriate part of the Geography Programme of Study. She did not use her assessment data to inform her planning, but saw it as a 'chore' imposed by the university. Some of this work was not completed. The class teacher had to prompt her to create displays and present the children's work. This was difficult as most of the work had been done on worksheets so was not in a form that could be presented easily.

She set broad general targets for herself and therefore found them difficult to achieve. She found critical evaluation impossible and instead used a time-consuming diary type approach.

The student did not meet her targets set at the midpoint review and was graded four. Her academic tutor then saw her after the practice, to discuss her next steps.

(Sheffield Hallam 1999–2000: 13–15)

The Sheffield Hallam handbook provides mentor-teachers with guidance on what to expect from students' planning of geography work. We have included here some pages from this handbook that relate to planning geography activities and lessons. Rather than add these sections to one of this book's earlier chapters on planning and policy, with which they are closely linked, we have kept them within the ITT partnership example. We do emphasise that while the pages are intended for link schools' mentors and student teachers, there is ample guidance for other early years teachers who may wish to refer to the following sections for their own planning or as part of a school's geography training or review process. The four handbook sections that are presented here concern:

1   Lesson Planning for Geography
2   Teaching and Learning Strategies
3   Fieldwork Planning
4   A Lesson Plan for a Y2 topic 'Making our Road Safer'

I   LESSON PLANNING FOR GEOGRAPHY

A good lesson plan for geography will have the following features:

- a clear, specific, relatively small-scale learning objective, derived from the PoS, which can be assessed;
- NC PoS from which the learning objective is drawn;
- a learning objective linked to assessment criteria;
- assessment criteria – which will often consist of the session objective turned into a question, for example:

Learning objective: the children will be able to draw a plan of the classroom.
Criteria for assessment: can the children draw a plan of the classroom?

- 'other purposes' identified if appropriate; for example, children co-operate in groups when involved in fieldwork;
- stimulating tasks and resources matched to children's experience and ability and informed by assessment;
- tasks and/or resources differentiated where appropriate, for example:
  - by outcome (painting a picture);
  - by resources (providing blank and partially completed base maps);
  - by task or method of recording (describing a feature or producing a labelled picture of it);
  - by intervention (extending more able children's learning through careful questioning);
  - by support (working with a group of children with particular needs);

- precise details of resources, for example scale of map.

Introduction

This section should include:

- telling the children what they are going to learn
- key teaching points or key questions, new vocabulary to be introduced
- how the children will respond

Development

This section should include:

- the task/s on which the children are engaged
- how the children are organised
- differentiation if other than by outcome
- how the teacher and children will interact

Conclusion

Students should always leave sufficient time at the end of a lesson to consolidate the learning objective. This can be done, for example, by:

- playing a game
- children sharing and discussing their learning
- the work being connected to future activities
- a similar question being asked in a different context

Extension

This section should only include geographical tasks which more able children or those who finish early will complete in order to extend their learning. These could include using different reference sources or applying a skill in a different context.

Students should avoid over-reliance on worksheets. Any worksheets produced should be well designed and word processed (and not be coloured in unless this is related to map work!).

Lesson plans are clearer if they are written in note form or using bullet points. It is also a good idea to attach a sheet containing relevant subject knowledge to the lesson plan.

(Sheffield Hallam 1999–2000: 20–2)

2   TEACHING AND LEARNING STRATEGIES

Children learn in different ways and have different needs. Students need to use a range of teaching and learning strategies in terms of organisation, approach and learning activities within a unit of work to ensure that geography is accessible, stimulating and interesting. This will also ensure children have the opportunity to provide evidence of their achievement in different ways.

Organisation

Whole class	a debate, listening to a story, watching a video
In groups	river fieldwork – measuring and recording, interpreting photographs, role play
In pairs	searching the WWW, measuring and recording the weather, carrying out a survey, using Roamer, using a map
Individual	drawing a map, reading a reference book, using a digital camera, writing a poem about the weather, drawing a graph

Approaches

fieldwork	experiential
creative	problem solving
enquiry	observing
describing	didactic
reading	drama
play	ICT

Learning activities

following a map	drawing a map
using a CD-ROM atlas	carrying out a land use survey

interpreting photographs

structured play

making a model

reading a reference book

designing a poster

undertaking a traffic survey

assessing environmental quality

searching the WWW

interpreting weather data

and many, many more!

orienteering

role play

sketching

producing a booklet

writing a newspaper article

measuring temperature

discussing a local issue

emailing other children

taking photographs

(Sheffield Hallam 1999–2000: 29)

3   FIELDWORK PLANNING

**FIELDWORK/VISIT PLANNER
RISK ASSESSMENT**

Responsibility for the safety of the children lies with the class teacher.
   A copy of this form must be left in the school office and given to all adult helpers.

Year group	Number of children
Details of adult helpers (name, role)	
Destination	Transport
Date	Timing
Preliminary visit YES/NO	Date
Adults briefed YES/NO	

Learning objectives

Activities

Resources

Hazard	Level of risk (high/medium/low)	Action to minimise risk

Children with special needs likely to affect ability to work safely

Action required

Emergency procedures

- secure safety of group
- contact emergency services if necessary
- contact responsible teacher

mobile phone number	school telephone number

mobile phone and medication will be held by

Signed	Date

After the visit, the reverse of this sheet should be used to complete an evaluation

4   A LESSON PLAN FOR A Y2 TOPIC: 'MAKING OUR ROAD SAFER'

Session title Making our road safer   Class Y2   Date   Time 1 hour
Objective(s) inc NC PoS
children will present a case in the
form of a letter writing
(2, 6a, 6c)

Resources templates, frames (hard
copy and templates on computer)

Assessment of outcomes

Criteria: can children use evidence to present a case in the form of a letter?
Mode: letter
Other purposes:

Time	What you will do/say	What the children will do
	Introduction and development	Indicate differentiation as appropriate
	Indicate differentiation as appropriate	
20	• ask children about survey results and ways of making roads safe	• recall previous work
	• discuss what would be appropriate in our road	• make suggestions with reasons
	• explain how decisions about local environment are made	• suggest writing to local council
	• ask/tell children about features of a letter	

30	• stress need to use evidence to support case • ask more able children for appropriate persuasive language they could use	• use template to produce letter • less able – use writing frame or • in pairs, word process letter using template/writing frame • more able include scanned pictures
10	Plenary/Conclusion • ask whether children have made sensible suggestions • ask whether letters are effective	 • selected children read out letters • respond with reasons • children identify use of evidence, etc.
	Extension	• produce map/diagram to accompany letter

Such comprehensive guidelines and support (and these are only part of a large handbook) are an important aspect of the partnership that exists between teacher training institutions, schools and students. It is unnecessary to add more than just a few comments to accompany the preceding documents that have been included to illustrate the work of just one ITT provider. We endorse Sheffield Hallam's approach to planning geography work so that it is not taught in isolation from other subjects and experiences. Indeed at Foundation Stage, it cannot be. Elements of the geography National Curriculum – associated with skills, places, patterns/processes and environment/sustainable development – are best taught in conjunction with each other where possible. As stated elsewhere in this book, skills should be offered and learned *alongside* knowledge and vice versa. Lesson plans that highlight other purposes to the learning, such as developing social skills or supporting work and play that has occurred elsewhere are a means of working towards a truly holistic means of learning. It seems important to add that the creation of documentation, planning sheets and review sheets is not advocated to the extent that paper work dominates early years' geography teaching and learning. Similarly, an over-reliance upon paper work for children should not be a part of students' practice; as the Sheffield Hallam handbook states, too many work sheets and too many colouring activities are not an effective means of geography learning. Geography work flourishes if set in practical and visual contexts, that make good use of fieldwork, classroom displays and variety in approach and activity. Hopefully, Sheffield Hallam students will begin to work with young children in such ways and provide inspiration for the schools in which they will work.

Local Education Authority Links – Staffordshire

Since 1997 Kate Russell has been Adviser for Geography for Quality Learning Services (QLS) in Staffordshire. QLS is the curriculum support and advice unit for the Staffordshire County Council, which consists of curriculum officers for all aspects of the curriculum. Information about QLS and a wonderful range of ideas and resources for geography teaching can be found at the Staffordshire Learning Net website (www.sln.org.uk/geography) and details of all QLS courses can be found on the QLS website (http:// www.qls/org.uk/cpd/htm).

First, we highlight the special needs teaching ideas and support that is provided by Staffordshire QLS. Kate's colleague, Chris Durbin, has placed on the Staffordshire Learning Net website some helpful suggestions for teaching geography to children with special educational needs. The website has initiatives for:

- a sensory room which is a resource for geography and literacy learning as well as a way to respond to and represent space and place;
- teaching geography to visually impaired students;
- making the most of opportunities to think about movement and travel;
- referring to the National Curriculum guidance for teaching geography to pupils with learning difficulties http://www.nc.uk.net/ld/ Ge_content.html;
- a Staffordshire Expanding Geography Scheme that reflects upon planning for geography teaching to pupils with special needs at Key Stage 1.

In terms of wider professional development, Kate provides a variety of programmes of assistance for teachers and practitioners, but in the short space available we focus on presenting an illustration of Kate's Geography in the Early Years/Foundation Stage courses that she runs each year. Useful resources offering more inspiration for teachers and practitioners can be found in Kate's articles in the Primary Geography publication (Russell, 2001, 2002a, 2002b).

Here, Kate presents a flavour of her Early Years Geography courses:

Sessions start with introduction about the Early Learning Goals and the contribution Geography makes (mainly to Knowledge and Understanding but also to other areas of learning). This is followed by a walk around the local area of the Kingston Centre in Stafford where the courses are held; the objective for this activity is to show practitioners how to make 'something' from an ordinary area which, on the face of it, has very little to offer. Also, this work helps teachers generate suitable open-ended questions to pose to children as well as stimulating observational work. The area does not have many special features; it is set in a typical residential area on the edge of a medium sized town.

Some of the activities put the practitioners into 'child' mode while others are at teacher level. The teachers undertake more activities than pupils would do in one session.

One of the 'pupil mode' activities involves giving each practitioner a photograph (often featuring a teddy bear) taken somewhere during the walk. Practitioners have to spot: where the photo was taken; where the photographer was standing; why the photographer took that particular picture. We finish off by talking a little about the place in the photo. This ensures that each practitioner or child has a turn. The activity is differentiated as more difficult photos could be given to more able pupils.

Practitioners are reminded that when they do the activity with children, they should try taking photographs which look up and down as well as being based at eye level. The photos are inevitably either man-made or natural features, thus there is opportunity to talk about the differences between them. Some photos could be of less pleasant features such as graffiti or litter so there should be some discussion of likes, dislikes and ways through which children could improve the environment.

Another activity where practitioners become pupils begins with each person receiving an 'emotions card' showing a variety of feelings or emotions in cartoon picture format; for instance there are cards showing approval, pleasure, happiness, disapproval, shock or disgust. Practitioners are asked to 'play' these cards in appropriate locations – where they find something they like or dislike and can talk about their feelings and ways to improve the place.

During their walk, practitioners in their 'child' roles are asked: what people are doing; what kinds of jobs they are doing; how many people they can see working; how many people are enjoying themselves (walking the dog, cycling, playing football for example). Types of transport or road signs or markings can also become the focus of observation. Sometimes, practitioners are involved in a sensory walk, so in certain places we stop and look, listen or smell and describe what we see, hear or smell. Practitioners are encouraged to take photos during their walks and they are reminded that even very young children can use digital cameras or disposable cameras during walks round their local areas.

Back in the classroom setting, we pull together what we have seen and talked about. The photographs can be placed on a large map of the area and captions are given to the photographs to create a kind of photographic record of the walk. In school or nursery settings, this activity could be extended to creating a book, where children provide the appropriate information for each stage and page.

We look at other materials which can help develop local area work such as some websites or simple software such as My World and Local Studies. We also use large-scale aerial photos (our local newspaper publishes some) or those from Wildgoose are very good (http:// www.wgoose.co.uk/index.htm). We talk about taking opportunities, when they arise, to experience at first hand the weather conditions and special events in the local area.

The afternoon activities focus more on studying places further away; this is often done through stories, visitors from other countries, using photo packs, food and artefacts from other places. Some of my favourite photo packs are from Action Aid – the Big Family series – they are very large, made from durable card with information on the back. They feature real families and everyday life in Bangladesh, Peru and Ghana. Another super photo pack is called Your World My World from Oxfam. This pack features 4 children from Ethiopia, India, Russia and Brazil (6 photos of each child) and all pictures of familiar situations at home and at school so that children in the UK can relate to the photographs even though the backgrounds and climate will be different. It can be an interesting activity to ask practitioners (or children) to 'sort' the photographs. I give no instructions; people just approach this task in different ways which enables some good discussion.

During my day with the early years practitioners, we also take a look at the role play or 'home corner' that is found in most Reception or Nursery classrooms. I find that many people have turned their corner into exciting places, like the seaside, the Arctic, a French café or an African village. Other ideas include making the corner into a travel agent, a train station or an aeroplane.

We usually have some food items during this session – perhaps some Bombay mix, tropical fruits, coconut ice or coconut ladoos I make from India. I also have a large bag of artefacts that we look at. For some of the items, it is very difficult to detect where they are from, and this places the teachers in a position so that they have to ask appropriate questions, as would children in their classrooms. Music from a particular country is often played during this session to generate a sense of place and we later look at stories from other countries thinking about how they can be used with young children.

The final session is spent looking at a range of resources. I ask everyone to review a book, photo pack, website, piece of software, artefact and then jot down some ideas about how it could be used. While practitioners are writing their evaluation forms, I quickly copy the reviews so that everyone receives all the reviews.

During most of these courses, I involved a practitioner from an Early Years setting to help out and provide something of the 'real experience'. A few years ago, I invited a teacher from a local private nursery who had strong links with Antigua; she creatively and imaginatively used this connection with much of her curriculum, bringing in art, music, language and PSHE as appropriate. During the sessions, I refer to the Geographical Association, pointing practitioners to useful articles in Primary Geographer. Overall, I find that teachers value this kind of course for practical ideas, seeing resources and meeting colleagues in different settings.

Some other aspects of Kate's activities that encourage practitioners to reflect on their own approach to geography teaching and learning are highlighted here, as they have potential for use in other INSET settings. For example, practitioners are asked:

- to state one interesting geographical feature in the locality of their own settings;
- to think of a resource for early years geography which they would like to recommend to others;
- to suggest one good geographical activity which they have seen in their own settings;
- to remember an early memory of a place, a local area, somewhere other than home;
- to remember their earliest memories from their own school geography, then positive and negative aspects of their school geography.

Kate sends teachers away with a very welcome resource: a set of poems that can be used for geography learning. A list of these poems can be found in Chapter 6, the Resources section of this book. One lovely example is June Crebbin's poem 'The Meeting of the Ways' which in its reference to motorways, high streets, avenues, closes, crescents, culs-de-sac, drives and footpaths is perfect for local study and development of geographical vocabulary.

Chapter 6

Resources

BEATING THE BUDGET

Successful teaching and learning in geography are inevitably dependent to a greater or lesser extent on resources; and with current and ever-increasing pressures on schools' budgets the acquisition of a wide range of useful items is no doubt a daunting, if not impossible, challenge.

This chapter begins, therefore, with some general comments on and advice aimed at reducing levels of anxiety in school budget holders, generated by the prospect of having to do conjuring tricks with cash before any worthwhile geographical education can be achieved.

In the first instance, schools may be surprised at the wide range of relevant materials that can be used from resource banks of other subject areas. Many general reading books, for example, commonly found in early years classrooms, are ideal for developing into geographical topics or for illustrating specific concepts and issues – more will be said about this later in the chapter. Many items purchased for science education are obviously transferable to geographical studies, notably equipment for collecting, observing and magnifying, and for studying the weather. Sand and water apparatus is highly relevant for investigatory studies and experimentation in various aspects of physical geography. Mathematics equipment, in the form of measuring devices, and material for reinforcing elements of size and shape, is necessary for many tasks relating to the teaching of geographical skills, and resources of technology and information technology are clearly important across the geography curriculum. It would probably be true to say that every infant school could ask its pupils to undertake a sophisticated range of geographical tasks without purchase of specialist equipment.

Furthermore, an impressive bank of resources for geography can be built up at little or no cost apart from effort on the part of staff – and all schools are encouraged to begin establishing such a bank now, if a collection is not already in place. For example:

- Make a school collection of maps of various scales, sizes and uses; consult the local Tourist Information Centre and travel agent, look out for maps in papers and magazines, and try to acquire a range of published maps, e.g. an Ordnance Survey map of the local area, a world map, an A–Z. Visit the local planning office, and ask whether any maps are available; the local studies section of the library may also be helpful.
- Make collections of objects/illustrative material from distant places. When abroad, or in distant parts of the UK, seek out photographs, posters, examples of local craft work, tapes of authentic music, items or pictures of national dress, details of special festivals, customs and traditional foods. Sketch or photograph homes and people. Suggest that every member of staff does this when going out and about or on holiday. Soon a large collection of objects relating to places will be assembled at comparatively little expense.
- Make a photograph bank. As with the above suggestion, each member of staff could be asked to add to a central collection after a holiday or visit away from the local area. One person could undertake to go out with a camera into the neighbourhood and make a specific collection of photographs of the locality. These could become useful for history topics in the future, as features of the local area inevitably change over time.
- Make a collection of interesting cuttings of geographical interest from local newspapers. This has the same potential as a photograph bank in terms of a future source of information about change.

Below is a checklist of general resources for geography and environmental work. This should be helpful to curriculum co-ordinators who are trying to build up a range of items to service teaching and learning. Some cost money, others are free and could well augment the budget-beating ideas set out above.

GENERAL CHECKLIST OF RESOURCES

People   Make a list of staff and contacts who have visited distant lands or lived in other places in the UK and who would be prepared to come and talk about them.

Make a list of people in the local community, perhaps elderly people, who could talk about aspects of life which have changed, or specialist workers (policeman, shopkeeper, vicar) who are knowledgeable about specific local buildings, places or jobs.

Keep these lists in 'file form' in a central place, so that staff can add to them, and the curriculum co-ordinator can check and update them regularly.

Places	Make an inventory of places (in the locality and further afield) of particular geographical interest for fieldwork, with a note of opening hours/special features if appropriate. Again, this should be kept centrally so that it can be updated. Maintain an associated box file, containing literature/brochures relating to the places.
Maps	Collect as wide a range of maps as possible. Also, acquire globes, atlases and air photographs. Local newspaper offices often have air photographs. Local studies sections of libraries usually have maps and photographs which can be copied; so too have planning offices. Ordnance Survey maps are an important aspect of the collection, and details about acquiring these are given below.
Books and written sources	Reference books about themes/topics, e.g. food, homes; also about distant places, world issues, festivals and customs. Newspaper cuttings, tourist brochures, leaflets, wallcharts. Stories set in distant places or about journeys. Recipe books from around the world, written sources about the local area (from the library, the planning office, etc.). Note that a school collection of books and other forms of written material should promote accurate knowledge about our multi-cultural world, and avoid images of stereotyping and bias.
Illustrative material	Photographs, posters, slides, filmstrips. Travel agents are often a useful source. The same cautionary note about accuracy as given for written sources obviously applies to illustrations. Try to keep a balance between familiar and unfamiliar people and environments.
Music	Collect tape-recordings/records of music from distant places, pictures or examples of traditional musical instruments.
Mechanical	Microcomputers and software, cameras, television programmes, radio programmes, videos of distant lands, films. Tape-recordings of current events or of people talking about their lives, their past, their jobs, etc.
Miscellaneous	Special equipment, e.g. for weather recording, pond dipping, soil studies, working out direction. Models, e.g. landscape models, stream channels. Objects, e.g. examples of clothing, craft work from distant places, menus from foreign restaurants.

Many of the above items will need careful selection, in order to strike an appropriate balance between items applicable to the various elements of content and authenticity and accuracy of knowledge. The task of the school co-ordinator will be to encourage the collection of, check and maintain up-to-date resources; also to help the rest of the staff make the distinction between that which is teacher resource material for study and appropriate interpretation, and that which is appropriate for the pupils themselves to use. Both have a place in the school collection and, as with all resources, staff will need to discuss and make decisions about how both children and staff access geographical materials so that an equitable arrangement benefits the school as a whole.

The remainder of this chapter is devoted to providing specific help and suggestions for resourcing geographical work in the early years.

STORY BOOKS SUITABLE AS STARTING POINTS IN GEOGRAPHY

The River Story, Meredith Hooper, Walker Books
The Drop that Goes Plop, Sam Godwin and Simone Abel, Hodder & Stoughton
Where the Rainforest Meets the Sea, Jeannie Baker, Walker Books
Katie Morag's Island Stories, Mairi Hedderwick, Red Fox
Rosie's Walk, Pat Hutchins, Bodley Head
Mr Gumpy's Outing, John Burningham, Random House
Little Bunny Bobkin, James Riodan, The Watts Publishing Group
The Little Boat, Kathy Henderson, Walker Books
Hue Boy, Rita Phillips-Mitchell, Penguin Books
Harry's Home, Lawrence Anholt, Orchard Books
Billy's Flower, Nicola Moon, Scholastic Ltd
Peter's Place, Sally Grindley and Michael Foreman, Belitha Press
The Long Long Journey, Tim Viner, WWF-UK
Billy Goats Gruff, Fran Hunia, Ladybird
Robin Hood, Joan Collins, Ladybird
Three Little Pigs, Fran Hunia, Ladybird
Goldilocks and the Three Bears, Fran Hunia, Ladybird
Little Red Riding Hood, Tony Ross, Penguin
Hansel and Gretel, Joan Cameron, Ladybird
The Lighthouse Keeper's Lunch, Ronda and David Armitage, Penguin
The Enormous Crocodile, Roald Dahl, Penguin
Don't Forget the Bacon, Pat Hutchins, Bodley Head
Postman Pat's Letters on Ice, John Cunliffe, Hippo Books
Topsy and Tim – Snowy Day, Jean and Gareth Adamson, Blackie
Let's Go to Sally's Place, Pat Edwards, Longman
Crafty Chameleon, Mwenye Hadithi, Hodder & Stoughton
Have You Seen Stanley?, Pat Edwards, Longman
Alfi Gets in First, Shirley Hughes, Bodley Head

Scragg's Flowers, Malcolm Yorke, Arnold-Wheaton
I'll Take You to Mrs Cole, Nigel Gray and Michael Foreman, Macmillan
My School, Sumiko, Heinemann
What-A-Mess, Frank Muir, A. & C. Black
There's No Such Thing as a Dragon, Jack Kent, Blackie
The Lion and Albert, Marriott Edgar, Methuen
Burglar Bill, Allan and Janet Ahlberg, Heinemann
Goodnight, Goodnight, Eve Rice, Penguin
Cops and Robbers, Allan and Janet Ahlberg, Heinemann
The Fox Went Out On a Chilly Night, Peter Spier, Penguin
The Tail of the Mouse, Joan M. Lexau, Ginn
On the Way Home, Jill Murphy, Macmillan
Dear Daddy, Philippe Dupasquier, Penguin
The Joggers, Pat Edwards, Longman
Just Awful, Alma Marshak Whitney, Armada
Weather, Jan Picnkowski, Heinemann
Can't Catch Me, John Prater, Penguin
Where the Wild Things Are, Maurice Sendak, Bodley Head
One World, Michael Foreman, Andersen Press
When Dad Cuts Down the Chestnut Tree, Pam Ayres, Walker Books
A Balloon for Grandad, Nigel Gray and Jane Ray, Collins
When Dad Fills in the Garden Pond, Pam Ayres, Walker Books
The World That Jack Built, Ruth Brown, Andersen Press
Ladybird, Ladybird, Ruth Brown, Beaver Books
The Twins in Greece/in France, Sally Kilroy, Orchard Books
Stories From Our Street, Richard Tulloch, Cambridge University Press
A Country Faraway, Nigel Gray and Philippe Dupasquier, Andersen Press
Where the Forest Meets the Sea, Jeannie Baker, Walker Books
A Garden in the City, Gerda Muller, Macdonald
Dinosaurs and All That Rubbish, Michael Foreman, Penguin
Will It Rain Today?, Althea, Dinosaur Publications
Lucy's Year, Stephen Weatherill, Two-Can Publishing
It's Mine, Leo Lionni, Hodder & Stoughton
Have You Seen Birds?, Joanne Oppenheim, Hippo
Deep in the Wood, Richard Bell, Little Mammoth
Oi, Get Off Our Train, John Burningham, Random Century
Tusk, Tusk, David McKee, Andersen Press
The Elephant and the Bad Baby, Elfrida Vipont, Penguin
How Can an Elephant Hide?, David McPhail, Methuen
Oxford Reading Tree
   The Dump, Roderick Hunt, Oxford University Press
   A Day in London, Roderick Hunt, Oxford University Press
   The Flying Carpet, Roderick Hunt, Oxford University Press
   The Emergency, Mike Poulton, Oxford University Press

The Journey Home, Joanne Flindall, Walker Books
In a Dark, Dark Wood, June Melser and Joy Cowley, Arnold-Wheaton
Four Fat Rats, Cathy Bellows, Macmillan
The Jolly Witch, Dick King-Smith, Simon & Schuster
The Invitation, Nicola Smee, Collins
Lost, David McPhail, Little, Brown and Co.
Once Upon a Time, Gwenda Turner, Penguin
How Stories Came into the World, Joanna Troughton, Blackie
The Shepherd Boy, Kim Lewis, Walker Books
Antarctica, Helen Cowcher, André Deutsch
Dr Xargle's Book of Earth Tiggers, Jeanne Willis, Andersen Press
The Hefty Fairy, Nicholas Allan, Hutchinson
Lost, Tony Kerins, J.M. Dent
The Mystery of the Blue Arrows, David and Chuck McKee, Andersen Press
Brave Babette and Sly Tom, Elzbieta, Faber
The Snowman, Raymond Briggs, Penguin
The Mousehole Cat, Antonia Barber, Walker
Pear Tree Farm, Cohn and Moira Maclean, Kingfisher
Bear's Adventure, Benedict Blathwayt, Walker Books
Bringing the Rain to Kapiti Plain, Verna Aardema, Macmillan
Odette, Kay Fender, Gollancz
The Jolly Postman, Janet Ahlberg, Heinemann
The Turtle and the Island, Barbara Ker Wilson and Frane Lessac, Frances
    Lincoln Ltd
The Playground, Diane Wilmer, Collins
The Worm Book, Janet and Allan Ahlberg, Armada
Feelings, Aliki, Pan Books
The Farmyard Cat, Christine Anello and Sharon Thompson, Hodder &
    Stoughton
Amoko and Efua Bear, Sonia Appiah, Deutsch
Ollie Forgot, Tedd Arnold, Heinemann
The Sandal, Tony Bradman, Andersen Press
Have You Seen My Cat?, Eric Carle, Hodder & Stoughton
Go Away, William, Margaret Carter and Carol Wright, Hodder & Stoughton
The Day of the Rainbow, Ruth Craft, Heinemann
The Weather Cat, Helen Cresswell, Collins
At the Café Splendid, Terry Denton, Oxford University Press
Charles Tiger, Siobhan Dodds, Armada
The Singing Sack, Helen East, A. & C. Black
Sid the Kitten, Mark Foreman, Andersen Press
Tom's Pocket, Sarah Garland, Reinhardt/Viking Kestrel
Wayne Hoskins and the Pram Lady, Jennifer Gubb, Meridor Books
Peedie Peebles' Summer/Winter Book, Main Hedderwick, Bodley Head
Sebastian: The Tale of a Curious Kitten, Vanessa Julian-Ottie, Heinemann

Geraldine's Big Show, Holly Keller, Julia MacRae
Lily Takes a Walk, Satoshi Kitamura, Blackie
UFO Diary, Satoshi Kitamura, Andersen Press
Tenrec's Twigs, Bert Kitchen, Lutterworth
Come Back, Hercules, Rob Lewis, Macdonald
Six Crows, Leo Lionni, Andersen Press
Albert and Albertine at the Seaside, Moira and Colin Maclean, Hutchinson
Katie's Picture Show, James Mayhew, Orchard
Farm Noises, Jane Miller, Dent
Rex – The Most Special Car in the World, Victor Osborne, Dent
We're Going on a Bear Hunt, Michael Rosen, Walker Books
Where Do the Wicked Witches Live?, Juliet and Charles Snape, Picture Corgi
Brave Irene, William Steig, Gollancz
Sophie's Bucket, Catherine Stock, Methuen
Spots, Feathers and Curly Tails, Nancy Tafuri, Julia MacRae
The Sandhorse, Ann Turnbull, Andersen Press
Great Gran Gorilla and the Robbers, Martin Waddell, Walker Books
The Park in the Dark, Martin Waddell, Walker Books
Casper's Walk, Cindy Ward, Macdonald
Max's Chocolate Chicken, Rosemary Wells, Collins
Teddy Bear Boatman, Phoebe and Joan Worthington, Penguin
Snappity Snap, Stephen Wyllie and Maureen Roffey, Macmillan
The Shell Dragon, Lynn Zirkel, Oxford University Press
Something is Going to Happen, Charlotte Zolotow, Collins

NURSERY RHYMES AS STARTING POINTS

Mary had a Little Lamb, Jack and Jill Went Up the Hill, The Grand Old Duke of York and Hickory Dickory Dock are all excellent starting points for introducing vocabulary relating to direction and movement. Classroom friezes could be made depicting the stories in the rhymes, annotated by appropriate words such as 'up', 'down' and 'hill'.

Dr Foster Went to Gloucester and Incey Wincey Spider can be used as the basis for discussion of concepts relating to water and the weather.

There Was an Old Woman, Baa Baa Black Sheep and Jack and Jill Went Up the Hill can be related to the origins and use of resources, and aspects of human geography.

POEMS

The list below has been compiled by Kate Russell of Staffordshire Quality Learning Services, an Education Unit of Staffordshire County Council:

Mango, Little Mango, in Wheel Around the World, Edited by Chris Searle, MacDonald.

Our Street, L.T. Baynton (Headteacher, Boulton Junior School Derby), Unpublished.

Jamaica Market, Agnes Maxwell-Hall, in Wheel Around the World, Edited by Chris Searle, MacDonald.

Wind, Shirley Hughes, in Out and About, Walker Books.

Mud, Polly Chase Boyden, Unpublished.

Seaside, Shirley Hughes, in Out and About, Walker Books.

Faraway Places, in Matt, Wes and Pete: Poems by Matt Simpson, Wes Magee and Peter Dixon, Macmillan.

Rhyming Roland, Richard Edwards, in Casting a Spell compiled by Angel Huth, Faber and Faber.

The Meeting of the Ways, Julie Crebbin, in Casting a Spell compiled by Angel Huth, Faber & Faber.

The Child in the Train, Eleanor Farjeon, in Collins Treasury of Poetry selected by Stephanie Nettell, Collins.

From My Window, Zaro Weil, Unpublished.

BOOKS FOR TEACHING GEOGRAPHY

Geography Picture Resource Book, Bill Marsden and Vera Marsden, Oliver and Boyd.

Rubbish and Recycling, Start Up Geography Series, Anna Lee, Evan Brothers Ltd.

Journey to School, Start Up Geography Series, Anna Lee, Evan Brothers Ltd.

Jobs People Do, Start Up Geography Series, Anna Lee, Evan Brothers Ltd.

Our Local Area, Start Up Geography Series, Anna Lee, Evan Brothers Ltd.

Traffic and Safety, Start Up Geography Series, Anna Lee, Evan Brothers Ltd.

Dolphins, In The Wild Series, Patricia Kendell, White-Thompson Publishing Ltd.

Our Street Our World, Exploring Environment and Development Issues with 4 to 7 year olds, Cathy Midwinter, WWF-UK.

COMPUTER SOFTWARE

Become a World Explorer (Dorling Kindersley)
All About Weather and Seasons (SEMERC)
Learning Ladder (Dorling Kindersley)
Where in the World is Barnaby Bear? (Sherston Software)
FirstLOGO (Logotron Software)
Lesson Maker (Eductech)

Geography Writing Frames (Folens Publishing)
My World (Structured Network Solutions)
Badger Trails (Sherston Software)
Local Studies (Soft Teach Educational)
The Oxford Talking Infant Atlas (Sherston Software)
3D World Atlas (Dorling Kindersley)

ATLASES SUITABLE FOR KEY STAGE 1

Hammond *My First Atlas* (2000)
Usborne Children's *Picture Atlas* (2003)
Kingfisher Books *First Picture Atlas* (1999)
Philip's *Children's Atlas* (1992)
Collins Longman *Keystart First Atlas (UK and Europe)* (1995)
Oxford University Press *Infant Atlas* (1998)
Longman, *Atlas of the British Isles* (1994)
Schofield and Sims, *A First Atlas of the World* (1991)

LINKS TO OTHER PROVIDERS AND PARTNERS

The Wildlife Trusts: http://www.wildlifetrusts.org/index.php?section=watch
Wildlife Watch, run by The Wildlife Trusts is an out-of-classroom environmental education programme and provides the junior club membership for The Wildlife Trusts. Environmental surveys, observation and experiments are promoted through Watch packs available to clubs and individual children and children in clubs, usually aged between 8 and 12 years.

SureStart: Government programme for early years child care and education: http://www.surestart.gov.uk/

The Earth Centre, Doncaster: http://www.townfield.doncaster.sch.uk/trips/earthcentre/senses.htm

The Sensory Trust is concerned with environmental design and management and is involved in promoting environmental education, access and participation: http://www.sensorytrust.org.uk/welcome.html

Learning Through Landscapes, school grounds charity: http://www.ltl.org.uk/

Bishops Wood: http://www.bishopswoodcentre.org.uk/ Bishops Wood is a centre for environmental education, consultancy and business training. It is based in Worcestershire and provides a range of environmental education programmes for children and adults of all ages. Bishops Wood centre can be contacted by email: jrhymer@bishopswoodcentre.org.uk or by telephoning John Rhymer on: 01299 250513.

Creeping Toad. Environmental Art and Celebration: Environmental Training and Workshops. Gordon MacLellan, 51d West Road, Buxton, Derbyshire, SK17 6HQ: http://www.creepingtoad.org.uk/toadhall.html

Scottish Natural Heritage can provide a free copy of 'Playing for Keeps – Ideas for Nature Activities with Pre-School Children' produced by The Scottish Environmental Education Council (SEEC), University of Stirling; Scottish Natural Heritage, Marks & Spencer, SPPA (Scottish Preschool and Play Association). Contact:
    Karen Smith
    Awareness and Involvement
    Scottish Natural Heritage
    Battleby, Redgordon,
    Perth
    PH1 3EW

TRAINING AND PROFESSIONAL DEVELOPMENT

National Curriculum site for planning, teaching and assessing the curriculum for pupils with learning difficulties: http://www.nc.uk.net/ld/Ge_content.html

Forest Schools: http://www.foresteducation.org.uk/index.asp

Links to the Geographical Association's web pages about research in practice: http://www.geography.org.uk/member/comm/bowles/bowlesd.html

Primary Geography training and Development in Staffordshire: http://www.sln.org.uk/geography/primary.htm

Eco Schools Handbook, Tidy Britain Group (now EnCams): http://www.encams.org/ or http://www.eco-schools.org/

Sheffield Hallam University School of Education Geography Handbook for Students, Mentors and Coordinators 1999–2000: http://students.shu.ac.uk/eds/course_info/geography/about.htm

Geography Through Play, Angela Milner, Geographical Association
7 by 7 Ways to be Creative with Geography, Chris Durbin, Geographical Association

MAPS AND MAPPING

Ordnance Survey's interactive web pages for Y2 children and older: http://www.mapzone.co.uk/ and for teaching direction at key Stage 1: http://www.ordnancesurvey.co.uk/education/schools/classroom/direction/index.html

Ordnance Survey maps, available from:

National Map Centre
22–24 Caxton Street
Westminster
London
England
SW1H 0QU
http://www.mapstore.co.uk/

Cook, Hammond & Kell Ltd
Whittington House
764–768 Holloway Road
London N19 3JQ
http://www.chk.co.uk/

The Goad Map Shop
Chas E Goad Ltd
8–12 Salisbury Square
Old Hatfield
Hertfordshire HL9 5BR
Telephone (01707) 271171

Trident Map Services
70 High Street
Houghton Regis
Dunstable
Beds LU5 5BJ
Telephone (01582) 867211
maps@tridentmaps.co.uk

AERIAL PHOTOGRAPHS

Wildgoose Catalogue
Getmapping Plc
Virginia Villas
High Street

Hartley Wintney
Hampshire RG27 8NW
United Kingdom
http://www2.getmapping.com/Catalog/ProductDetails.asp?ProductId
= 3463 and: http://www.wgoose.co.uk/frm/index2.htm

Aerofilms
Gate Studios
Station Road
Borehamwood
Hertfordshire WD6 1EJ
http://www.bnsc.org/wouk/html/contacts/aerof.htm
Will take aerial photographs to order and have a library of photographs
available.

Photo Air/SKYPLAN
22 Townsend Way
Folkesworth
Peterborough
PE7 3TU
Telephone: 1733 241850
http://www.skyplan.fsnet.co.uk/about.htm
Have a wide range of aerial photographs in stock and can only deal with
specific individual orders.

Mulitmap.com provides links to online aerial photograph suppliers. The
website also provides some online aerial photographs: http://www.
multimap.com/

PROFESSIONAL ASSOCIATIONS

Readers are encouraged to subscribe to two professional associations which
publish journals containing a wealth of practical guidance for primary
teachers, including material relevant to teaching and learning in the first three
years of school. Both also produce a range of other publications. Further
details are available from their national headquarters:

The Geographical Association (primary membership): http://www.
geography.org.uk/index.asp
Email: ga@geography.org.uk
Geographical Association
160 Solly Street
Sheffield S1 4BF
United Kingdom
(Journal: *Primary Geographer*)

The National Association for Environmental Education: http://www.
naee.org.uk/
Email: info@naee.org.uk
University of Wolverhampton
Walsall Campus
Gorway Road
Walsall
West Midlands
WS1 3BD
(Journal: *Environmental Education*)

FURTHER WEB RESOURCES

Staffordshire Learning Net Geography web pages: http://www.sln.org.uk/
geography/

Geography pictures – photographs may be found online at: http://www.
geogpix.co.uk

Pictures – art and the environment. Andy Goldsworthy web pages
compiled by the Centre for Global Environmental Education, Hamline
University Graduate School of Education, St. Paul, MN, USA: http://
cgee.hamline.edu/see/goldsworthy/see_an_andy.html

Hopscotch Books lesson ideas – information for ordering packs about
seasides, Geography and Literacy and Geography and ICT: http://
www.hopscotchbooks.com/

Action Aid: http://www.actionaid.org/supportusnow/supportusnow.shtml
Resources produced by Action Aid, Chataway House, Leach Road, Chard,
Somerset TA20 1FA Tel: 01460 62972/238000 Fax: 01460 67191 or email:
deved@actionaid.org.uk

Your World My World is an Oxfam pack designed for teachers to use with 4
to 7 year olds. Ordering information, sample lesson plans and photographs
can be viewed online: http://www.oxfam.org.uk/coolplanet/teachers/ywmw/

Global Dimension – DFID (Department for International Development)
website, 'Bringing the world to your classroom, an essential resource for
teachers': http://www.globaldimension.org.uk/

Curriculum Online: Department for Education and Skills online catalogue of
multimedia and educational resources: http://www.curriculumonline.gov.uk/
Curriculum + OnLine/cover.htm

Postscript

It is hoped that this book has shown how building upon first-hand experiences, practical investigations and interactions with the natural and built environments, and helping children to begin to appreciate the complex inter-relationships between people, culture and biophysical surroundings are essential starting points for teaching and learning in geography and environmental education. Indeed, the most valuable and readily available resource is the environment itself. Young children are fascinated by their surroundings and have a tremendous capacity to build upon natural learning experiences that take place within them. A wealth of secondary resource material – books, audio- and video-tapes, television programmes, computer software and web resources, archives, maps, illustrative material, poems and plays about the world, about people and environmental issues and inter-relationships – is not just desirable but an essential focus of successful classroom work. These will combine with experiences derived from the environment itself to ensure progress in, and give structure and meaning to learning tasks.

If a primary school's co-ordinated approach to the inclusion of geography and environmental education is to be successful, it depends as much upon the attitude of those designing and implementing it as on the content of what is being taught and learnt. The importance of developing pupils' attitudes has been discussed, but the critical importance of educators' attitudes has so far escaped attention. Central to geography and the study of the environment is the importance of attitudes and values, especially if a fundamental aim is to change people's attitudes from exploitation and dominance to global protection and care. This is, of course, a deeply personal issue and every individual has to be responsible for his or her own attitude changes and concern for future generations. Nevertheless, the teacher's role cannot be over-emphasised. If a real impact is to be made, environmental awareness in the school as a whole is surely essential. In part this involves the successful implementation of programmes of work and progressive topics of a geographical and environmental nature, incorporating those components which this book has highlighted. It also takes account of the *whole* school environment, its ethos, its approach to caring for people and other living things, and, of course, the overall personal development of each child as an individual.

This book opened with some comments from young learners. It will conclude with some of the thoughts of Nicola, aged 4, from Stanford, California:

Nicola	I'm going to tell you something that's very awful – we are trying to save trees . . . they're trying to chop down the trees in this beautiful place, but you know what, we're trying and trying to save them from not being chopped down . . . but they're sick, but we're trying to save them even though they're sick.
Researcher	I'm so pleased you're trying to save them. Who told you about them?
Nicola	My dad . . . my mommy, I meant.
Researcher	Right. So some people really try to spoil our world, but we can help to take care of it. Can you think of any ways that you and I can help to take care of our world, and help to keep it beautiful?
Nicola	Not to chop down the trees . . . and my grandma always does . . . um . . . if someone throws litter around, you want to know what she does? She picks them up.
Researcher	And what's the right thing to do with litter?
Nicola	Keep them until you put it in the trash can. That's what I do.
Researcher	That's right – and, do you know, sometimes litter can get used again . . .
Nicola	Uh-huh.
Researcher	Do you know what we call that? When waste . . . garbage gets used again?
Nicola	Recycling.
Researcher	Well done, Nicky.
Nicola	Do you know why I know? The um . . . trash can up there says recycle. I even saw it on this programme . . . that's . . . um . . . recycle. And I even saw how you can do other things . . . um . . . with trees on the programme.
Researcher	Well, that's very good. Do you know why we must recycle?
Nicola	Yes. To make new things and . . . um . . . save the bad . . . em, not . . . um . . . save the used things.
Researcher	Right – so we can use used things to make new things. And that's important for our world.
Nicola	I know.
Researcher	What are we saving if we use things over and over again?
Nicola	Um . . . saving trees.
Researcher	Right. And do you always recycle your things – your family recycles?

Nicola	Uh-huh. We used to recycle these little glass bottles me and my brother used to use. And now we don't use them any more, but my brother still uses a bottle . . . and it's a different kind of these plastic ones.
Researcher	Well, Nicky, you told me you were smart, and you are right. You know a lot about these things, so you understand that our world is very beautiful, and we need to take care of it.
Nicola	Mmm.
Researcher	Why do you think you really want to take special care of the world?
Nicola	Because I love this world, even though it gets too cold in the winter.
Researcher	Why do you love the world? What's really special about it?
Nicola	Um . . . that it's . . . that it . . . gets to be warmer as the year comes, and it gets to be colder as the year comes.
Researcher	Right. Why is our world . . . why do you love it?
Nicola	Because it's so beautiful and the leaves turn to colours . . . and in the summer . . .

No child in school is too young to begin to stand in awe of the world and to reflect upon the glories of the natural environment and the achievements of human life, or to take those first steps along the path towards individual concern, responsibility and action.

References

Alderson, P. (2003) Sign of the Times. *Nursery World*. 10/09/03 Retrieved from the World Wide Web 16/09/03 http://www.nursery-world.com/

Appleyard, D. (1970) Styles and methods of structuring a city. *Environment and Behavior* 2, 101–17.

Atkins, C.L. (1981) Introducing basic map and globe concepts to young children. *Journal of Geography* 80, 228–33.

Bell, P.A., Fisher, J.D., Baum, A. and Greene, T.C. (1990) *Environmental Psychology*. Fort Worth: Holt, Rinehart & Winston Inc.

Blades, M. and Spencer, C. (1986) Map use in the environment and educating children to use maps. *Environmental Education and Information* 5, 187–204.

Blades, M. and Spencer, C. (1987a) Young children's recognition of environmental features from aerial photographs and maps. *Environmental Education and Information* 6, 189–98.

Blades, M. and Spencer, C. (1987b) The use of maps by 4–6 year old children in a large-scale maze. *British Journal of Developmental Psychology* 5, 19–24.

Blaut, J. (1997) Piagetian pessimism and the mapping abilities of young children. *Annals of The Association of American Geographers* 87, 168–77.

Bluestein, N. and Acredolo, L.P. (1979) Developmental changes in map reading skills. *Child Development* 50, 691–7.

Catling, S. (1988) Using maps and aerial photographs. In D. Mills (ed.) *Geographical Work in Primary and Middle School*. Sheffield: The Geographical Association.

Claxton, G. (1997) *Unconscious Learning: Hare Brain, Tortoise Mind. Why Intelligence Increases When You Think Less*. London: Fourth Estate.

Cornell, E.H. and Hay, D.H. (1984) Children's acquisition of a route via different media. *Environment and Behavior* 16, 627–41.

Cornell, E.H. and Heth, C.D. (1983) Spatial cognition: gathering strategies used by pre-school children. *Journal of Experimental Child Psychology* 35, 93–110.

Cousins, J.H., Siegel, A.W. and Maxwell, S.E. (1983) Way finding and cognitive mapping in large-scale environments. A test of a developmental model. *Journal of Experimental Child Psychology* 35, 1–20.

Darvizeh, Z. and Spencer, C.P. (1984) How do young children learn novel routes? The importance of landmarks in the child's retracing of routes through the large-scale environment. *Environmental Education and Information* 3, 97–105.

Department for Education and Employment (DfEE), (1999) *The National Curriculum. Handbook for Primary Teachers in England. Key Stages 1 and 2*. London. H.M.S.O. www.nc.uk.net

Department for Education and Employment/Qualifications and Curriculum Authority (DfEE/QCA), (2001) *Curriculum Guidance for the Foundation Stage*. London: QCA.

Devlin, A.S. (1976) The small-town cognitive map: adjusting to a new environment. In G.T. Moore and R.G. Golledge (eds) *Environmental Knowing*. Stroudsburg, PA: Dowden, Hutchinson & Ross.

Donaldson, M. (1978) *Children's Minds*. London: Fontana.

Donaldson, M. (1992) *Human Minds*. Harmondsworth: Penguin.

Ellis, B. (1997) Working Together – Partnership in Teacher Education. Sheffield: Geographical Association.

Evans, G.W. (1980) Environmental cognition. *Psychological Bulletin* 88, 259–87.

Garling, T., Book, A. and Ergezen, N. (1982) Memory for the spatial layout of the everyday physical environment. *Scandinavian Journal of Psychology* 23, 23–35.

Garling, T., Book, A. and Lindberg, E. (1984) Cognitive-mapping of large-scale environments: the inter-relationship between action plans, acquisition and orientation. *Environment and Behavior* 16, 3–34.

Hart, R. and Chawla, L. (1981) The development of children's concern for the environment. *Zeitschrift für Umweltpolitik* 4, 271–94.

Hart, R.A. and Moore, G.T. (1973) The development of spatial cognition: a review. In R.M. Downs and D. Stea (eds) *Image and Environment: Cognitive Mapping and Spatial Behavior*. Chicago: Aldine.

Huckle, J. and Sterling, S. (eds) (1996) *Education for Sustainability*. London: Earthscan.

Jaspars, J., Van der Geer, J., Tajfel, H. and Johnson, N.B. (1963) On the development of national attitudes in children. *European Journal of Social Psychology* 2, 347–69.

Laurendeau, M. and Pinard, A. (1962) *Causal Thinking in the Child*. New York: New York International Universities Press.

Martin, F. (1995) *Teaching Early Years Geography*. Cambridge: Chris Kington Publishing.

National Curriculum Council (1990) *Curriculum Guidance 7: Environmental Education*, York: NCC.

Palmer, J.A. (1994) *Geography in the Early Years* (First Edition). London: Routledge.

Palmer, J.A. (1998) *Environmental Education in the 21st Century: Theory, Practice, Progress, Promise*. London: Routledge.

Palmer, J.A. and Suggate, J. (2004) The Development of Children's Understanding of Distant Places and Environmental Issues: Report of a UK Longitudinal Study of the Development of Ideas between the Ages of Four and Ten Years. *Research Papers in Education* 19, 2.

Piaget, J. (1954) *The Construction of Reality in the Child*. New York: Basic Books. (Original edition, 1937).

Piaget, J. (1960a) *Judgement and Reasoning in the Child*. New York: Harcourt & Brace. (Original edition, 1928).

Piaget, J. (1960b) *The Child's Conception of Physical Causality*. Totowa, NJ: Littlefield, Adams, Patterson. (Original edition, 1927).

Piaget, J. and Inhelder, B. (1956) *The Child's Conception of Space.* London: Routledge & Kegan Paul.

Piaget, J. and Inhelder, B. (1967) *The Child's Conception of Space.* New York: Norton.

Piaget, J., Inhelder, B. and Szeminska, A. (1960) *The Child's Conception of Geometry.* London: Routledge & Kegan Paul.

Piché, D. (1981) The spontaneous geography of the urban child. In D.T. Herbert and R.J. Johnson (eds) *Geography and the Urban Environment: Progress in Research and Applications* Vol. 4. Chichester: John Wiley.

Pick, H.L. and Lockman, J.J. (1981) From frames of reference to spatial representations. In L.S. Liben, A.H. Patterson and N. Newcombe (eds) *The Life Span.* New York: Academic Press.

Portugali, J. (ed.) (1996) *The Construction of Cognitive Maps.* New York: Kluwer Academic Publishers.

Qualifications and Curriculum Authority (QCA), (1998) *Geography: Teacher's Guide. A Scheme of Work for Key Stages 1 and 2.* London: QCA.

Qualifications and Curriculum Authority (QCA), (2001) *National Curriculum in Action: Geography.* www.naction.org.uk/subjects/geog/levels.html

Qualifications and Curriculum Authority (QCA), (2002) *Education for Sustainable Development.* www.nc.uk.net/esd/index.html

Royal Society for Nature Conservation (1993) 'Enviroscope', Lincoln@RSNC.

Russell, K. (2001) Early Years Environmental Experiences. *Primary Geographer,* April 2001, 28–9.

Russell, K. (2002a) Bring out the globe. *Primary Geographer,* January 2002, 32–3.

Russell, K. (2002b) Stories of place. *Primary Geographer,* April 2002, 24–5.

Scoffham, S. (ed.) (1998) *Primary Sources: Research Findings in Primary Geography.* Sheffield: The Geographical Association.

Siegel, A. and White, S. (1975) The development of spatial representations of large-scale environments. In H.W. Reese (ed.) *Advances in Child Development and Behaviour* 12, 167–82.

Somerville, S.C. and Bryant, P.E. (1985) Young children's use of spatial co-ordinates. *Child Development* 56, 604–13.

Spencer, C. (1998) Aerial photographs and understanding places in Scoffham, S. (ed.) (1998) *Primary Sources: Research Findings in Primary Geography.* Sheffield: The Geographical Association.

Spencer, C., Blades, M. and Morsley, K. (1989) *The Child in the Physical Environment.* Chichester: John Wiley & Sons.

Spencer, C., Blades, M., Hetherington, D., Sowden, S. and Craddock, S. (1997) Can young children use aerial photographs as cues for navigation? *Proceedings of the Royal Institute of Navigation. Oxford Conference,* Oxford: Royal Institute of Navigation.

Stea, D., Blaut, J. and Stephens, J. (1996) Mapping as a cultural universal. In Portugali, J. (ed.) *The Construction of Cognitive Maps.* New York: Kluwer Academic Publishers.

Stillwell, R. and Spencer, C. (1974) Children's early preferences for other nations and their subsequent acquisition of knowledge about those nations. *European Journal of Social Psychology* 3, 345–9.

Storm, M. (1984) Teaching about minorities. In N. Fyson (ed.) *The Development Puzzle*. Sevenoaks: Hodder & Stoughton/CWDE.

Tajfel, H. (1981) *Human Groups and Social Categories*. Cambridge: Cambridge University Press.

Tidy Britain Group (1994) *Litter and Waste – Towards a Sustainable Lifestyle*. Leaflet. Tidy Britain Group.

Vosniadou, S. and Brewer, W.F. (1992) Mental Models of the Earth: a Study of Conceptual Change in Childhood. *Cognitive Psychology* 24, 535–85.

Vygotsky, L.S. (1979) *Mind and Society*. Cambridge, MA: Harvard University Press.

Welsh, R.L. and Blasch, B.B. (eds) (1980) *Foundations of Orientation and Mobility*. New York: American Foundation for the Blind.

Wiegand, P. (1992) *Places in the Primary School*. Lewes: Falmer Press.

Name index

Acredolo, L.P. 15
Appleyard, D. 10
Atkins, C.L. 13

Bell, PA. 11
Blades, M. 13–16, 88
Blasch, B.B, 12
Blaut, J.M. 10
Bluestein, N. 15
Brewer, W.F. 10
Bryant, P.E. 14–15

Catling, S. 87
Cornell, E.H. 11, 13
Cousins, J.H. 11

Darvizeh, Z. 11, 15
Department for Education and
    Employment/Qualifications and
    Curriculum Authority (DfEE/QCA)
    30
Devlin, A.S. 10
Donaldson, M. 9
Evans, G.W. 10

Garling, T. 10
Geographical Association 102

Hart, R.A. 11
Hay, D.H. 13
Heth, C.D. 11
Huckle, J. 33

Inhelder, B. 10

Jaspars, J. 18

Laurendeau, M. 8
Lockman, J.J. 12

Moore, G.T. 11

National Curriculum Council (NCC) 35

Palmer, J.A. 19, 33
Piaget, J. 8–12, 14, 17
Piché, D. 17
Pick, H.L. 12
Pinard, A. 8

Qualifications and Curriculum
    Authority (QCA) 59, 60, 72, 154

Russell, K. 189

Siegel, A. 11
Somerville, S.C. 14–15
Spencer, C. 11–16, 18, 88
Stea, D. 10
Stephens, J. 10
Sterling, S. 33
Stillwell, R. 18
Storm, M. 18
Suggate, J. 19

Tajfel, H. 17

Vosniadou, S. 10
Vygotsky, L.S. 9

Welsh, R.L. 12
White, S. 11
Wiegand, P. 10

Subject index

action research 175–176
aerial photographs 13, 94, 195, 203–204
analysis (of children's work) 169–172
animals 26, 35, 57, 104–106, 113
assessment 153–164, 167–169
atlases 68, 201
attainment target in geography 32, 126, 154–155
attitude development 17, 19–20, 36, 39, 69

bananas topic 80, 82–84
bias 17, 19, 113
bird life 26, 57
books and written sources 16, 61, 124, 195, 200; *see also* story, use of; story books
breadth of study 32, 34, 80, 81, 111

causality 9
citizenship 73, 145–146
cognitive maps 10–12
communication, organisation of 139
community links 147–152
compass directions 13, 95
computer programs and software 200–201
concepts and recording acquisition of 26, 37, 73
conceptual development 8–19
concern for the environment 19–20, 26
content and structure 28–43; *see also* national curriculum for schools
co-ordinate reference systems 14–15, 57, 94–95; *see also* grid reference systems
country: idea of 17–19; *see also* distant places

cross-curricular integration and links 39, 58, 63, 70–71, 83, 127–147
curriculum co-ordinator 44, 47, 119

decision-making 45, 114–115
desert areas 112
development of policy 49–50
developmental theory 9–11
direct experiences 10, 16, 38, 40, 56, 114, 126
direction, understanding of 13, 88, 95
distant places, understanding of 12, 16–19, 38, 61, 111–115, 166, 191
drama 98
dwellings 106

Eco-schools 119–127
education for sustainable development 33–37, 44, 73, 119–127, 146
egocentrism 10–11
emergent environmentalism 19
enquiry skills 96–97; *see also* thinking skills, problem-solving approach and geographical enquiry and skills
environmental cognition 8–27
environmental concern 19–20, 26
environmental education 9, 19, 28–43, 104, 119–127; *see also* education for sustainable development
environmental issues 8, 26
Euclidean stage of cognitive mapping 88
evaluation of policy 49–50

fieldwork 38, 63, 107–111, 185–187
first-hand experiences; *see* direct experiences
food 113, 191; *see also* bananas topic

foundation stage 28–30, 61, 62, 66–67, 80, 85, 96, 103, 117–119, 122, 128, 152

gardens of school 99, 120, 123, 148; *see also* school grounds as a resource
geographical enquiry and skills 30–31, 34, 63, 81, 82, 87–103, 108
geographical vocabulary 100, 136–140, 175
global dimension 62, 71–74
global warming 20, 22–24, 26
globes 13, 61, 95
Graduate Teacher Training Registry 173
graphicacy 13–14, 56, 58, 96
Great Outdoors Project 151–153
greater reciprocity 8
grid reference systems 14–15, 87, 94–95; *see also* co-ordinate reference systems

habitat surveys 106
holidays 57, 61, 166
homes 104–107, 130, 132
human environments 64, 105–107, 115–117

information technology 63, 70, 83, 130, 147
initial teacher training 173–189
invertebrates (case study) 42, 111–115

journeys 96, 118, 135–140

Key Stage 1 30–37, 59, 61, 67–68, 72, 80, 129
Knowledge and Understanding 19–27, of environment change and sustainable development 32, 34, 81, 82, 108, 119–127; of patterns and processes 31–32, 81, 82, 108, 115–119; of places 31, 81, 82, 104–115, 108

landmarks, use of 11, 13, 15–16
learning tasks 59
level descriptions 32–33
listening and the assessment process 156–162, 167–169
literacy 83, 129, 132, 140, 144
Local Education Authority Links 189–192
local environment 101–102, 107–111, 129, 192

maps 10, 13–19, 56, 61, 63, 87–96, 140, 194–195, 203
mapwork 13–19, 56, 87–96, 140
maze 16
media 10, 16–19, 57
mentoring 176–184
misinterpretation, erroneous understandings 9, 17, 19, 26, 57, 113
moths 99
multi-cultural education 71
music 191–192, 194–195

national curriculum for schools – organization 28–37, 63, 65
near and far 12–19; *see* also places
newspaper cuttings 194–195
numeracy 83, 129, 140, 144–145, 147–148
nursery rhymes 199

objectivity 9
observation and the assessment process 156–162
organization and potential partners 74, 151, 201–202
orientation of maps 15, 89

parental links 147–151
partnership schools 173–189
personal, social and health education (PSHE) 63, 71, 83, 132
photographs and pictures 10, 20, 61, 74–75, 94, 101, 114, 190–191, 194–195; aerial 13, 94, 195, 203–204
physical education 95
physical environment, conception of 8–9
physical systems 8
place(s): concept of 8–10, 12–19, 39, 87; *see also* distant places
planning and organisation 9, 39, 43, 50–60, 61–85, 182–184
plans 89–94
play 117–119
poems 192, 199–200
polar lands 20, 22–24
policy, whole-school 44–50, 60–85
policy into practice 46–50
prior knowledge 58
problem-solving approach 69–70
professional associations 204–205
professional development 165–192, 202

progression in learning 58–59, 66, 68, 72, 92–93, 153–155

Qualifications and Curriculum Authority – Exemplar scheme 59
questioning and the assessment process 156–162

rain forests 20–22, 26, 40–42, 52–54, 57, 61, 112
rationale for teaching and learning methods 48–49
realism 8
reality, construction of 9–12
reciprocity 9
record-keeping 156–164
record sheets 162–164
relief 95
resource(s) 39, 74, 191–192, 193–205
review of policy 49–50
river case study 107–111
rocks 116–117
route learning 11–13, 16

scale, concept of 51–52, 54–56, 87–88
school grounds as a resource 61, 99–103
school policy 44–50, 60–85
sensory trail 153
skills, recording acquisition of 81; see also assessment
space, concept of 8–12, 39, 87

spatial relationships, knowledge and understanding 8–19
staff development meetings 165–173
stereotyping 17–19, 26, 61, 73, 113, 166
story, use of 61, 88, 101–102, 124, 127, 132, 135–140, 148, 172–173
story books 17, 101–102, 124, 195–199
symbols, identification of 13–14, 87–88, 92–93

tape-recordings for assessment purposes 158, 167–169
television 16–17, 57, 102
thinking skills 70, 83, 96–99, 104; see also problem solving-approach
topic webs 80, 166–167
topic work planning 57, 82–85
topological stage of cognitive mapping 88
training sessions, in-service 165–173, 202

values 36, 39, 73
views, use of 115–116

waste materials 20, 22–24, 26, 35, 124, 128, 151
web resources 205
wetlands 20, 25
whole-school policy 44–50, 60–85
word associations 18
world events 61
written work, analysis of 169–172